Health
Freedom

Health Freedom

The Greatest Freedom of All

Diane Miller, JD

HEALTH FREEDOM
THE GREATEST FREEDOM OF ALL

iUniverse books may be ordered through booksellers or by contacting:

iUniverse
1663 Liberty Drive
Bloomington, IN 47403
www.iuniverse.com
844-349-9409

ISBN: 978-1-6632-2019-6 (sc)
ISBN: 978-1-6632-2020-2 (e)

Library of Congress Control Number: 2021906160

Print information available on the last page.

iUniverse rev. date: 04/23/2021

Contents

I lovingly dedicate this book to my daughters, Johanna and Theresa, who were sweet young girls when their mother headed down the health freedom trail and who continued at my side throughout the journey, all the while maturing, inspiring, and becoming beautiful women and friends. Their flexibility, patience, tolerance, understanding, support, and love, in the face of our many challenges and adventures as a family, will forever warm my heart and fuel my eternal gratitude.

To Calvin and Herb, who brought me full force into my role in the health freedom movement. I am grateful for Herb's patience and his willingness to heal in the face of personal risk. I am grateful to Calvin, who wielded a depth of skill, expertise, and passion for the law that would benefit the entire world. I am forever grateful for the opportunity provided to our team to voice the truth. They knew, before I knew, that I had a mission. Their encouragement and admiration gave me the courage I needed to walk the path of health freedom and find my voice. Our work together was divine destiny, and my hope is that the simplicity of our message of health freedom, and the passion that we continue to experience about health freedom, will ring true for others.

To my valiant Minnesota colleagues and dear friends, some of whom are introduced in this book, who had the vision, the spark, and the dedication to design and successfully pass the new safe harbor practitioner exemption law, Minnesota Statute 146A, which freed the herbalists, homeopaths, traditional naturopaths, and so many more healers, from the jurisdiction of an outmoded criminal law so that they could practice freely and happily and be available to all Minnesotans.

To my siblings and family members, especially Marylu, who traveled with me, listened to me, encouraged me, and even housed me during some of these amazing years of health freedom work. Without my gold dust twin, the challenge would have been unsurmountable.

To my mentors and heroes in the health freedom movement who have passed on before me: Clinton Miller, Whendell Whitman, Robert Irons, Elissa Meininger, Lily Rott, Berkley Bedell, Dan Haley, Herb Struss, Jim Jenks, and Arthur Miller (former chief justice of the Florida Supreme Court), among many others. And to my friends and colleagues, John Melnychuk, William Lee Rand, David Amrein, Jackie Pinkham, Joan Vandergriff, and Kirk Bashaw, who provided critical and significant guidance and support for my work and for the initial launch and work of National Health Freedom Coalition and National Health Freedom Action and who continue their passionate support to this day. And to my current inspiring peers, the leaders of so many amazing organizations and groups around the country working hard to protect health freedom. To state leaders working in their respective states for health freedom, to leaders monitoring federal issues, to the members and attendees of the United States Health Freedom Congress, and to the many citizens keeping the flame of hope alive for the protection of our bodily autonomy and our right to make health decisions.

To Jerri Johnson and Leo Cashman, my dear friends, colleagues, and fellow founders of National Health Freedom Coalition and National Health Freedom Action. Without these two angel beings as partners, who tirelessly gave their hearts and talents to make it possible for all of us to establish a new voice for health freedom in our country, we would not have existed at all.

And to all the remarkable NHFC and NHFA board members who joined us in our passion for health freedom, for their leadership and commitment over these past twenty years of health freedom adventures. I deeply thank you.

Foreword

Among us, a giant is leading mere mortals to freedom, liberty, and justice.

You will see how she has learned the art of manifestation for a future that has now become a golden age. With a brilliant mind, and humble to a T, she flashes a smile, with her beautiful dark brown eyes, that melts resistance. She calms as she leads us all to a new world where privacy, healing, and the right to declare and claim our medicines to survive and thrive are recognized as fundamental and statutory.

She was the other attorney on the very famous Herb Saunders case, of the Odin farmer who used colostrum and mammal medicine developed right here at the University of Minnesota.

Herb was offering fresh bovine colostrum, age-old animal medicine, to human beings. For years he honed the art of using milk immunized to balance common bacteria and pathogens that caused harm. Hundreds of people from all over the country came to this simple dairy farmer who understood the gift that moms create in their milk.

When Diane Miller, Herb Saunders, and I were alone, an incredible vortex of energy formed because of our presence, the three of us together.

The first time this happened for me, we were standing outside on a large gravel driveway connecting the farmhouse (the size of my cabin), the machine shed (where thirty to forty people arrived every night to sit upon upside-down five-gallon buckets—Mrs. Saunders did not permit customers in her house), and numerous outbuildings, with a large barn and holding pen to round out where we stood. The feeling was unmistakable. We were three old chiefs gathered for our mission. The stars were lined up with my client willing to fight for his right to heal another. Once we got him false teeth (Herb had one pearly white tooth in the front of his mouth when I met him), he was downright handsome.

This was our mission, each one of us specializing in a way to allow the blessings to flow. The case took six years, as Judge Dempsey loves to remind me. (Diane recounts three years.) The first time Herb and his wife visited my office, before Diane's involvement, Herb asked, "What's with all the crows?"   ·

Going outside, we saw thousands upon thousands of crows gathered in the trees down the block. It was ominous. My heart raced, hoping this was not portending danger or doom. Then, every time when the case got interesting, be it finding a good witness, making a significant medical discovery, going to trial or to the Court of Appeals, or entering the second trial, the birds returned. The local paper even reported the crows' presence.

When all was done, and the case was dismissed and my client was a free man, we gathered in a large circle of healing souls created by Diane Miller. They were all women. Herb and I were the lone males. Again, Herb asked, "What's with all the crows?" Then we detailed our visual sightings to the others.

Someone brought out the *Animal Speak* book. This is what I remember it said: Crows manifest spiritual law into the physical plane.

Diane Miller's story shows you what that looks like. In reading her words, you will discover within your being a newfound freedom. Diane gives us the confidence to understand that even if it's just one, we are enough when the goddess thread of the divine weaves us into the future.

Please enjoy this read. Prepare to be inspired.

Calvin P. Johnson
Attorney at Law

Preface

One autumn day in September 1993, I arrived home from work and trudged up the stairway to my bedroom; the phone in the hallway was ringing, ringing, ringing. I was so depressed, I could hardly drag myself forward. That very day, my first job out of law school had unexpectedly ended, giving me short notice to find a new job with no other work lined up. What would I tell my children after I had already moved them out of their hometown to the big city? How would I make ends meet as a single parent? I was numb with fear. Why had I left my wonderful farmhouse? How would I pay rent? I plopped on the bed after grabbing the ringing phone.

"Is this Diane Miller?"

"Yes. Who is this?"

"I heard that you are kind of an unusual lawyer."

All I needed to top off this day was a crank call. Before I could hang up or burst into tears, the caller quickly proceeded to ask me not to hang up. He was an attorney, he explained, who had employed one of my best friends from law school as a clerk in his practice. My friend had recommended me for a special case that they were working on involving natural health. My heart skipped a beat and my near tears began to evaporate into hope. *Thank you, God!* Could it be that I was getting a job offer this very day?

The stranger continued, "Before we talk further, I'd like you to answer a question for me. What do you think about antibiotics?" I paused, wondering why he had asked. I didn't know what to say. My first legal job had been in a family law firm doing divorce work; I hadn't had a case about antibiotics.

I had graduated from law school a year and a half earlier as a second profession while raising my children. Previously I had earned a chemistry degree and a medical technology degree; I had done graduate courses in immunology and hematology, but I hadn't worked as a licensed medical technologist in a hospital lab for more than ten years. Interestingly, though, I had studied medical law and had hoped to find a job in that area.

I suppose my reputation could have been considered "unusual" by my colleagues because they knew I had used homeopathic remedies and dietary supplements throughout my years at law school. And, yes, I sure had an opinion about antibiotics since I, as a parent, had been round and round with my doctor about how to deal with my daughter's chronic ear infections. Ultimately, I had helped her myself with garlic oil and elimination of dairy products. I had also learned to get rid of my own chronic strep throat with homeopathy.

My mind was racing with a potential answer. What if I were to say the wrong thing? What if I then were to lose a job opportunity? My anxiety was countered by the knowledge that I did not have the energy to work for a new employer who did not support my lifestyle choices. I needed to find a supportive job with all my cards on the table.

"Do you want a technical answer, or do you want my personal opinion?"

"I really want to know your thoughts about the use of antibiotics."

So, I went into a three-minute diatribe about how I believed that the overuse of antibiotics was one of the most dangerous practices in our medical model, especially for children. "Antibiotics are being used prophylactically, people are depending on them, and they are weakening people's immune systems. Pharmaceutical companies are making large profits from sales."

Once I'd started, I couldn't stop myself. "Doctors don't have enough time to spend with patients to find out what is really wrong with them or why their patient got sick in the first place—or teach them about how to get well without drugs and keep their bodies and immune systems strong."

I am sure I barely paused to take a breath. When I finished, there was a long silence.

And then the man said, "I'm smiling." He added, "I just found the lawyer that I have been looking for!"

That moment was the beginning of a challenging adventure that would change my life forever and bring me to writing *Health Freedom*.

I agreed to help the attorney who had called. The first thing I did was to transition from my former law position to the establishment of my own law practice in family law. I would now be able to do independent projects on a contract basis.

State v. Saunders

The attorney was Calvin P. Johnson from Mankato, Minnesota. I agreed to help him write an omnibus hearing brief for a criminal case, *State v. Saunders*. Mr. Johnson was defending Herbert Cecil Saunders pro bono. The charges being brought by the State of Minnesota were for the practice of medicine without a license, for swindle, for fraud, and for cruelty to animals. The charge of unlicensed practice of medicine was a gross misdemeanor; swindle was a felony charge in Minnesota. I would be working on a memorandum with arguments to defend and protect Mr. Saunders.

The case forced me to delve into the complexities of healing law. I was in disbelief as to why a local farmer would be criminally charged for helping people get well from their ailments when there had been no consumer complaints. I spent hours at the library of my law school alma mater, Hamline University School of Law, researching the constitutional issues of healing practices. Some nights I left the library when the midnight bell rang, while my teenage daughters were home patiently awaiting their immersed mom.

The page limit for the brief was supposedly thirty-five pages; in my passion, I had drafted an eighty-page memo and was not finished. We eventually ran out of time and I had to quit writing.

During those months I had the distinct feeling that I had been called to do this task. It seemed to resonate with my life story. Since I was young, I wanted to become a doctor. In 1967, at age seventeen, I left my family farm and went to college for premed and a chemistry degree, but my studies were never as important as my singing at local coffeehouses, working in the hollers of Appalachia, or protesting in peace rallies. When I did finish college, I went to California for a twelve-month hospital internship in medical technology. After I became licensed as a medical technologist, I still thought someday I would go to medical school. But instead of pursuing med school, I let my young life take its course, getting married and settling down. My husband and I had two beautiful daughters. Through birthing and raising those children, I learned much about the natural healing arts and the politics surrounding healing. One instance was when my firstborn daughter began to have reoccurring ear infections with high fevers and screaming pain. After many bouts accompanied by rounds of antibiotics and sleepless nights, our doctor recommended that we agree to have tubes put in her ears for drainage purposes. I was not wanting my baby to have surgery, so I started in-depth research into the topic. I found a lot of information, mostly in sources discussing natural ways to cope with health concerns. It was fascinating to me. I learned that a drop of garlic oil in the ear was sometimes used to cope with ear infections. I also learned that sometimes dairy and concentrated sugars could cause congestion or effect immunologic health. Around this time, my father read the book *Sugar Blues* and offered it to me to read. I was convinced I could help my daughter. The next time my daughter had an earache, with my doctor monitoring her, I helped by decreasing pasteurized dairy and concentrated juices and using the garlic oil drop. She never had an ear infection again.

From the use of natural remedies to becoming involved in natural childbirth and working for better birthing environments for parents, to participation in the organic food co-op movement, I slowly became part of a growing movement in our country to reclaim natural health. When I approached the age of forty, I decided to set aside my longtime dream of becoming a doctor; that dream was often overshadowed by my continual involvement in political issues and my passion for the politics of medicine and healing. I entered law school, hoping someday I might be involved in an alternative healing center or work in the area of natural health. I am grateful now that my background brought me to Calvin Johnson and farmer Herbert Saunders.

Initially, I jumped in to the analysis of the case wearing my mother hat instead of my attorney hat. "Well," I said, "of course it's legal to sell colostrum. It can't be defined as the *practice of medicine*! How else would mothers and sick people get fresh colostrum? Not everyone owns a cow!"

The irony was that I had been a nationally certified Lamaze instructor for a number of years. I had attended many births. I had been active with La Leche League, had nursed my own daughters, and had taught mothers and fathers the value of colostrum and early nursing. When I was growing up, my family had two milking cows on the farm; the value of colostrum and nursing was common knowledge.

But as I began the legal research on this case, I had to have my attorney hat firmly in place. I was appalled that the definition of the practice of medicine could be used to stop ordinary people from healing or giving healing advice. Minnesota law defined the practice of medicine to include anyone who "offers or undertakes to prevent or to diagnose, correct, or treat in any manner or by any means, methods, devices, or instrumentalities, any disease, illness, pain, wound, fracture, infirmity, deformity or defect of any person."[1] I imagined what the impact of this broad law must have been on all of Minnesota when the law was originally passed, decades ago. The seemingly innocuous statute slowly made its way into every health care setting in the state, potentially making criminals out of mothers, natural healers, and helpers, and allowing only medical doctors to practice any of the healing arts.

No wonder people eventually considered natural healing and alternative health care to be weird. The practices were not only weird; they were downright illegal. As I became increasingly aware of the impact of this law, I shivered at its ramifications, especially on the female population, who had always been the natural primary caretakers of the sick. It appeared that they were gradually relegated to caring for the sick at the behest of a licensed doctor, usually male.

Interestingly, the criminal law that Saunders had been charged under was passed in 1923, just three years after women obtained the right to vote. Who were the economic interest groups that might have lobbied to pass such legislation? How did women deal with this change? What about other segments of the culture, the Native American medicine men, the midwives, the herbalists, the homeopaths, the naturopaths? Were they all as vulnerable as Herb Saunders? Would that mean that my very own homeopath could be charged with practice of medicine without a license?

Because I, too, was from a farm in southern Minnesota, I was especially empathetic and saddened by the shame and hardship I knew these charges brought to Herb's farm family. However, I also knew how rural farm families and their friends and relatives stick together. They have a lot of common sense too. I knew that Herb was being flooded with support from family, friends, and neighbors while the State of Minnesota proceeded.

Calvin P. Johnson Esq.

In January of 1994 I had the legal memorandum ready for review; it would be the basis of the final brief. It was a cold and snowy night, the Minnesota roads were bad, and Calvin Johnson made his way to my office in Stillwater. This would be our first in-person meeting, although we had spent hours in conversation on the phone. I sat in my small office waiting, watching the snowstorm gather force.

My office was humble. I had not been able to afford furniture yet, so I had stacked two columns of boxes and put a door across them as a desktop. I had one chair. I pulled in a second one from another office to use for our meeting.

When Mr. Johnson finally arrived, he immediately sat down without taking off his heavy winter coat and began talking about the case. The photo that I had viewed of Mr. Johnson had not prepared me for the experience of his physical presence and energy. His bustling short robust stature and his darting blue eyes were just as intense as his phone presence. It seemed natural to this man, whom I had never met in person before, to sit right down amid my boxes and start talking, without skipping a beat, with intensity and laser focus on our case. An hour later, at the end of the review, he stood up, still with his coat on, and said, "I want you to be cocounsel on this case. I have no money to pay you right now. Think about it." Calvin Johnson had been chief public defender in Blue Earth County for over ten years; I was just getting started with my legal profession. What an opportunity for learning! I would be honored but needed to think about it. Then he headed back into the night and the cold for his drive back to Mankato.

As I drove home that night through the blustery snow, I felt the warmth and safety inside my car, like a soft blanket of stillness enveloping me, quiet enough to invoke in me a certain knowing. I remember it well. I was entering my destiny. The Saunders case ultimately led to my role as a leader in the health freedom movement in the United States and to the writing of this book about health freedom.

The past twenty years have given me continual opportunities to explore the different aspects of health freedom. As problems were presented to me, I had to delve into each new area of law affecting health freedom, from dietary supplement law, health claims, and the suppression of truthful speech, to international United Nations Codex Alimentarius meetings regulating vitamins across country borders, to licensed professionals losing their medical licenses for practicing holistic medicine, to pandemic flu laws and the right refuse vaccines, to parental rights to make health care decisions for their children, to truth in labeling legal concerns and the need for labeling of genetically modified foods and products, to notice laws for spraying of dangerous chemicals, and much more. *Health Freedom* is about my journey into the breadth of health freedom law and the general health freedom principles that I have observed along the way. I now offer these principles to you with the hope and belief that they will contribute to the overall health and well-being, and even the survival, of the human family.

Acknowledgments

I would like to acknowledge my many friends and family who took the time to read my writings and provide me comments over the course of the past fifteen years. The many starts and stops of versions were a sign of the ups and downs of the journey. Their willingness to give me straightforward feedback gave me the confidence to continue to pursue the desire to write a book about health freedom.

I would also like to acknowledge the first official editor of this book in 2016, Patricia Manzi, of New York, for her remarkable talent to give me line-by-line editing as well as subjective content direction for the story herein. Her guidance was immeasurably useful in my efforts to improve my writing and storytelling.

And I would like to acknowledge my daughter Theresa for her final comprehensive reorganizing and editing guidance and her overview of my book writings. Her clarification and extensive edits, showing me that I really had two books within my writings, one nonfiction and one memoir, were instrumental in helping me take the leap to write this first book, a nonfiction book, for my health freedom health seekers.

Finally, I would like to acknowledge those people involved in the substantive victories for health freedom mentioned herein, giving the world great news to write about and report as we work to preserve health freedom. You know who you are, in the trenches, working toward and reporting on the evolution of protection of health freedom in our country. You are my heroes.

Introduction

The world of medicine and technology is evolving at record speed. Historic and sometimes age-old healing knowledge and cultures are cast aside, forgotten, or marginalized as new medical technology, pharmaceuticals, and surgical procedures come into use. Along with the speedy development of technology come laws that are changing just as rapidly dealing with how the technology will affect people. We are now challenged with balancing how to retain protection of basic human rights and freedoms with our expectations, use, and interface with modern technology and health practices.

Health Freedom begins with the Farmer Saunders case and gives an introduction to the very simple, straightforward legal question of whether the US Constitution supports the concept that humans have a fundamental and inalienable right to make their own health care decisions, including the right to heal themselves and each other in ways that they themselves prefer. But this very basic question ripples out and leads us to asking the same question in almost every other area of law, including laws pertaining to environment, agriculture, food and drugs, telecommunications, advertisements and marketing, commerce, administrative agencies, and professional licensing, among many others.

No matter where you stand on human rights issues regarding health, you will notice that all areas of life and health law are affected by the expectation of individuals to have the right of self-determination, that is, to have a say in what they experience with their bodies.

Health Freedom explores the many ways that the right of self-determination in health matters is affected by the laws that have been enacted in our country. In the founding of our country, there was intense debate about the role of government in people's lives. The harsh history of personal sufferings under British rule was spelled out boldly in the Declaration of Independence. The very reason for establishing a new form of government was to create a government that would not lead to the oppression of individual people; equal opportunity for life, liberty, and the pursuit of happiness for everyone was the goal.

This vision of freedom was a defining characteristic of a new community. Out of debate came a founding premise that freedom is not a privilege given to people by governments or royal families; freedom arises out of a person's birth and existence and their participation in life's experiences and conversations among other humans.

After the Constitution was passed, the founders added ten amendments to the Constitution entitled the Bill of Rights. These additions address specific individual rights. They include a protectionary amendment, the Ninth, reminding everyone that all other inherent freedoms not listed are not to be infringed upon.

Amendment IX

The enumeration in the Constitution, of certain rights, shall not
be construed to deny or disparage others retained by the people.

Health freedom is a personal freedom that is not laid out in the Bill of Rights. Sadly, this freedom is now at the core of much upheaval and suffering in our country.

Over the years, working to protect health freedom, I developed my own understanding and definition of health freedom. It is this:

Health freedom is the internal and intentional steering mechanism within a person and within a community that guides us in life-and-death decisions. It is the freedom to make decisions for oneself and one's community about survival and health. It is rooted in the naturally occurring drive and commitment within people to keep themselves and their loved ones alive. Health freedom is a fundamental natural right of survival and personal sovereignty.

Americans exercise their health freedoms every day. For example, many Americans work to keep themselves and their families healthy by eating healthy foods each day. Many also use dietary supplements, including vitamins, minerals, and herbs. Access to dietary supplements was once in jeopardy in our country, but because of a very important law brought forth by citizens and passed in 1994 (the Dietary Supplement Health and Education Act), broad access to these products has been protected. If it weren't for those courageous citizens who worked hard to get those products taken out of the jurisdiction of restrictive drug law and put under the jurisdiction of food law, we would be like many other countries that treat vitamins like drugs without good access to these products. In the United States, dietary supplements are recognized as food and are generally regarded as safe. Government has to show harm before restricting access to them. International United Nations Codex Alimentarius meetings have attempted to make regulations to block large doses of vitamins and minerals, such as those we have access to in the United States, from being shipped between countries. But health freedom advocates and the National Health Federation attend these meetings on a regular basis and provide a strong voice for the values of American health freedom.

The areas of law and the people's stories in *Health Freedom* are very diverse. And basic principles of health freedom emerge throughout. Eventually I set forth these principles with examples of how each health freedom principle might apply in a particular situation.

Health Freedom describes the many areas where health freedoms are affected, especially focusing on the ability of people to have access to the practitioners and products they deem beneficial for their health, the protection of the right of persons to make their own health care decisions without coercion from outside sources, the right of practitioners to practice their professions, and the role that government has in our lives when it comes to the health of citizens and the act of making health care decisions. I will also discuss the overarching nature of freedom itself as an important ongoing conversation as our world evolves. As I have concluded: "Freedom is not something just to be had but, rather, something to be lived. Freedom is a conversation." May *Health Freedom* inspire you to live in health freedom and be an active participant in the health freedom conversation.

Chapter 1

The Arrest of Herbert Saunders

In June of 1993 five squad cars came out to the Saunders farm in Odin, Minnesota, to arrest Herb Saunders. A television news helicopter flew overhead as Herb worked in the field on his tractor. Nine state police officers came to Herb's farm that day with a search warrant. The officers called Herb into his house and interrogated him and his wife about his sale of colostrum to his dairy customers. The officers went through the farm and confiscated whole freezers full of bottles of colostrum that Herb was keeping for people who had been out to his farm. On the day of the raid, Herb's walk-in freezer was left open and the generator burned out.

What had Herb Saunders done? He had sold colostrum from his dairy farm to local people for addressing their health concerns, a practice he had engaged in for many years. But the state was claiming that he was practicing medicine without a license; committing swindle and fraud; and being cruel to animals. Before that day, the Federal Drug Administration had investigated Herb for two years but found no jurisdiction. Then the Minnesota Bureau of Criminal Apprehensions investigated Herb, including sending a local undercover agent to his farm posing as a person with lung cancer. The undercover agent was wired for sound. Two investigators sat in their car, two miles down the gravel road, listening to the tape-recorded conversations. During one visit, the state sent a local physician, also wired for sound, in with the undercover agent to draw the undercover agent's blood to give to Herb to put into a pregnant cow. Herb would inject the person's blood into a cow's udder and then collect the cow's colostrum for use to help the person get well. The undercover agent had purchased the cow from Herb with state funds.

1

Herb had learned how to work with his cows to strengthen their colostrum's immunological strength, a practice he had learned from academic researchers. Colostrum is the first three days of serum milk that a mother cow provides right after she gives birth to her calf, before her regular milk comes in. The first milk colostrum is essential in programming the immune system of offspring to fight against disease long term. Pregnant cows naturally develop antibodies to organisms that they are in contact with in their environment, and they produce antibodies in their colostrum to those organisms for their offspring. When offspring ingest the first milk colostrum, they are then protected from the things in their environment that might otherwise cause them illness.

Researchers have learned to stimulate a cow to produce antibodies to any disease-causing organism by injecting the organism into a cow's udder and then collecting the colostrum for use against that organism.[1] Herb, who had learned this process and discussed how the process could be applied to human health, had gained a good reputation for providing strong "immune colostrum" to people who were seeking it.

The First Trial

The big old courtroom of Watonwan County, Minnesota, was toasty warm on a subzero February day in 1995. Cocounsel Calvin Johnson and I were prepared and sitting at the front of the courtroom at the huge oak counsel table with our client Herbert Cecil Saunders, waiting for proceedings to begin. We were defending this dairy farmer on the criminal charges of practicing medicine without a license, swindle, fraud, and cruelty to animals. Since the raid, Herb was out of jail on bail.

What had Herb Saunders done? He had worked to produce hyperimmune colostrum from his dairy cows and had sold it to people for their ailments, including cancer, multiple sclerosis, AIDS, arthritis, asthma, and immune diseases. It was obvious to Herb's customers that he was not holding himself out as a doctor or practicing medicine like a licensed physician. He did not call himself a doctor or wear a white coat. He was a simple dairy farmer. And he was selling his cow's colostrum to people who had remarkable results in terms of their ailments, many of them serious

2

conditions. It was disingenuous to accuse Herb of swindling people out of their money since many of the customers often came back to his farm and because his lifestyle was simple with extremely meager accommodations. Herb had a big heart. He took good care of his dairy cows. Since there were no known victims of the alleged crimes Herb had been charged with, the state actually advertised for victims. Herb Saunders was taken to trial based on the statement of one alleged victim, an undercover agent.

I was asked to join the efforts of the criminal case team to draft a constitutional brief to protect this dairy farmer healer. In addition to my legal career, my degrees in chemistry and medical technology would prove helpful. The brief would attempt to protect the rights of citizens to make their own health choices and the rights of Minnesota farmers to sell the nutritious products from their farms.

We prepared the defense for Herb Saunders for two years. Some of the most memorable experiences during our trial preparations were of meeting with our amazing experts and listening to their stories about life and work.

Our meeting with Dr. Hugh Fudenberg was one such experience. In May 1994, Mr. Johnson's secretary booked me on a train to South Carolina with attorney Johnson and Herb Saunders. We were going to have an expert witness interview with Dr. Hugh Fudenberg. I was honored to be given the opportunity to meet *the* Dr. Fudenberg, the Pasteur Award–winning, internationally acclaimed top immunologist in the world.

My role would be to review medical records with Calvin while traveling on the train. The records were of people who had been healed by Herb's colostrum. I would also be part of the interview with Dr. Fudenberg.

It was on the train that I learned Calvin was from a farm in Wisconsin. He talked about his family and his ancestors and of how his young wife had died of cancer just three years before. Their son was now twelve, and his daughter was eight years old. During our train conversations, we shared a deep motivation to expand the options that people have for healing beyond the conventional medical system. Those conversations in the train observation deck were anchor points for me. The long train ride also enabled me to learn much from Herb about the complexity of the process that he used to provide people with the colostrum they wanted. The history of colostrum therapy and the process have since been memorialized and described in detail by former New York State legislator Dan Haley in his book *Politics in Healing.*[2]

Calvin and Herb had brought a large trunk aboard the train that held volumes of medical records, charts, and histories of patients who had used colostrum. I read then about many special people who had been deathly sick and who had recovered. The papers included incredible testimonies of the people who had visited Herb's farm. The medical charts included people who had extensive medical surgery, an array of medications, bad blood counts, abnormal blood chemistries, and a lot of pain, and who had been helped by Herb. Some had a diagnosis of MS; others, of diabetes; and others, of cancer. It was amazing.

One obvious absence in the medical records was that of knowledgeable comments or notes by the medical doctors about the colostrum alternative their patients were using. Oftentimes, a patient did not tell their doctor about the colostrum they were using.

Cal and I had to match a patient's personal notes about when they secured colostrum from Herb and when they took it, with the dates in the medical records in order to follow the patterns. In some records in which it was indicated that the medical doctor knew of the use of alternatives, there were comical or cynical comments written by the doctor. There were rarely doctor comments when wellness was achieved.

I remember in particular one case record describing a man who had severe erythrocythemia, the making of too many red blood cells. His condition was so severe that he had been having a pint of blood taken every week in an effort to keep the number of red blood cells down and keep him alive. When he used the colostrum, as noted in the medical record, his need to have his blood drawn decreased. Within three months, he no longer needed to have his blood drawn at all, but there was no comment in the medical chart of the reason or even curiosity about the cure.

The cross-country train ride gave Calvin and me an opportunity to discuss the individual cases and talk about the theme of Herb's court case. Calvin was committed to putting forth the truth about the power of immune colostrum, including the scientific underpinnings and testimonials from cured individuals.

We switched trains in Chicago with sleeper cars and arrived in Spartanburg, South Carolina, at 4:30 a.m. the following day. The meeting with Dr. Fudenberg was to be that very morning. Calvin, Herb, and I met in the hotel lobby and decided to walk to Dr. Fudenberg's office, which was not too many blocks away. When we arrived, we were surprised: the office was completely boarded up with crisscross planks. It looked as if the building had been condemned. We were confused.

Within minutes, a car pulled up next to the curb: it was the head homicide detective of the Minnesota Bureau of Criminal Apprehensions. Having had no idea he would be there, we were increasingly confused.

The detective rolled down his window and motioned to us. He said he knew where Dr. Fudenberg was and offered to drive us to the doctor's location. He explained that he knew we were going to interview Dr. Fudenberg and requested that we allow him to observe the interview and give him permission to tape it. He had brought along from Minnesota all the taping equipment necessary, which was in the trunk of his car. He did not offer any explanation as to why he had shown up there, why the building was boarded up, or how he knew the location of Dr. Fudenberg.

Calvin stepped back and took Herb and me aside for a moment to assess what to do. This was a star witness for us; we had every right to decline the request from the Minnesota Bureau detective. On the other hand, Calvin had a profound desire to get the truth out about colostrum and Herb's work. He thought it would be good for the detective to hear for himself from a world-renowned scientist the truth of what Herb was doing and how people had gotten cured, even if it was before the trial. And it would be good to have it on tape. Calvin decided we should agree to the request.

Calvin approached the detective's car again and let him know of our decision. Then we all got in the car, and the detective escorted us out of town to a small remote rambler where we would find Dr. Fudenberg.

As we entered the home, I was shocked to see the small humble surroundings for this world-famous immunologist. Having only seen photographs of Dr. Fudenberg when he was a young scientist, I was humbled and honored as he entered the room, a weathered dignified elder moving slowly with shoulders bent and thick round-rimmed glasses. After introductions and an explanation for the presence of the detective and his videotaping equipment, Dr. Fudenberg graciously agreed and led us into his office at the end of the hallway.

His office was a small room with a large desk and a long leather couch; the walls were covered with plaques and awards of all kinds. Herb, Calvin, and I sat next to each other on the couch directly in front of the imposing desk. A chair was brought in for Mr. Berg, the detective.

The video camera was set up, and the interview proceeded with Calvin directing the questions. Dr. Fudenberg was extremely articulate and forthright about his work involving the immune system. He showed us a short film he had produced explaining how the various T cells and B cells, along with many other cells, work together in a complex way in the immune system to maintain balance in the body. He enthusiastically shared his knowledge about the immune system with us. A profound four-hour tape of the interview is available in our archival files; it includes a discussion of colostrum and cancer. That day we learned in fact how and why the people who came to Herb's farm had gotten better. And we were glad that the detective had heard such explanations of the truth of this colostrum process. We returned home confident in our use of the defense of truth at the upcoming trial.

When the trial finally began, we had our national experts travel to Minnesota to prove to the jury the truth of the efficacy of the colostrum healing method. We spent five days picking a full twelve-person felony jury.

Much to our shock, before the jury was sworn in, the State of Minnesota notified the court that it had dropped all charges against Herb Saunders, except the charge of practicing medicine without a license. Since the charges of swindle, fraud, and cruelty to animals were dropped, the defense of truth would no longer be needed. The state argued that the testimonies of our experts was no longer relevant because they would not be relevant to the legal elements of the remaining charge, practice of medicine without a license.

The remaining charge was based on a portion of the Minnesota Medical Practice Act, which defines the practice of medicine in part as follows:

> For purposes of this chapter [147.081], a person not exempted under section 147.09 is "practicing medicine" or engaged in the "practice of medicine" if the person does any of the following: ...
>
> (3) offers or undertakes to prevent or to diagnose, correct, or treat in any manner or by any means, methods, devices, or instrumentalities, any disease, illness, pain, wound fracture, infirmity, deformity or defect of any person.

The law was so broad that it could include anyone, such as people offering medical treatments in the conventional health care world and also regular citizens with vocations in other healing practices such as herbalists, homeopaths, and traditional naturopaths. The language of the law was so broad that it could even mean a person giving comfort to another, such as offering chicken soup to a neighbor when he is sick. It was at the moment when the other charges were dropped that we came to know the magnitude of what we were up against. The whole dynamic of the trial changed. It became an intense battle and a fight for the freedom to heal.

We worked to get our experts on the stand to educate the jury about what was really happening on Herb Saunders's farm and how people could have recovered from such serious health conditions, but the testimonies of our experts were continually cut off as not being relevant to the definition of the practice of medicine. Calvin and I continued to help our experts have the opportunity to get as much testimony into the record as possible amid objections.

I found myself in that big St. James courtroom assisting the unfolding of an incredible story—a story that made me wish the whole world could hear it. Could it be true that the basic act of healing itself was relegated to only a few, those who were licensed physicians? My medical training, legal training, and personal journey now needed to come together to protect freedom and truth. The cured people were there, silently watching the trial, often tearful. They watched their friend Herb be ridiculed and discredited—a healer treated like a common criminal. The lay witnesses were not allowed to take the stand on Herb's behalf or talk about their cures to the jury. We diligently made offers of proof for these witnesses, but the jury never had the opportunity to hear their stories.

The intellectual warfare taking place in that courtroom was intense, but I found moments to look around myself and absorb the blessings of the illumined faces of the Minnesota natives. I let myself feel the warmth of their presence amid the weathered hues of the courtroom and the hot clanging water radiators. I remembered my farmer elders and my childhood on the farm on the plains of Minnesota.

Our experts in the case were powerful testimonies to the dilemma that Herb was in under this very broad law. Dr. Regelson, our nationally known oncologist expert witness and author of over two hundred cancer and immunology research articles, shared with the jury that he thought our farmer was a hero. Former congressman Bedell testified that Herb should not be convicted of making illegal claims that something can help someone be well because colostrum is not a drug but is milk—food—and that drugs need to get approved before their manufacturers may make health claims. And it takes millions of dollars to get a new drug approved. Berkley Bedell had worked with Congress to establish the new Federal Advisory Board on Alternative Medicine. He said he would never have been able to be cured of his Lyme disease without Herb's colostrum. Dr. Fudenberg had published more than eight hundred articles on immunology and was a leader in the international immunology research community. He testified that he used colostrum transfer factors for remarkable cures and said that colostrum transfer factors were used in China on six million people to prevent hepatic cancer. Dr. Clifford in Colorado, formerly employed in the United States military, testified about bacteria and the workings of the immune system. Dr. Herbert Struss from the Department of Agriculture explained to the jury that colostrum and its effect on the immune system is our survival organism rather than simply nutrition for our young and that its role in the development of a strong, long-lasting immune system is crucial. His vast research regarding colostrum brought him to the conclusion that our knowledge of colostrum is small like Columbus's vision of North America. Dr. Struss produced hyperimmune milk and a journal focusing on immune milk thirty years before the trial, and the process was patented at the University of Minnesota, where he worked. Later the patent was sold to a company in Iowa because of the political climate at the university. The trial involved an immense amount of information.

The jury deliberated two days, and then the judge called a mistrial, ending the case with a hung jury. We considered the result a victory.

We read in the newspaper the following day that one of the jurors was a schoolteacher who understood that the Minnesota definition of practicing medicine was so broad that she could feasibly be prosecuted for putting a Band-Aid on a student's knee. She refused to convict Herb for two days until the judge called a hung jury mistrial.

Certified Question for Appeal

After the trial, the State of Minnesota threatened to bring Herb to trial again. But we were concerned that the law regarding practicing medicine was both so broad that anyone could be accused criminally and unconstitutional. So, we explored options and decided to prepare a motion to the district court to certify constitutional questions to be presented to the Minnesota Appeals Court to give the higher court an opportunity to review the constitutionality of the statute in case we faced trial a second time.

District court judge Dempsey denied our motion to certify the questions of freedom of speech, privacy, and liberty; about the Ninth Amendment; and about the Farmers Amendment, protecting a farmer who seeks to sell the products of their farm without a medical license. But Judge Dempsey did certify the questions as to whether the law was vague or whether the law was overbroad. The certified questions were sent to the appeals court.

The appeals court reviewed the law and ruled that the law was not too vague and, thus, the statute was constitutional. But the appeals court declined to review the issue of whether the statute was overly broad in its wording. The appeals court indicated that in order to rule on the topic of overbreadth, it typically would need to address the issue of freedom of speech. And the lower district court had denied our request to certify review of freedom of speech, so the appeals court did not have the issue of freedom of speech in front of it. Thus, the issue of whether the language of the law was written too broadly was not addressed.

The appeals court sent our case back down for retrial. The news media missed the significance of the appeals court's ruling and its lack of decision about overbreadth, saying the law was constitutional and not vague, and not mentioning the overbreadth dilemma.

Second Trial

After the appeals court ruling, the state announced it would retry the case.

The second time we were more seasoned warriors. We began to prepare for another battle. The charge was again practice of medicine without a license. We had received strict orders from Judge Dempsey that we were not to talk about the efficacy of using colostrum for cure, that the law did not care what the substance or method of healing was and that cure and knowledge of colostrum were irrelevant to whether Herb was practicing medicine without a license.

We had gotten permission to bring in experts to testify as to whether they thought a person doing similar behaviors as Herb was practicing medicine. We expected the experts to change the whole dynamic of the trial. We were up in the large courtroom again, but this time the winter had passed, the trees were budding, and the jurors were anxious to get in the fields and plant their crops.

We began by bringing forward some of our former expert witnesses because of their knowledge about the behaviors that Herb was doing, and to demonstrate that these were not the practice of medicine behaviors similar to what a licensed physician would be doing. Dr. Struss described the practice of immunizing cows and the concept of how we all are naturally immunized in many ways in our daily lives. Dr. Struss explained that creating immune milk is a natural process and that it can be enhanced to make specific immune milk. Dr. Struss had owned a dairy farm years before and produced immune milk from his cows and sold it in grocery stores in Minnesota. It was known especially to help people with arthritis. He even had a copy of a legislative journal that recognized his work producing immune colostrum. He was not allowed to speak about the benefits of immune milk.

Dr. Regelson came back to testify because he had been the director of the Virginia Commonwealth University Medical School's oncology department and he had extensive experience teaching medical students. He was able to describe what it looks like to practice medicine as a doctor. He taught students how to be cancer doctors and about the role of supportive healing people in patients' lives to aid in the process of healing. Dr. Regelson said a person such as Herb was participating in healing behaviors but was definitely not practicing medicine as thought of in the Medical Practice Act of Minnesota.

The state's expert witness, Dr. Goodman, indicated that the more knowledge a person has and the more she acts on that knowledge to obtain a cure, the more likely that she is practicing medicine under the Minnesota statute, even if it is healing of herself. On cross-examination, my cocounsel and lead attorney Calvin Johnson suggested that possibly ignorance is bliss. Dr. Goodman said that a person doing similar behaviors as those done by Herb is practicing medicine and that only doctors could do these behaviors without being prosecuted. However, Dr. Goodman did not know of any doctors working with cows to provide immune colostrum.

We believed it was important to call an expert witness who did not have a vested interest in the definition of the parameters of the practice of medicine. We called Dr. Ray DeVries, a medical sociologist from St. Olaf College in Northfield, Minnesota. Dr. DeVries explained to the jury that citizens make laws to divide up the task of healing and that these laws are made in the context of political and social forces. He said that a person doing similar actions as those done by Herb Saunders is participating in the tasks of healing and not practicing medicine under a Physicians and Surgeons statute.

The second trial was powerful. It focused squarely on the heart of the issue: the difference between the practice of healing by ordinary citizens and the practice of medicine. The secondary theme was that of medical choice. We worked to portray the practice of healing as those actions that are part of the experience of being human, inalienable rights that people engage in that are generally regarded as safe, along with the fact that not all healing is the practice of medicine. Examples would be herbalism, homeopathy, traditional natural healing arts, and cultural traditions such as offering chicken soup. We also argued that the broad legal definition of the practice of medicine made it seem as if all those healers could be prosecuted unfairly.

A significant event occurred that allowed us to put our cured lay witnesses on the stand. The state had attempted to destroy Herb's character by making statements such as "snake oil salesman" and "scam artist." We brought the plain witnesses forward to repair Herb's character. Again, we had strict orders from Judge Dempsey that the witnesses were not to talk about their "cures." But they could tell the jury how they had met Herb. The jurors astutely listened as witness after witness took the stand, all of them describing their search for medical options for survival after exhausting all other avenues and eventually finding Herb. They vouched for him in terms far from derogatory.

After the closing arguments, the jury deliberated for two days. The jury sent a total of nine messages to the judge for clarification, including questions such as "Can we have the definition of practicing medicine from the law book?" and "Can we have the definition of practicing healing?" and statements such as "If we decide by the law solely, our decision will be different than if we base it on the testimony we heard during the trial. If we are to decide on the law only, it would seem that the testimony was useless." They also said, "We can reach a decision, but some of us would have to go against our beliefs. Is that what you want? We want to be able to live with our decision." Finally, at the end of the second day, the jury was deadlocked and Judge Dempsey once again called a hung jury mistrial. We considered it a victory.

Dismissal

In the days following the second hung jury, our tenacity did not waver. We were ready to go at it again pro bono if the state so chose. And then we received the news. The charge of practicing medicine without a license against Herbert Cecil Saunders was dropped by the State of Minnesota on May 28, 1996, three years after Herb's arrest.

This marked the end of just one chapter in the story of preserving our right to heal ourselves in the way we see fit. Herb Saunders was a necessary eruption in the controversial paradigm shift of the healing world.

For us, this was only the beginning. There was no going back. The truth about our lack of health freedom demanded a voice. The law in Minnesota was still active and overly broad, threatening Herb and a myriad of healers across the state.

During our three-year trial, we had protected Herb against an unjust law. We had asserted that we as Americans have the right to survive, including the right to choose the way in which we heal ourselves and the right to choose the people who help us heal ourselves.

In addition, I had also learned that there was a potential cure for a damaged immune system, and that cure needed to be freed from political bondage. My life experience had perfectly brought me to this trial.

This case brought all of these experiences together and gave me the foundation for the challenge that came next: changing the law in Minnesota.

At the trial in Wantonwon County. *Left to right*, veterinarian expert witness Dr. Tony Eckstein, farmer Herb Saunders, Dr. Hugh Fudenberg, attorney Calvin Johnson, former congressman Berkley Bedell (Iowa), and attorney Diane Miller.

Chapter 2

Changing the Minnesota Law

I had worked on the Saunders case for almost three years. Five days after the Saunders charges had been dropped, I received a call from an attorney in Minneapolis who had heard that Dr. Helen Healy, a local doctor of naturopathic medicine, had been served cease and desist papers by the State Board of Medical Practice for practicing medicine without a license!

When I heard those words, *practicing medicine without a license*, I cringed. My first thought was that this case might be even harder to win than the Saunders case because this case was civil instead of criminal, which would mean a lower court's standard of proof. In addition, it was presumed that the plaintiff called herself a doctor, which Herb Saunders had not done.

Since no clients had been harmed, I viewed this as another turf battle in the healing arts. Once again, consumers were going to suffer by having their natural health options restricted.

Although Helen Healy had already retained an attorney, there was no question that I would be responding to this case in some form or other. I contacted Calvin Johnson, and we agreed that we could prepare an intervening case on behalf of Helen Healy's patients if a patient were to come forward who wanted to assert their right to access her services.

Calvin and I knew that the only way to stop these prosecutions and persecutions of healers was to find legal avenues that would protect the rights of consumers to access healers of their own choice. Ideally, I knew we needed new protective laws for the practitioners. Since we didn't have time to go to the legislature to change the law before this new case, my job was to assist in this pending court case on behalf of the consumers.

In addition to the involvement in the immediate Healy matter, Calvin and I were determined to reform the bigger picture of unfair prosecutions of healers. We began the work of establishing a new nonprofit organization to offer information to the public about alternative health.*

Healy Hearings

On August 21, 1996, the first public hearing of the Healy case was held. The consumer movement had been mobilized, and they showed up in numbers. A public rally was scheduled to be held outside the courthouse before the hearing began. I arranged to meet the plaintiff, who had come forward for our intervening case before the rally.

There were more than three hundred activists gathered. Powerful speeches about health freedom were given. One of the speakers was Senator Janet Johnson. Her words were filled with both common sense and eloquence. She was candid and direct. She told the story of a family member who suffered from severe asthma. One year, her father purchased bees and became a bee farmer. As a result, the family began enjoying their own honey. By

---

* We wanted to change the law and bring the healing arts and trades back into the public domain. Our first step in bringing more public awareness to the issue was to found a nonprofit corporation to promote alternative health and to protect alternative health practitioners' rights to practice. We named it NOAH, the National Organization for Alternative Health, Legal Defense and Education Fund.

NOAH's founding board of directors included former congressman Berkley Bedell, who had been cured of Lyme disease by Herb's colostrum and who had testified at Herb's trial. Congressman Bedell had been instrumental in setting up the first Office of Alternative Medicine in the federal government after having been transformed by his own healing.

The board also included Dr. Tony Eckstein, a native Minnesota veterinarian; Mr. Jerry Grings, the father of a young woman who had been cured of permanent disabilities by the use of immune colostrum; Dr. Janice Henry, a southern Minnesota medical doctor interested in alternative care; Dr. Jacob Mirman, an internal medicine doctor practicing homeopathy in Minnesota; Carol Hamilton, an administrative assistant and homeopath; and Herbert Struss, PhD, the scientist who had done the original research in Minnesota on immune colostrum in the 1950s and 1960s.

the end of the year, and to their surprise, her sibling's asthma disappeared. The senator explained that since the honey was from local flowers near their home, it provided immunity against the local pollen allergens. She said this was the reason why she became involved in alternative health. She was a dedicated senator and spoke of a bill that she was carrying before the Minnesota Legislature to demand a study by the State of Minnesota on complementary and alternative medicine. Ultimately, she wanted alternative practices to be more available to consumers. I was excited to hear about her work.

After the speeches, the crowd moved to the Ramsey County courthouse. The judge entered and made a few brief remarks, including encouraging the parties to work out their differences ahead of time, then set the case for a contested hearing on October 3.*

Finding My People

Back at my law office, I made a commitment to myself to meet more of the freedom activists in the metro area and to find the support that I needed to make the vision of health freedom a legal reality. I needed to find a community of support.

No matter the outcomes of Helen's and Herb's cases, the most frustrating thing for me was the injustice of not allowing citizens to heal each other when there had been no harm done to clients. These honest, helpful persons and professionals were being stopped from practicing their vocations during a time when these very vocations were needed to turn the tide of chronic disease and to teach people age-old wisdom and holistic means to wellness.

That night, I went to the community meeting for the Healy supporters. I told the group my conviction that all healers, not just naturopathic physicians,

---

* Contested hearings are hearings that are held when the parties cannot reach an agreed-upon solution and the case then needs to go to a formal trial with evidence exhibits, witnesses, and testimony. Setting a date in the future gives the parties time to work out their differences. If they do come to an agreement, they can then sign a stipulated agreement and have the judge sign it as an order, thereby avoiding going to trial.

should be free to practice as long as they were not being fraudulent or causing harm.

After the meeting, two of the women from the group came over and introduced themselves. They were Jerri Johnson and Nancy Hone. They were both RNs, now homeopaths. Nancy had been tracking the Saunders case. I was very surprised and happy to meet someone who was interested in the case and had followed it. After that night, I felt renewed energy, a new ray of hope, knowing that I was not alone in my quest. With a concerted effort, the Saunderses and the Healys of the world would surely be accessible to me as a health care consumer when I wanted them or needed them. I would help make sure they had the freedom to practice.

Back in the office that week, I received another call for help from a well-known medical doctor and author whose name I need to treat as confidential. He had been served papers for, among other things, departing from or failing to conform to the minimal standards of acceptable and prevailing medical practice. I couldn't believe a well-known medical doctor was being investigated who was considered an expert in his field. I advised this good doctor to stay with the attorney who had represented him in the past. But it was another sign of the need for legal support for holistic health doctors and practitioners.

Need to Change the Law

In September 1996, I completed the preparation of the motion to intervene in Helen Healy's case. We were ready to proceed. Then on September 26, before we filed our motion papers, word came by phone from Healy's attorney that the case had been settled out of court. We would not need to file the motion to intervene after all. Helen Healy was free under a stipulated conditional agreement. She would be able to practice in a limited capacity as a naturopath under the agreement, which was signed by the judge, according to what the Minnesota Medical Board would allow her to do. But the broad law would remain in place for everyone else.

We still needed to change the law!

Meetings continued to be held by Helen Healy supporters focusing on how to protect practitioners like Helen Healy in the future so that her colleagues could also practice and so she would not have to practice under a narrow stipulated agreement. These supporters planned to work to get naturopathic physicians licensed in the state of Minnesota.

But I was not comfortable with their plan to obtain licensure for naturopathic physicians because I did not want to have all naturopaths in Minnesota be required to go to a particular government-endorsed medical school to become medical naturopathic doctors. There were so many nonmedical traditional naturopaths and herbalists who had secured their education from a wide variety of educational programs and who did not use the title of doctor and did not participate in any medical procedures.

I had read over the Minnesota professional licensing laws and realized that the way licensing laws are written, licensure gives a particular group of people who go to particular schools permission from the state to practice a profession that is broadly defined and described in statute, just like the definition of practice of medicine. Licensing laws also give exclusive permission to use specific titles for that profession. Those persons without the license would not be able to practice that broadly defined profession or use any of the listed exclusive titles. Persons without a license would end up like Herb Saunders, being charged criminally with practicing without a license.

If the naturopathic physicians were to be licensed, it would provide a new law that would allow for an unlicensed naturopath to be criminally charged for practicing without a license. Not only would the unlicensed naturopaths be charged with the practice of medicine without a license under existing law, but also, more specifically, they would be charged with the practice of naturopathy without a license. They could also be charged under a new law for the use of the title *naturopath* or the term *naturopathy* in their practices.

The naturopathic bill being promoted for licensure would be restrictive to many kinds of unlicensed natural health practitioners and healers such as herbalists and homeopaths because it would allow only licensed naturopathic physicians to practice many natural health modalities and systems such as the use of "food, food extracts, vitamins, minerals, amino

19

acids, enzymes, digestive aids … [and] homeopathic preparations."[1] The bill also had language prohibiting the use of the terms *naturopath* and *naturopathy.*

Safe Harbor Exemption Support

Minnesota has a large number of naturopaths, herbalists, and homeopaths, and many other types of practitioners, who use only natural substances and practices and who do not use conventional medical treatments such as prescription drugs and surgery. During this time Minnesota had only a small number of naturopaths who were trained medically and wished to be licensed as physicians by the state. If one group of naturopaths were to be licensed, then all the other practitioners from a wide variety of schools of naturopathy would be put out of business.

Rather than licensure, I thought we should simply create an exemption to the Medical Practice Act for those unlicensed healers who were not committing fraud or hurting anyone. In that way, all practitioners could practice.

My newfound friends, who were not only healers but also activists in the politics of natural health, were eager to begin a new project as health freedom advocates. We set the goal to protect access to all different kinds of healers and to prohibit their unwarranted prosecution. We began by researching the laws. We soon confirmed that licensure was the most restrictive type of regulation available for occupations; it could lead to the exclusive use of titles and the shutting down of thousands of wonderful healing practitioners. We wanted to design a better solution to protect access to all healers.

We called a meeting of citizens who were speaking up to voice their concerns about the impact of proposed licensing on other unlicensed healers such as traditional naturopaths, herbalists, homeopaths, nutritional consultants, and energy healers. About twenty persons attended, some seasoned activists, some practitioners wanting protection, and some citizens wanting their access to their practitioner protected. We discussed the simple concept of exemption from licensing requirements for those healers who were not licensed and who did not pose any harm to the public. A straightforward exemption law would preserve access to the practitioner and practice of one's choice, and the right of healers to practice as long as they posed no harm by avoiding performing certain prohibited acts such as administering prescriptions drugs, puncturing the skin, or doing surgery. We also wanted to protect licensed practitioners such as medical doctors who were already practicing complementary and alternative medicine approaches and were being investigated for practicing holistic medicine.

After our position was solidified to oppose licensure for noninvasive healers, our next task was to defeat the proposed licensing bill that had been introduced into the legislature by the naturopathic physician licensing advocates. Our group members went to the state capitol, where we learned how to do grassroots lobbying, attended hearings, and testified in opposition to licensing. We learned a lot about the political process and worked hard to defeat the licensing bill. Finally, at the end of a very important hearing, the licensing bill was tabled and would not be moving forward in the session.

Our original group began to grow. Even after the licensing bill was tabled, our members spent a lot of time at the Capitol Building getting to know the legislators and the legislative process. We learned that Senator Janet Johnson, who had given a speech at the rally to support Helen Healy's cause, continued to consider other solutions in support of natural health. Thanks to her efforts as a strong senator and natural health advocate, she had sponsored a bill to study complementary and alternative health care. The bill had passed and was signed into law at the end of the 1996–1997 session.

The Study of Complementary Medicine in Minnesota

The new law authorized the Minnesota Department of Health (MDH) to conduct a study based on existing literature, information, and data on the scope of complementary medicine in Minnesota.[2] As part of the lengthy list of study topics in the bill, the commissioner of health was mandated to make recommendations on whether or not the state should credential or regulate any of the complementary medicine providers. The commissioner was to appoint an Advisory Council Task Force to provide expertise and advice.

The council was to include health care providers, including providers of complementary medicine; health plan companies; and consumers. An appropriation of $20,000 was provided. The commissioner was to report the task force findings by January 15, 1998.

We requested that a consumer and a practitioner be on the task force. Jerri Johnson, our activist and homeopath, was invited by MDH to be on the task force. We hoped that the study would support our new concept to create an exemption to current violation laws and allow practice by unlicensed health care practitioners and natural healers.

The Study Advisory Council Task Force met with the Minnesota Department of Health staff and public meetings were held. Some task force members had strong biases toward one type of healing over another or one type of health care delivery system over another, or even toward specific financing allowances for health care. At the end of a series of meetings, the task force garnered agreement on some recommendations that our group thought were reasonable. When the recommendations were published, we saw that there was some understanding of our position. The report, entitled *Complementary Medicine: A Report to the Legislature*,[3] is available online.

The final MDH report is one hundred three pages of important comprehensive information about complementary and alternative medicine, including a glossary of terms. We cited the report at the Capitol Building a number of times to support our work to promote our complementary and alternative health exemption bill. The section of the report we used reads as follows:

> Freedom of practice legislation, which allows providers to
> continue providing services as long as the service is not shown
> to be dangerous or harmful, should be considered as a possible
> alternative to licensure or registration when appropriate. This
> may require making some changes in the Medical Practices Act
> or other licensure laws or health practice acts.[4]

Minnesota Natural Health Coalition Is Born

In the spring of 1997, our small group working for health freedom, having gained official organizational status, founded the political fund called

Minnesota Natural Health Coalition Action Network. The establishment of the Minnesota Natural Health Coalition Action Network was a political start toward our legislative goal. We were able to lobby but were unable to accept corporate donations. We soon understood that we needed a legal platform through which we could accept donations, both from individuals and from corporations.

We made plans to become a Minnesota-based educational nonprofit and seek 501(c)(3) federal tax status. We decided on the name, Minnesota Natural Health Coalition (MNHC), and the organization was incorporated on August 11, 1997. Its first board members were Leo Cashman, accountant; Lyman H. Coult, traditional naturopath; and President Marillyn Beyer, nurse.

Nancy Hone, with her great passion and ability to mobilize the forces, wanted to start having open educational meetings with speakers to educate the public about our movement. Our good friend and supporter Dr. Keith Sehnert said we could hold our public meetings in the basement of the church he attended.

We organized the first public meeting for August 4, 1997, right before we filed our incorporation papers. We invited a well-known health freedom advocate from New York, Monica Miller, to speak. She was completely inspiring. I remember sitting in the audience listening intently to every word she said. It was during this speech that she said words that resonated deeply with my own being:

> Regular people like you and me, we can make laws. We really can. And when you say we are going to do this for ourselves and our children, and all these people, this isn't a law about a trade organization. This will be a law about people's rights, about how we can determine, according to our own belief system, how we will deal with illness and health.[5]

Monica's words gave me the personal confidence that I needed as a regular citizen to participate in the lawmaking and lobbying process itself.

The discussions about what to submit to the MDH task force had forced us to clarify the hard-core legal issues of what kind of exemption we wanted.

We decided for sure that we did not want to have a mandatory permit or registration requirement for all healers.

I spent many hours drafting different versions of what would eventually be called the Minnesota Freedom of Access to Complementary and Alternative Health Care Act. During those months, October through December, I generated fourteen different drafts of our bill. The input I received was invaluable. I was grateful anytime a local attorney volunteered to help.

1998 Session: Bill Draft Concepts Finalized

The 1998 legislative session began in January, and although we were not ready to introduce our own bill, the group needed to be vigilant to make sure that the naturopathic physician bill did not move forward again. After having learned that the naturopathic doctor licensing bill was resurrected and still alive in early January 1998, our group began working hard to defeat it. We were worried that if the licensing bill were to pass, it would be difficult for us to move forward with an exemption bill. In early February, I was asked to draft protective amendments to put on the licensing bill to exempt unlicensed healers from the naturopathic licensing bill just in case the bill did get close to passing. We never needed those amendments! On February 12, the licensing bill was withdrawn.

Stopping the naturopathic licensing bill from going forward again allowed us to lay a broader foundation for health freedom. It was essential to our vision for health freedom in Minnesota. We were clear that we were not opposed to licensing naturopathic physicians as long as the unlicensed practitioners would be able to practice too. Since the licensing bill did not allow for such an exemption, we were relieved that the bill was stopped.

One question that continually arose in our group discussions was whether our bill should be limited to the protection of practitioners who were not licensed health care professionals or if we should also include a section in the bill to allow holistic medical doctors to practice without fear of losing their licenses for practicing holistic unconventional or alternative approaches with their patients.

There had been legal cases where holistic dentists and doctors were investigated for practicing alternative treatments. One such case was that of Doctor Stanislaw Burzynski in Texas. He had cured a young Minnesota boy of a brain tumor. We had met the boy's mother. The Texas Medical Board had investigated the physician. We wanted to make sure to protect consumer access to these professionals. In the end, we decided to draft a bill with two sections, one for each group, namely, the licensed holistic professionals and the unlicensed practitioners. I contacted attorneys from around the country to review the language of our proposal; four replied with excellent feedback.

There was not a lot of hope from persons living outside of Minnesota that we would ever pass an exemption for unlicensed practitioners, but there seemed to be belief that the section for licensed professionals would pass. That type of medical bill had already passed in a number of states other than Minnesota thanks to Monica Miller's work. We kept both sections in the bill.*

Finally—a wonderful feeling—we had our first draft ready to present to our legislators!

On September 18, 1998, we had the great honor of having former congressman Berkley Bedell come up from Iowa to address our public health freedom meeting. His presentation was immensely inspiring and encouraging. Congressman Bedell earned a grand round of applause when he said, "If you—I shouldn't say 'if'—when you pass that legislation, Minnesota is going to set a standard for all of the rest of the nation."

Congressman Bedell's passion and leadership for holistic healing is unsurpassed. After his healing with Herb Saunders, he founded the federal Office of Complementary and Alternative Medicine. His reputation as a bipartisan congressman with a great deal of integrity made all the difference in the world.

---

* As part of our preliminary lobbying work, we shared our draft language with other interest groups in Minnesota who we thought might have an opinion if it were to be introduced at the capitol.

Congressman Bedell was seventy-seven years old when he came to address our group—and as vibrant as could be. I marveled at his accomplishments during his many years in Congress. I learned that his long-term illness had interrupted his work in government. I listened to the story of the healing path that led him to Farmer Saunders and to his own restored good health. I thought to myself as I bid him goodbye, *What an amazing health freedom hero this man is for our country!* After that September evening meeting in Minnesota, there was renewed excitement and hope that we would reach our goal.

Bill Sponsors and Lobbying Team

Our learning curve continued. We learned that one of the most important decisions we would have to make would be our choice of chief sponsors of the proposed bill. We needed one sponsor from the House of Representatives and one from the Senate. We discussed this at length in our Monday night meetings and finally decided on which legislators to approach, one from each of the majority parties in each body. Members of our group volunteered to schedule meetings with them and discuss the possibility of their support. To our joy, the meetings went well. We received confirmation of support and sponsorship from both our selected sponsors by mid-October.

Our sponsor in the House would be Representative Lynda Boudreau from southern Minnesota, a Republican and an avid supporter of personal freedoms. Our sponsor in the Senate would be Senator Steve Morse. Senator Morse had been raised in a large family on an orchard farm in southeastern Minnesota; he was a Democrat and an avid supporter of personal choice in health care. We were very grateful to these two legislators who were fully supportive of our vision.

Our sponsors were both warm, friendly communicators who proved to be great teachers as well. They were eager to help us and teach us what we needed to do to help them pass our bill. They let us know that our next step would be to meet with key legislators in their home districts to garner their support and ask them to be cosponsors of the bill. Meeting our sponsors involved my first face-to-face meetings with legislators.

The work to defeat a bill had forced us to figure out how the legislature works. And we understood, by watching and learning, that passing a bill would be a lot more work and a very different process from defeating a bill. Passing a bill would be like building new home, requiring us to know every detail of the legislative process, including providing and overseeing the language at all times; knowing each legislator, their positions on the bill, and their positions of authority in the legislature; and knowing all the rules and deadlines of the legislative process—among many other things. As the weeks unfolded, I learned that I could do many things that I otherwise thought I could not or would not ever do.

For one thing, I learned that I didn't need to know how to do everything myself. The members of our group had the range of talents that it was going to take to do this project. It would be a totally collaborative effort.

Nancy was a well-known naturopath and homeopath who had a terrific gift for keeping a political group together. She kept our group meetings happening; she kept the public informed about key issues through public speaker meetings; and she kept us all moving our project forward. She had a passion for natural health, which she demonstrated in her experience and her expertise with her clients.

Jerri had an amazing gift for building and maintaining relationships, including relationships with legislators and people in the outer community. She had a talent for strategizing and analyzing situations based on faithful tracking of political relationships inside the community. She was a great listener and a homeopath in private practice.

Leo had been an activist in several political campaigns. He, too, was a brilliant strategist with a great wealth of information. Leo had been involved in a number of advocacy nonprofits, including working with the team at Dental Mercury Awareness to educate about mercury in dentistry. He was also an advocate and activist in the food co-op movement. Leo has a BS degree in physics from San Diego State University and an MA in mathematics from the University of California, San Diego (UCDS). He was an accountant by trade.

Marillyn was a retired nurse and nurse educator, and a strong personality and spokesperson, advocating for natural healing on all levels. She was our first president and a strong foundational leader to our new nonprofit, the Minnesota Natural Health Coalition.

LaDonna was the wife of a holistic medical doctor who had been investigated for providing holistic health services. They had survived the ordeal of those investigations together. LaDonna lent a steady, nurturing hand to each of us by providing undivided commitment to the cause and her home in which to meet every Monday night.

Greg showed a remarkable ability to track words and articulate the concepts of health freedom on behalf of citizens. He was a strong businessman, local contractor and carpenter, and owner of a local company that provided residential historical renovations. Most importantly for us, Greg was an avid raw foodist. And it was uncanny how he could repeat, word for word, what had been said in meetings.

Barbara was an assertive, strong advocate of health freedom who singlehandedly protected the right of massage therapists and bodyworkers to practice by opposing overly restrictive statewide licensing regulations. Barb was an educator, a public speaker, and president of the Massage Therapy Network. She led the preparation of handouts and informational packets for legislators.

Libby was a graphics design artist at a local university and a strong health freedom advocate. Libby designed our first corporate logo and worked with me in 1999 to launch our first website. She maintained that website throughout the entire legislative process.

Matt was a world-renowned herbalist and author. He owned his own herb farm an hour from the city. Matt could speak about his vocation as an herbalist with great honor and knowledge. He was one of our chief testifiers at the hearings.

David was a traditional naturopath, a minister, and an articulate strategist. He had a strong client base of supportive consumers who wanted their access to his broad understanding of energy, spirit, and nutrients protected.

Jan had exceptional administrative and organizational skills, honed through her work as an administrator at the Northwestern School of Homeopathy. An avid historian and researcher of the healing arts, Jan provided us with documents for our work.

For me personally, the biggest lesson was to be on top of the location and language of our bill at all times, whether it was being introduced on the floor and, if so, by whom; whether it was headed to committee and, if so, when; and whether there were amendments that people we did not know were trying to get on our bill. Also involved were the tasks of negotiating amendments with others and keeping track of what kind of time deadlines the bill had to meet to keep it alive and keep it moving. Missing a deadline could actually table a bill for an entire year or even cause the bill to die.

The list of talented people who added to the success of our group could go on. The individuals whom I describe here suffice to provide you with a sense of the amazing diversity and skills of our team.

A national group, the Coalition for Natural Health, heard about our efforts and became interested in passing health freedom legislation too. They had opposed the Healy licensing bill. One of their lobbyists, a Minnesota attorney, contacted us, wanting to attend our weekly meetings. He joined our meetings. His extensive experience and good reputation as a Minnesota lobbyist proved to be a great asset to our discussions and strategy.

Our Bill Introduced

On February 11, 1999, Senator Steve Morse introduced our bill on the Senate floor. We received the bill number and title, Senate File 689, the Complementary and Alternative Health Care Freedom of Access Act.[6] It was a great day for us all. Part of the process of introducing a bill is to secure supportive cosponsors. We took the bill in its introduced form and walked it around to legislators who we thought might support our efforts. We went to their offices and requested their signatures of support for cosponsorship. The supporting Senate authors were Senators John Hottinger (D); Don Samuelson (D); Linda Berglin (D); and Michelle Fischbach (R).

Earlier, on February 8, Republican representative Lynda Boudreau, our key House chief sponsor, introduced the bill in the House: House File 537, the Complementary and Alternative Health Care Freedom of Access Act.[7] We had worked hard at the capitol, making meetings with legislative offices and tracking down legislators wherever we could find them to gain their signatures of support. We found the following supportive legislators to be our House cosponsors: Representatives Wejcman (D); Bud Nornes (R); Mary Ellen Otremba (D); and Karen Clark (D).

We were officially launched!

Having bill numbers of our own was very exciting. I felt protective of the actual language of the bills. I did not want any changes to the bills, and I was ready to discuss them word for word with anyone with whom we could get a meeting. The bill, for the first time, would put many new terms into Minnesota health law. It created a safe harbor exemption for many healing arts, sought an exemption for generally regarded safe practices from licensing requirements and criminal charges of practicing medicine without a license as long as the practitioners avoided the prohibited conduct and provided proper disclosures. The protected practices in the original version of our introduced bill included, but were not limited to, the following:

- acupressure;
- anthroposophy;
- aromatherapy;
- Ayurvedic medicine;
- craniosacral therapy;
- culturally traditional healing practices;
- detoxification practices and therapies;
- energetic healing;
- environmental medicine;
- folk medicine;
- healing practices utilizing food, food supplements, nutrients, and the physical forces of heat, cold, water, touch, and light;
- Gerson therapy and colostrum therapy;
- healing touch;
- herbal medicine;

- homeopathy;
- iridology;
- bodywork, massage, and massage therapy;
- meditation;
- mind–body healing practices;
- naturopathy;
- noninvasive instrumentalities;
- traditional oriental practices, such as Qigong energy healing; and
- other health care and healing practices and resources pursued by clients for the purpose of preventing or treating illness or promoting health and well-being.

Our bill had been introduced in both the House and the Senate. I wondered whether we would have to lobby in the House and Senate simultaneously to move our bills forward. We decided to focus our lobbying efforts in the House of Representatives, based on a suggestion from our Senate sponsor.

On February 18, 1999, two hundred people came to our public educational meeting. Speeches were given by Representative Boudreau and Senator Morse. After the meeting, Nancy called me and said the meeting had raised $2,600. It seemed like a million dollars to us. We were ecstatic.

Our bill was presenting a new concept to attorneys and legislators, namely that instead of the government endowing a practitioner with the privilege to perform a healing act by setting out a licensing statute, we were claiming the fundamental right to heal and asking for protection with an exemption to licensure, certification, or registration laws as long as the practitioner avoided prohibited acts and gave out disclosures.

And instead of holding a medical doctor to a conventional standard of care that required, for example, the doctor to give a particular drug, we were saying that in some medical and health circumstances, the medical doctor could use gentler, noninvasive treatments and not be disciplined for not giving out a drug. I had to work hard to help people understand this new legal architecture and feel comfortable with it.

Minnesota Natural Health Legal Reform Project Is Born

> Never doubt that a small group of thoughtful, committed
> citizens can change the world; indeed, it's the only thing that
> ever has.
>
> —Margaret Mead

Now we needed to lobby more aggressively, so we began to consider having a paid lobbyist. We would have to raise funds, and that would require us to set up a lobbying organization!

The coalition was an educational organization that allowed for a limited amount of professional lobbying and a lot of volunteer lobbying. But we knew that we needed to lobby a great deal more to reach our goals.

In June 1999, we launched a sister organization to the educational coalition to focus on our lobbying efforts. We chose the name Minnesota Natural Health Legal Reform Project. On June 7, 1999, the organization was officially incorporated as a Minnesota nonprofit with a future federal tax status of 501(c)(4). It was a grand day. The first board members of the Minnesota Natural Health Legal Reform Project were Leo Cashman, Greg Schmidt, and Kathy Schurdevin.

Minnesota has 67 senators and 135 representatives. Our goal was to talk to each of them individually to convince them to pass our bill. We would start by meeting with the legislators serving on the committee where the bills would be heard first. The group developed official three-ring binders of information to explain our goals. It was a very impressive collection of documents supporting complementary medicine. It included excerpts from the *Minnesota Department of Health Study on Complementary Medicine*, which was published in 1998.

We also drafted one-page handouts explaining our bills, and made a five-minute audiotape about health freedom. We had a website address. The logo that Libby designed was beautiful! We proudly used the logo as a full cover page on our binders. The large binders provided good reference material for legislators who wanted to learn more.

Early Setbacks and Movement

Although our bill was introduced in the Senate in February 1999, it wasn't long before we learned that Senator Morse, our chief sponsor, would not be able to carry it forward. Senator Morse had been offered a position by the governor's administration as a deputy commissioner for the Minnesota Department of Natural Resources. Since natural resources and wildlife were his true passion, he had accepted the position. We were very sad to lose him; he had been such a help and support to our bill. We were left with the reality that we needed to find a new sponsor, so we went to work.

We decided to ask Senator Janet Johnson to sponsor the bill. Her passion for and commitment to natural health was apparent in her carrying the bill that had authorized the *Minnesota Department of Health Study on Complementary and Alternative Medicine*. Senator Johnson was very supportive of our goal and agreed to be our chief sponsor.

We were excited to have such a senior legislator on board with us and hopeful that our bill would pass with her support. On March 11, Senator Morse's name was taken off the bill; Senator Johnson's was added; and the bill was referred to the Health and Family Security Policy Committee in the Senate.

The bill in the House of Representatives also began to move. After it was introduced in the House on February 8, 1999, we learned that it was to be referred to the House Health and Human Services Policy Committee. We also learned that before the bill would be heard by the full committee, it would be assigned to a subcommittee for consideration. The subcommittee would vote on the bill and make a recommendation to the full committee. We were delighted to learn that Representative Lynda Boudreau would be the chairperson of that subcommittee.

On February 25, 1999, Lynda presented the bill to the full committee and requested it be referred to her subcommittee. I was called to that full committee hearing to answer questions about the bill. It was the first time that I had ever testified at a hearing. The full committee did refer our bill to the subcommittee, and Lynda let us know that she planned to give it a hearing in the subcommittee.

The House subcommittee hearing date was set for March 11. I kept doing research to make sure I could answer all the questions that I knew would be asked. I spent a lot of time at the capitol giving presentations to legislators and answering questions about the bill. I went to related hearings so that I could observe and become more comfortable with the hearing process and with other health care issues, including pharmacy and dental hygienist bills.

One day in March I met representatives from the Minnesota Department of Health. Later I met with one legislator who was upset with us for having stopped the naturopathic licensing bill. It was a difficult meeting. One thing that was hard for the representative was that some of the people who had come to her office during the naturopathic licensing bill lobbying were so angry at her for introducing the bill that they had been very rude and hostile. I listened to her carefully. I was very sorry to hear that she had been offended, and I made a mental note always to remind our citizen activists to be respectful when expressing their passionate opinions. I had compassion for the legislator because she had wanted her bill to move forward. At the end of the conversation, I felt satisfied that we each had been heard and that things had gone well.

I also met with a legislator who despised homeopathy; he thought it was a fraud. He claimed that homeopathic remedies were so diluted that there was nothing in them. On the other hand, he said they could be dangerous. He did not support the concept that they had any "energetic" qualities. There was no convincing him, even though he knew that I had both a medical technology and chemistry background and had used homeopathy all my life for myself and my family. I encouraged him, saying that even if he did not believe in the value of homeopathy, he should allow others the choice of what they deemed best for themselves. He was not convinced.

I was disappointed that some legislators did not fully support the right of each citizen to have health care options protected by allowing legal access to alternative healers. The legislators who were opposed to our bill seemed to focus on current standards that limited options to the state-condoned medical practitioners. It was disheartening.

Then I went to meet with one of our most avidly supportive legislators. She had been diagnosed with cancer and had complemented her cancer therapy with alternative options. She believed in the right of all people to be able to access whatever source they wanted for their health. I was encouraged.

We began to plan the testimonies we would offer at our first hearing. We asked Matt Wood, herbalist and author, to testify about his decision to become an herbalist and the work that he does growing his own herbs and providing herb-based services to clients. He had a client who was open to testifying; she had been severely ill for twenty years with Crohn's disease and had spent most of those years in emergency rooms. She had recovered in a matter of months after seeing Matt and using herbs. In addition, we knew that our wonderful president, Marillyn, would testify. She was a well-respected registered nurse and a strong voice for patient freedom.

We also invited attorney Michael Meyers from South Dakota Law School to be an additional testifier for us. He had worked as an executive for major health care systems in Rochester and Minneapolis and was an avid health freedom educator, law school faculty member, and radio announcer. He made presentations all over the country about health care reform and natural health.

During the hearing, I had the task of fielding many concerns. When a representative challenged the use of homeopathy, I responded by saying that the bill was not about making judgments of someone's choice or what they think works or doesn't work. Rather, the bill protects treatments that are generally regarded as safe, and it should be up to the consumer as to whether they want to use something or not. I told the representatives that I had raised my children with the use of homeopathy, a noninvasive option, and had only selectively used antibiotics when my doctor indicated it, adding that such was my right.

When a legislator asked about dentists who were "scamming consumers" by removing mercury fillings from teeth, I responded by saying that people have a right to live without toxins, adding that it was my understanding as a chemist that mercury is one of the most toxic substances on the planet and that in some countries it has already been banned for use in dental fillings.

When attorney Michael Meyers testified, he generated some challenging discussions. He stated that, literally, given the way the laws have been structured, if a person is diagnosed with cancer and chooses not to undergo chemotherapy, radiation, or surgery, the only other option available legally to them is to go home, sit in a rocking chair, stare out a window, and wait to die. I carry the memory of that moment, and I repeat Michael's comment often in my work today. It was simply and straightforwardly put.

On March 11 the bill passed the subcommittee! We were very happy. Our first passage! Since our bill was referred back to the full committee for a vote, we kept the pressure on at the capitol. Shocked to find out that it would be heard again in just a few days in the full committee, we scrambled to prepare additional testimony. We knew the full committee would be a serious challenge, especially with Representative Huntley, a biochemist from Duluth, adamantly opposed to homeopathy, which he considered a major fraud.

On March 15 the bill was heard by the full committee. A key question was whether this would be a bill that protects access to both licensed and unlicensed persons. The Board of Medical Practice testified in opposition; they said that they did not have a bias against complementary and alternative health care per se, but they did not think it appropriate for a consumer group to be bringing forward a change to their Medical Practice Act for their own physicians. At the close of the hearing, the bill passed, but not before it was adversely amended to remove protection of the rights of already licensed professionals such as physicians and nurses to provide holistic services. The rest of the bill, for unlicensed practitioners, remained intact. Representative Wejman made strong remarks on the record to hold the Board of Medical Practice accountable in the future for their promise to address the freedom of their professionals.

We thought that the Board of Medical Practice and the Minnesota Medical Association would be in support of their doctors' right to provide complementary and alternative health care services to their clients, since a 1993 study had shown that one in three patients in the United States regularly used complementary and alternative therapies[8] and since we were aware that many were seeking out holistic physicians. Instead, in the House we would be going forward with a bill solely to protect access to unlicensed traditional healers. This also meant that the Senate and House language would no longer be identical. The Senate might pass the bill in its original language and send it back to the House floor for adoption. We were certainly learning the complexity of things as we went along.

At the end of the hearing, the committee passed the bill as amended and re-referred it to the House Civil Law Committee. We had won another victory for freedom!

Civil Law Committee, 1999

The House Civil Law Committee was our next big hurdle. The hearing was set for March 19, only four days away! We had to get our bill passed in the committee and to the floor before the deadline passed. We had to move quickly to lobby that committee. As a lawyer, I felt that this committee hearing would be daunting for me because the committee of seventeen was made up of mostly lawyers.

As we continued to lobby, we considered legal groups that might weigh in on the bill in civil law, such as the County Attorney's Association. We also got a summary from the executive director of the Board of Medical Practice, Mr. Leach, to determine whether or not they had had any complaints during 1998 against unlicensed complementary and alternative health care practitioners. There had been five "nonjurisdictional" complaints. Mr. Leach said three or four of those were against clinics. It was rare, he said, for a complementary and alternative health care person to be shut down. That was a good statistic for us since licensing boards often had hundreds of complaints against their own professionals.

As we spent more time at the capitol, we kept track of who would vote for us and who would not. It did not look like we had the vote. Even though the committee chair supported our efforts, we didn't believe that he wanted the bill to come to a vote because it may be voted down.

We worked very hard to negotiate the language of the bill to accommodate concerns and garner support. We were about to get an unexpected break— and continue to learn the intricacies of politics. The chairman of the Civil

37

Law Committee, Representative Steve Smith, made a motion to lay the bill over until summer, saying it was an important topic that should not be rushed. This is called *tabling the bill.*

We quickly learned what tabling a bill meant. We were told that a tabled bill neither moved out of committee nor was voted down but was still alive—but stalled. We were told that we could work during the summer to gain more support for the bill and make some changes that would make it more acceptable. But for this session, it was finished. Although we were stopped in our tracks, we were very glad that our bill had not been voted down. We were determined to make the changes necessary to bring it back.

As we spoke with other legislators, though, we learned that tabling a bill is often a bad sign. Often, legislators do not bring back tabled bills because they are too controversial or do not have a chance of passing. Tabling, it seemed, was a polite way of saying, *Go away.* We were not going away! Although it was a shock to us, there was some relief in knowing we could take a breather for a bit.

We stayed in touch with the legislative aide to the chairman of the Civil Law Committee. The chairman was an attorney and a Republican colleague of the author of our bill. We asked the aide how to keep our bill alive and moving forward. There was one specific hurdle we learned that needed to be jumped. On the committee sat an attorney who became pivotal in the story of health freedom in Minnesota. He was a well-respected attorney and formerly had served as Speaker of the House for fifteen years. He and his colleagues carried a lot of weight on the Civil Law Committee although they were Democrats on a newly elected Republican committee. Even though the committee chair supported our efforts, this Democrat was opposed; he made it clear that he preferred a licensure type of bill. When the bill was tabled, I saw that we would have to make it past Representative Carruthers and his colleagues, or else our efforts would end in a defeat. I made a decision to get a meeting with him during the summer and talk the whole thing over in person.

Three Great Health Freedom Heroes Pass On

Some years after the Saunders trials, Herb Saunders had become ill. The stress of the trials had really taken a toll on him. He had been receiving medical help from his local doctors. In June 1999, I learned that Herb was growing weaker and more incapacitated. We had also gotten the sad news that Dr. Keith Sehnert had become ill. Then in July, we received more devastating news that the chief author of our bill, Senator Janet Johnson, had become ill. By the end of that summer, we were forced to experience the passing of all three of these great heroes of health freedom. They were grave losses for Minnesota and for all of us.

Herb Saunders died on June 20, 1999. The funeral for Herb was in St. James, Minnesota. It was a beautiful tribute to his great spirit and kindness to all. On the way home from Herb's funeral, I received a call that Dr. Sehnert had passed. A very sad day. Dr. Sehnert was an avid supporter of our group and of health freedom. His patients loved him, and his research, writings, and books in the area of holistic health were known far and wide. It was a final deep sadness then in August of that same year when we received the very unbelievable news that Senator Johnson had passed away. The shock went through the entire community. We had been honored to have her for our author and friend and would miss her deeply. I attended the public service for Senator Johnson that was held in North Branch, Minnesota. The large crowd of bipartisan dignitaries, and the outpouring of respect and love for this community leader, was profound.

I knew that this would mean that we would need to find another author for our bill, but that seemed inconsequential in the midst of our deep sadness.

Summer and Fall 1999—Keeping On Keeping On

In June I made an appointment to meet with Representative Carruthers from the House Civil Law Committee—the representative who opposed us. My goal was to be myself and speak our truth. During our meeting, he and I shared a lively exchange of ideas, although it was apparent that we were not in agreement on the bill. I would have to think long and hard to figure out how we would be able to come to some mutual understandings to make this happen.

In June my colleagues and I talked to representatives in the Minnesota Department of Health to let them know that we were going to proceed in the coming session of the legislature. We continued our Monday night meetings for the remainder of the year, focused on building relationships and helping people understand our bill.

There was some talk regarding the Civil Law Committee holding an early summer or fall hearing on the bill in 1999, but we learned later that it would only be set for hearing in the upcoming January 2000 session. That gave us time for meetings with the Department of Health and the attorney general to establish the best enforcement language in the bill.

We also organized and traveled to outstate meetings in legislators' state districts to give constituents avenues to publicly tell their legislators what their wishes were. During these meetings, people came forward and told of how they had been healed by nonconventional natural approaches to health. Some told of recovering from lifelong illnesses through their complementary or alternative therapies. One particular story I remember was from a doctor who had been severely ill with itchy sores and lesions all over his legs and abdomen for which he could find no reason and from which he could find no relief. His health and business were seriously failing. He met a holistic doctor who said it might be gluten intolerance, so he began a diet without gluten. His condition cleared up within three weeks. This story caught my attention and amazed me because I myself had experienced itchy sores on my legs and abdomen. I took the story to heart and got tested. Ultimately I tested positive for gluten intolerance. I have been on a gluten-free diet for twenty years and have had no further problems. While listening, I silently applauded the committed health seekers and healers willing to share their experiences and knowledge to further health care options for all of us.

The outstate meetings were held in Mankato, the home of the senator John Hottinger, chairman of the Minnesota Senate Health and Family Security Policy Committee; Rochester, home of Senator Sheila Kiscaden, a leading legislator regarding health care issues; and four northern Minnesota cities, including Moose Lake, Virginia, Cloquet, and Duluth. These meetings and travel to outer Minnesota were highlights for me because we got to meet local people and hear their profound healing stories. We also got to be immersed in the truth and facts about what was transpiring in our communities and our country.

After the Mankato public meeting, Senator Hottinger indicated that he would consider giving the bill a hearing in his Senate committee when session began. He asked that we contact his aides about the language of the bill. This was great news. Of course we immediately followed up with his office.

We continued building our base. We met with the director of the University of Minnesota Spirituality and Healing Center and explained our bill. We gave a presentation to the Complementary and Alternative Medicine Task Force for Allina Health Care Systems. We toured and gave a presentation to the Integrative Wellness Center in Rochester, Minnesota. We set up a lobbying training day for volunteer lobbyists to help us at the capitol. We kept in close touch with our sponsor, Representative Lynda Boudreau, who helped us rewrite and amend our bill as suggestions and new ideas came in to sharpen its content. We met with Representative Bradley, chairman of the Minnesota House Health and Human Services Policy Committee, a committee through which we expected our bill would need to pass. Also, we explored potential options for a new author in the Senate. And, of course, we kept fundraising to keep our movement strong.

In November 1999, Twyla Ring, a personal friend of Senator Janet Johnson, won the Senate race in her district in a specially held election. Members of our group met with her to learn if she would be interested in carrying our health freedom bill forward as part of Janet's legacy.

When we met with her, I learned that Senator Ring was a strong woman, extensively traveled, an environmentalist, an educator, a teenage advocate, and a dear friend of Senator Johnson. She told us a story about a time when she had become deathly ill while traveling in China. She was offered a red fluid by a Chinese native to help her feel better. Twyla accepted the help and said that she was better "in no time." Later on, she learned that it was turtle blood that she had drunk! She had stories of how she had gained respect for the broad range of cultural healing practices all over the world. She was extremely supportive of our cause and promised to take it forward in the Senate.

We had used our time well in 1999. Support was growing. In late November, I was honored to be invited to the state of New York to give a presentation on our Minnesota efforts to the New York Natural Health Coalition. They were a new group who were launching a campaign in New York to pass a bill similar to our Minnesota bill. I left for New York in early December. The trip was a new experience for me, giving a presentation out of state. I was able to meet with two New York attorneys and meet many health freedom activists in New York City. Kathy, their leader and owner of a school of homeopathy in NYC, was a wonderful host who helped us really experience New York City.

The speech I gave in New York is one I will always remember because I took the liberty of sharing about the recent loss of our three Minnesota health freedom heroes and what they had meant to me and the health freedom movement, along with the contributions they had made. The trip energized me! I was more motivated than ever when I returned home to voice the truth of health freedom.

Session 2000 Begins with a Bang

We started the new year with a bang, even before session began. On December 15, 1999, the House sponsor of our bill, Representative Boudreau, received a memorandum from the Board of Medical Practice with the board's formal written opposition to our legislation. All the legislators had received the memo. It was a lengthy and hostile document that we thought misrepresented how our bill would work. When I read their memorandum, it appeared that they did not understand the legal structure of a safe harbor law or possibly did not want to understand that structure. I will describe some of their concerns here.

Representative Boudreau was upset with the board. She knew that our organization had made many attempts to communicate with them. We wanted the board to discuss their detailed objections to the bill with us directly so that we could address them. However, now that this debate was going to be public, we needed to respond formally, in writing, before the session started in January.

I let Representative Boudreau know that our organization would start working on a formal response to the board's memorandum and that we would get it to her as soon as we could. My holidays were colored by the stress of getting such an important responsive public document prepared.

The board document had articulated many of the board's concerns. For example, they were very concerned that our bill would allow "some twenty-three ... alternative and complementary health care professions to practice" (twenty-three professions had been listed as examples in the bill). We agreed that it would and that actually this bill would affect many more practitioners than were on the specified list, including but not limited to the hundreds of different traditional healing tradespeople, artists, and practitioners who were practicing in the community from all different walks of life, belief systems, and cultures. Each would need to abide by the safety parameters of the bill. For example, the bill made it clear that practices under the bill did not include surgery or giving out prescription drugs, or anything that included puncture of the skin or manipulation of joints or the spine.

We explained that importantly, and in addition, the bill would provide fair and reasonable legal avenues of recourse for the government or clients against unlicensed practitioners in the event of potential harm. It also incorporated legal concepts of expanded informed consent by establishing mandated additional disclosure and notices to clients, and practitioner ethical responsibilities.

The board was concerned that we were not setting up a licensing body or educational standards. We had to explain that we had not designed it as another licensing statute asking permission to do dangerous acts. Licensed professionals are given the privilege by the state to perform potentially risky practices as long as such professionals have a state-mandated education. And those persons not licensed who do those activities can be charged criminally for not having a license. This bill, however, was for activities that were generally regarded as safe and not requiring a particular set of educational standards. The bill was not a permission request but rather a protective harbor where those activities were protected as long as prohibited acts were avoided and disclosures were given. We reminded the board that the state cannot just mandate state licensure and education for any vocation and jeopardize the right of others without a license to practice their vocation. Under Minnesota law (Minn. Stat. 214.001 Subd. 2[a]), before licensing a profession, the state must first consider "whether the unregulated practice of an occupation may harm or endanger the health, safety and welfare of citizens of the state and whether the potential for harm is recognizable and not remote"[9]

We reminded the board that we are a free society where people can follow their vocations. Many people follow their professions without government licensing. If it doesn't pass the harm threshold, then licensure along with the criminal charges for practicing without a license may not be deemed necessary to protect the public.

Many healing arts, including natural health practices, have not been licensed because they do not fall within that harm or endangerment standard. They are age-old arts that have a broad variety of origins and trainings, and in fact they are practiced successfully in many communities. So why are they illegal? Sadly, years ago the Board of Medical Practice acquired language in the law that defined the practice of medicine as literally all healing practices, all of them requiring a medical license. By this definition, instantly all the natural health practices became illegal with criminal consequences. The Minnesota law stated that if a person were to practice any of the following without a medical license, then they would be guilty of a gross misdemeanor unless specifically exempted. This included anyone who "(3) offers or undertakes to prevent or to diagnose, correct, or treat in any manner or by any means, methods, devices, or instrumentalities, any disease, illness, pain, wound, fracture, infirmity, deformity or defect of any person."[10]

Our response to the medical board was to remind them that even though many healing practitioners continued to practice under this oppressive law, they practiced in fear! They could be charged in most states, in criminal proceedings, even when no harm or fraud had occurred. Just like Farmer Saunders. This because they were healing without a medical license. We explained that consumers had lost options and would continue to run the risk of losing more of their practitioners as more biases were developed against them. Consumers were demanding a stop to prosecutions and asking for the protection of access to healers of their choice.

The board claimed that our bill did not have an effective form of public protection, but we knew this was false. Under the proposed bill, consumers had far more protection than they did under existing law, including a lengthy client bill of rights and a clear list of prohibited acts.

The medical board did not want a consumer to choose to go to a complementary and alternative practitioner and delay a diagnosis or treatment by a licensed doctor. However, in our bill, civil sanctions could be brought by any consumer based on harm. We reminded the opposition that consumers have the right to delay conventional treatment if they so choose and the right to seek other options for care. Statistics show that for most clients with severe ailments such as chronic musculoskeletal pain, they visit their conventional care providers before trying complementary or alternative therapies.[11] Again, consumers were demanding that their options and rights be protected.

The bill was designed to answer the basic question "Should an unlicensed practitioner have to choose between not practicing, or practicing at the legal risk of being criminally charged, when no harm or fraud is being done and when a consumer is exercising their fundamental human right of health freedom?" The bill addressed this important question by making a protected exemption for practitioners who were performing treatments that were generally regarded as safe, listing twenty-seven paragraphs of prohibited acts and providing strong mandates for expanded statutory disclosures. If a client wanted to go to a licensed professional, then they could seek such services at any time, of course.

The board document went so far as to say that our bill would open Minnesota to forms of sheer medical quackery, a term which Representative Boudreau had publicly asked them to refrain from using. Their memorandum was a publicly distributed misinterpretation of the actual language of the bill. In addition, it reflected bias against the greater culture of the healing arts.

Our bill was addressing a great debate in the culture, challenging the right of the government to make the conventional medical health care system the only option available to citizens. Our bill assumed that it is the consumers who ultimately decide whether something is beneficial to them or not. We believed that it was appropriate that all noninvasive and truthful practices be legal and free from discrimination. To articulate what we perceived as noninvasive and truthful, we included a list of prohibited acts in the bill such as no surgery, puncturing of the skin, or use of prescription drugs. In fact, Minnesota has a law still on the books that originated in 1927 and was amended in 1974 that clearly shows legislative intent regarding systems of healing. It reads as follows:

> The several boards or other officers whose duty it shall be to administer or carry into effect the provisions of this chapter shall, while exercising such authority, in no manner discriminate against any system or brand of healing.[12]

We included a statement in our response stating that the healing arts community is diverse and includes competent practitioners who bring clients into a state of wellness. The fact that they acquire their talents and vocations in a variety of ways from a number of sources and cultures does not mean they are not providing a valuable service and legitimately practicing their profession or vocation. We believed that the natural health community was preserving age-old wisdom and cultural truths and adding a legitimate element of caring to our society. We were determined to protect access to this type of healing experience for consumers who wanted to choose it.

We knew from experience that the Board of Medical Practice had a powerful voice in the legislature. We sent our responsive document to all legislators. I believed our response to their objections was equally powerful.

In mid-January, we learned that Senator Hottinger, the chair of the Senate Health Committee, was concerned about the medical board's memorandum. He invited us to a special meeting with him and the medical board so that he could hear both sides of the debate. We were concerned that the board might sway Senator Hottinger to withhold our bill from a Senate hearing. We needed his support, or at least his open-mindedness, to allow our bill its fair hearing. After the two-hour meeting, we learned that Senator Hottinger planned to give our bill a fair hearing.

In January we were preparing for the bill to be heard in both the Senate and the House. We learned that we were set for a hearing on February 7 in the House Civil Law Committee and for a hearing in the Senate on February 8 in Senator Hottinger's Health and Family Security Committee. Our vote-tracking notes showed that in the House Civil Law Committee, there was a close vote count of seven to seven. We did not have the count in the Senate, but we were lobbying the members of the Health Committee.

One important member of the Senate Health Committee was Senator Sheila Kiscaden from the Rochester area. She was well-known in the Senate for her work in health care, and she appeared to be the senators' go-to person on these issues. When we first met with her, she did not agree with the approach of our bill. However, we kept returning to her with our thoughts and changes to the bill. We were very glad when she became a supporter of our bill. In fact, it was Senator Kiscaden who was the one to eventually volley our bill into a large Senate omnibus bill and get it passed in the Senate.

In January 2000 we had meetings with the Nursing Association; the Chiropractor's Association; the medical board staff; chairs of possible future committees such as Senator Jane Ranum, chair of the Senate Judiciary Committee; and lobbyists for the Minnesota Medical Association. No matter how grueling a meeting was, my colleague Jerri Johnson, who was most often with me, would sit down and debrief with me and find the best interpretation and movement from each meeting. Debriefings, in my opinion, are the secret ingredient of lobbying. And Jerri was awesome at it!*

---

* One important note about weather: The legislative session in Minnesota takes place in the coldest, snowiest months of the year. And one day in the middle of a January snowstorm, I drove three and a half hours to accomplish the fifteen-minute drive to the capitol. No stopping us.

Civil Law Committee 2000

On February 7, 2000, Chairman Representative Steve Smith heard our bill in the House Civil Law Committee for our first hearing of the session. Members from both the Minnesota Natural Health Coalition and the Minnesota Natural Health Legal Reform Project showed up in great numbers, all wearing yellow buttons for health freedom. Many of them were allowed to testify and tell their stories.

I sat at the testimony table with Representative Boudreau and answered questions. The lead Democrat Representative made his opposition very clear. The Minnesota Medical Board, the Mayo Clinic, the Hospital Association, and a number of other testifiers stated their concerns about the bill, a number of which I believed we could address. Representative Boudreau did an excellent job of speaking to our bill. After lengthy debate, no vote was taken and we were told another hearing would be set. We heard that it was unusual to take so much time with one bill, so we were guardedly optimistic. Later that week I called Representative Carruthers, the lead Democrat in that committee who opposed our bill, and he and I discussed the bill by phone.

On February 14 the second House Civil Law hearing was held. We went to the hearing, and much to our surprise, Representative Carruthers, whom I had spoken with, presented an amendment in the form of a delete-all bill that would have deleted our entire bill and replaced it with language that was not in any way acceptable to us. Our bill was a fairly short three-page bill. But the delete-all amendment included many pages of general regulation for unlicensed practitioners: eighteen paragraphs of notices and disclosures to clients, twenty-seven paragraphs of prohibited acts, mandatory reporting of abuse, self-reporting requirement for noncompliance, and most importantly setting up a special office in the Department of Health to take complaints instead of using the current system already set up for unlicensed practice violations, which would require the government to allocate money for the bill to pass.

The delete-all amendment was put up for a vote. We held our breath. The delete-all amendment got a tie vote, so it did not pass, but the tension was so great in the room, it was nerve-racking.

The full bill was still alive, so the debate on the bill continued. There was so much tension in the committee room that day because of the tie vote and so much confusion with the introduction and failing of that long amendment that the chairman called a five-minute recess to speak with Representative Boudreau. When the committee reconvened, the chairman asked that I not sit at the testifier table with Representative Boudreau. As they continued, they did not call for a vote on the full bill; the chair encouraged the parties to work out differences. Yet another hearing, the third and final hearing of the bill, was set for February 26.

Our organization met and discussed at length whether we should accept the opposing representative's long regulatory delete-all model amendment. We thought maybe we could take it and make some amendments to it to make it more acceptable to us. We also discussed whether or not we should ask for the bill to be withdrawn.

In those next hours and days, I went through the long delete-all bill that had been proposed by the opposition just in case it was introduced in the committee again, seeing if there were ways we could amend it to protect our interests. At our weekly meeting, the health freedom leaders talked long into the night about a potentially revised delete-all amendment. We finally agreed to go with the delete-all bill, but our own amended version of it. The reasons we decided to agree to it were that we made sure that our amended delete-all would not have any registration component, it would not have a board, it would not give the Department of Health any rulemaking authority to mandate certain types of educational requirements, and it would not have any mandatory interface with the government before a practitioner could perform a healing act as long as such practitioner stayed within the safe harbor parameters of the bill.

The day of the hearing came. The room was packed with supporters on both sides of the debate. Representative Boudreau and we were ready to proactively introduce the opposition's lengthy delete-all amendment with some of our own changes. I hoped it was the right thing to do, and I hoped the opposition would agree to it.

Well, we did it, and it happened very quickly. We introduced the new lengthy bill as an author's amended delete-all. Everyone was surprised. And positive. It was put to a vote and passed the House Civil Law Committee *unanimously*! We had arrived at a win-win situation and had gotten through the bottlenecked House Civil Law Committee.

The bill was then re-referred to the House Health and Human Services Committee because of the extensive changes. That hearing was on March 1. We lobbied all three days. The Monday night organizational meeting was lively with discussion of our huge and monumental decision to change the language of our bill. The hearing was at 6:00 p.m. The new bill passed the full Health and Human Services Committee again! We were on our way again.

Our HF 537 bill was then referred to the House Health and Human Services Finance Committee for appropriations evaluations. However, this is what happened. The chair of the Finance Committee was Representative Goodno. He was also author of the large omnibus finance bill, HF 2699, which was currently in the Ways and Means Committee. On March 6, Chairman Goodno moved to have HF 2699 re-referred to his Finance Committee from Ways and Means, and thereafter, his House Health and Human Services Finance Committee amended HF 2699 to include our complete new health freedom language. Our bill language was now amended onto the large omnibus health finance bill that had passed in the Health Committee. We quickly learned that having language in a large omnibus bill, a bill that many interest groups wanted to pass, was very significant and increased the chances of getting our language into law.

Senate Movement: The All-Out Movement

By this time, it seemed as if all we did was breathe, eat, and sleep health freedom. Jerri and I spent almost every day, all day, at the capitol. Nancy was grand central and kept all the leaders of the Monday night steering committee informed of everything at all times. On the days close to hearings, the steering committee members would lobby together. We were an amazing team of players and supporters. It was a true honor for me to be part of this dedicated band of health freedom advocates.

Many days legislators were not in their offices but were in session in the full House or Senate chambers. I was shocked to learn that legislators could actually leave the floor chamber during a floor debate and that we could send in a note by way of a floor clerk and ask legislators to come out and speak with us in the chamber foyer. I started to understand how much information they were juggling and why they depended on each other and lobbyists for quick conversations outside chambers. For example, during the year we were there, 3,422 bills were filed in the House of Representatives with Senate companion legislation. Only 188 of these bills became law in the 1999–2000 biennium, exclusive of resolutions.

Everyone heard that we had made it through the House Civil Law hearings and the House Health Committee. Therefore, our bill started to move in the Senate, for which three Senate hearings were scheduled, one right after the other! March 7 was the Senate Health and Family Security Committee hearing; March 8, the Senate Judiciary Committee hearing; and March 9, the Senate Government Operations and Veterans hearing.

March 7: Senator Twyla Ring re-presented our bill in the Senate Health and Family Security Committee with the new language. We agreed to have her introduce the long amended delete-all language in the Senate so that the bills would be similar in both the House and the Senate. She did a great job as a new senator, speaking eloquently of the value of complementary and alternative health care. Senator Kiscaden and Senator Weiner, both of whom were looked to for guidance on health issues by other senators, supported the bill. The bill passed the committee.

March 8: I stayed up late into the night following our Senate committee success preparing the hearing in the Senate Judiciary Committee. I made a side-by-side table of our new bill language as it compared to Minnesota law for unlicensed mental health care practitioners. That document proved very helpful to the Judiciary Committee members. I was very glad I had made the effort.

The next day there were intense discussions in that committee around whether practitioners had a duty to recommend that a person also go to a licensed doctor if they needed, and discussions about whether any enforcement actions would be private or public information. Our language

Diane Miller, JD

was acceptable to all, and the bill passed out of judiciary. We were very relieved and happy!

March 9: The Senate Government Operations and Veterans hearing was next. The bill had to go to this committee because it included the creation of a special state office to take complaints, instead of the medical board taking complaints as they had always done with unlicensed practice. We lobbied in the morning, but I was so exhausted from the preparation for the past two hearings that I went and found a quiet Senate conference room, lay down on the floor near the wall behind some chairs, and fell asleep. Luckily, I awoke in time for the hearing!

Chairman Senator Metzen conducted the hearing. Before the hearing, many lobbyists had approached me regarding new amendments from the medical doctors. The doctors wanted language in the bill so that no medical doctor, dentist, or chiropractor could give up their license and practice as an unlicensed healer. The committee adopted this amendment, and the bill passed.

It was all we could do to keep up. It was challenging to keep my eye on every single amendment and conversation that came up to evaluate them. As the bill moved forward, we drafted an updated one-page summary with the changes, a list of endorsing organizations, and *Ten Good Reasons to Support HF 537 and SF 689.*

On March 15 the bill was heard in Senator Linda Berglin's Senate Human Resources Finance Committee. In that hearing, when the chairman asked the Minnesota Department of Health how much money they would need, they said that they were not really sure what they would need because this was such a new bill concept. The bill passed with no appropriations allocated at the time.

Senator Berglin's committee was the final committee to hear SF 689 bill in the Senate. On March 20, 2000, Senate Bill 689 moved onto the Senate floor and passed, 47–13. Yippee. The Senate then sent it over to the House, and the House floor referred it to the House Health and Human Services Finance Committee. We were very happy.

That very same day, we got another great surprise. The House floor took up Representative Goodno's large finance omnibus bill that had our bill language in it. An amendment was introduced on the floor by one of our opposing legislators requesting the removal of the complementary and alternative health care portion of the large HF 2699 finance bill. A heated debate ensued. The hostile amendment was soundly defeated 111–18, and HF 2699 passed on the floor with our language intact. We were ecstatic that our health freedom bill language had passed on the floor in both bodies!

The language was in two separate bills and was not identical because the House floor debate had generated some new amendments to the House version. And we knew that the language needed to be identical from both Senate and House before it could be sent to the governor, so there would hopefully be a joint House Senate Conference Committee in the future to decide how to get the language identical. But we were almost there.

Complexity of the Legislative Process

Things were getting very complicated. The original House File 537 was still active and headed to House Finance hearings. But since the House floor had adopted and passed the omnibus HF 2699, the House Health and Human Services Finance Committee now had the option of putting the amended SF 689, which had been sent over from the Senate, forward in committee. Or they could put forward the original HF 537. On March 21, Chairman Representative Goodno decided to put SF 689 forward in his House Finance Committee. Representative Boudreau presented the bill by amending SF 689 with the preferred language, and the bill passed out of Chairman Goodno's committee. Now it was referred to the Rules Committee.

Putting it mildly, the legislative process was extremely complicated. Even as I am writing, I have a hard time tracking it. I found a diagram of the path of our bill that I had drawn in my diary notes, and decided to include it here, for purposes of amusement as much as for clarification!

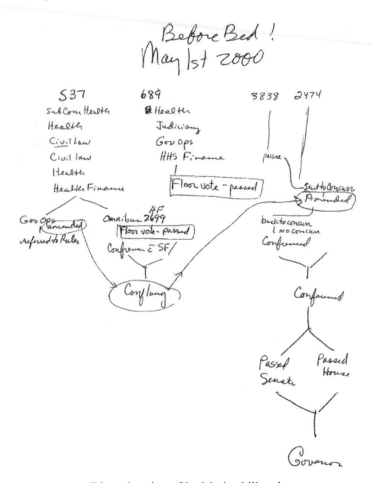

Diary drawing of legislative bill path

Why was the amended SF 689 bill referred to House Rules? Because House Government Operations wanted to hear the bill that had been sent over from the Senate and there was some question about whether they should be able to.

On April 10, SF 689 as amended was heard by Chairman Pawlenty's House Committee on Rules and Legislative Administration. The bill passed the Rules Committee and went to the House floor, where Representative Boudreau moved that SF 689, now on the General Register, be re-referred to the House Committee on Governmental Operations and Veterans Affairs Policy.

On April 17, 2020, when the bill was eventually heard in Government Operations, two very important amendments were added to make the rulemaking capabilities of the Minnesota Department of Health (MDH) much narrower. We were opposed to giving the Minnesota Department of Health any rulemaking capability to determine what type of education or qualifications a practitioner would need to have in order to practice, similar to conventional licensing law requirements, because our bill was based on concepts of safety and prohibited acts rather than what type of education a person might have. It was acceptable to us that rulemaking capability was limited to making rules about the investigation and complaint process only. There was also language added that mandated that MDH provide a report to the legislature in three years to assess the implementation of the bill. We were very glad and impressed that Representative Carruthers from the Civil Law Committee came over to the Government Operations Committee hearing to lend support for the bill, stating to the committee that it had gone successfully through the House Civil Law Committee.

As I left the Government Operations hearing room, I met Senator Kiscaden in the hallway. She said that she had managed to support putting our bill language into the large omnibus bill in the Senate that morning and that it had successfully been put in! I almost fainted. Our language was now in an omnibus bill in the Senate and an omnibus bill in the House.

Since omnibus bills are large bills that often pass all the way to the governor, we now had our language in other vehicles other than our stand-alone bills. I was very excited. The news spread. But then we learned that the House had not adopted the Senate version of the omnibus bill and that there would be a conference committee for the omnibus bills to resolve the differences.

Conference Committee

Conference committees are where the legislators, some from the House and some from the Senate, sit down to resolve differences in Senate versions and House versions of bills that have passed both bodies. Side-by-side documents consisting of between one hundred and three hundred pages per bill are provided so that each interest group can track the section of the bill that holds its language and track the differences between the House and Senate language. Stakeholders can testify about their section(s) while the conference committee listens. Hour by hour, with lobbyists moving around the room and a myriad of notes being passed, the process unfolds and new laws are made.

Although our stand-alone HF 537 made it out of the House Government Operations and Veterans Affairs Policy Committee and was on its way to the House floor, we began to focus on tracking the omnibus bills because we were close to the end of session.[*]

We spent long days in April at the capitol, attending lengthy conference committees remaining vigilant. The last few days of session, we were so exhausted that we camped out in the balcony of the Senate and House chambers to watch the floor debates on the large omnibus bills, hoping our language would remain intact. Finally, on May 1, 2000, the lengthy HF 3839 omnibus bill was voted on in the House and passed. And then on May 5, 2000, the identical HF 3839 was voted on in the Senate and passed. Our language was safely part of that omnibus bill, and we were on our way to the governor!

Our grassroots lobbying team

---

[*] We learned that the comprehensive omnibus bill number would be HF 3839.

Governor Jesse Ventura Signing

Waiting to hear whether or not the bill with our Complementary and Alternative Health Care section had been signed was more stressful than I could have imagined. At that point, I was taking nothing for granted. But on May 11, 2000, we got the news that Governor Ventura had signed the bill!

The aftermath of the signing was sheer jubilation and exhaustion. The bill would go into effect the following year, on July 1, 2001, as Minnesota Statute 146A[13] (see appendix A).

We planned a big public celebration to thank the many supporters and celebrate the good news. We wanted a photo with Governor Ventura and our crew, but this proved harder to procure than any of us thought it would be. LaDonna and Nancy called the governor's office every day for dozens of days until they got the yes from his office. On June 20 we gathered at the capitol and had our picture taken with Governor Jesse Ventura, just as we wanted.

After we left the governor's office, we walked out onto the West End steps of the capitol. I spread my arms and shouted happily, *"We did it!"*

That was the end of one long adventure. But of course, later I learned it was just the beginning of many more to come.

Governor Ventura with our grassroots team

Victory Celebration

I was honored to speak at the celebration of the passage of MN 146A. In part I said:

> *We have crafted a gift to Minnesota consumers that will forever protect their access to the healers and practitioners [who] mean the most to them.*
>
> *We have created an arena for natural health practitioners to practice and be exempt from arbitrary charges of practicing medicine without a license.*
>
> *So here we are: Natural health—free at last!*
>
> *...*
>
> *We have been pioneers, and so we have had to be creative. Our greatest strength was in the perspectives on health care that we brought to the drawing board.*
>
> *We were convinced that:*
>
> 1. *An individual's right of self-determination and search for wellness is a key element in the healing process and that people and their friends and families are their own best resources during illness.*
> 2. *Healing is a multifaceted miraculous process that can be facilitated by a wide range of helpful events, people, and circumstances.*
> 3. *The government's interest to protect the public and the individual's interest to have access to their favorite healer do not need to be in conflict. Those interests can exist in harmony given a thoughtful approach to the problem.*
> 4. *Change can be incredibly uncomfortable.*
> 5. *The days of perceiving the human body as simply a mechanical device are over, and the days of persecution of healers who see the human body as responsive to nature, touch, energy, and spirit are over.*

6. *The process of changing laws is not unlike the process of healing a wound or righting a wrong.*
7. *The process takes a lot of love, a lot of support, a lot of information, a lot of patience, a lot of meetings, a lot of discernment of what to do next, a lot of forgiveness, a lot of water, a lot of prayer, and a lot of research, study, and talent, but most of all, a lot of integrity and love.*

One of the most important lessons I have learned at the legislature and in my own healing journey is to keep putting one foot in front of the other in the face of all odds.

Eventually, since I never really knew what was going to happen at the legislature each day, I lived by the motto "Show up, pay attention, and tell the truth."

Chapter 3

Health Freedom Going Forward

> Health freedom ... the freedom to make decisions for oneself
> and one's community about health and survival. It is rooted in
> the naturally occurring drive and commitment within people to
> keep themselves and their loved ones alive and healthy. Health
> freedom is a fundamental natural right of survival and personal
> sovereignty.
>
> —Diane M. Miller, JD

National Health Freedom Coalition

After the Minnesota bill passed, we were all exhausted. I wondered if I
should go back to working as a family law attorney and mediator full time.
But my heart had been captured by the desire to continue health freedom
work. And we began to receive calls from across the nation asking us how
we had done it and whether we could help others get similar bills passed in
their states. I deeply wanted to respond and to expand the health freedom
work nationally.

I had always been under the impression, and very proud of the fact, that
as a citizen of the United States I was assured of my inalienable right to
survive and to be let alone to make my own health care choices if I was
able. Yet I had learned through my legal and legislative experiences that
the numbers of people working to protect this freedom are small. I'd also
discovered that millions of Americans participating in the existing health

care system will not, or cannot, bring themselves to act outside that system on their own behalf, even in the face of potential loss of life, to utilize this important freedom. As health seekers, we have limited options and limited access to information other than those options provided by conventional care. This includes a reliance on a narrow selection of specialists who sometimes do not have knowledge outside their own areas of expertise and, often, specialists who do not encourage health seekers to seek health options beyond the specialists' offered protocols.

In short, millions of health seekers are not empowered to make their own decisions because they have been conditioned to believe that the conventional medical system is the system that will protect their lives and that there are no other valuable options.

I had a deep yearning to continue to be involved in health freedom issues. I especially wanted to found an organization that would address broader health freedom issues on all levels and be available to educate or assist citizens calling us with their concerns.

Three months after the Minnesota bill passed, we jumped in. On August 8, 2000, Jerri Johnson, Leo Cashman, and I founded the National Health Freedom Coalition, a 501(c)(3) educational organization. Soon thereafter, we were honored to add two board members, Dr. Norm Shealy and William Lee Rand of Reiki.org. Our mission was, and still is, as follows:

> To promote access to all health care information, services, treatments, and products that the people deem beneficial for their own health and survival; to promote an understanding of the laws and factors impacting the right to access; and to promote the health of the people of this nation.

National Health Freedom Action

It wasn't long before we were asked to be involved in lobbying health freedom issues around the country. Since lobbying was done in addition to our educational efforts, on November 9, 2001, we also founded a 501(c)(4) lobbying organization, National Health Freedom Action. Its first board members were Jerri Johnson, William Lee Rand, Marylu Miller, Michael Meyers, JD, and Bonita Yoder, JD. Its mission was, and still is, as follows:

> To promote access to all health care information, services, treatments, and products that the people deem beneficial for their own health and survival; to promote legislative reform of the laws impacting the right to access; and to promote the health of the people of this nation.

Responding to the Call

Within the frameworks of these two amazing organizations, I worked as the director of law and public policy, a position I have continued in for the past twenty years. NHFC and NHFA board members are hands-on active health freedom advocates, and the organizations have a courageous small staff including two full-time attorneys who travel; do public speaking, educating, and lobbying; and help to strengthen the health freedom movement.*

Polarization

As I went forward with working for health freedom, I observed that the most prominent aspect of the United States' health culture affecting health freedom was the polarization of society. The dominant health care culture has strong messaging, that is for sure. But Americans have their own thoughts about their personal freedoms. Emotions run deep regarding

---

* NHFC and NHFA have had the honor of assisting citizens and promoting health freedom in forty states. In the beginning, NHFA efforts focused on working to pass safe harbor practitioner exemption laws for homeopaths, herbalists, traditional naturopaths, and other such healers. Over the years we have overseen the drafting of many safe harbor practitioner exemption bills, thirty of which were introduced into a state legislature and nine of which were successfully passed. We have testified in many states and have worked with groups on-site at eighteen state capitols. NHFC has met with leaders in Washington, DC, our nation's capital. We have supported the protection of access to dietary supplements by attending meetings at the United Nations Codex Alimentarius in Geneva and Rome. NHFC and NHFA have attended many conferences and meetings of our colleagues' organizations across the country working for health freedom. We regularly offer workshops and public presentations on health freedom.

what people think that they, or the government, should or should not do regarding health care.

Over the years I have been given the opportunity to provide comment on cases and bills that are shrouded in controversy and polarization. Even though NHFC and NHFA are not law firms and we do not take private clients, we are often called on to share our thoughts about a case or to offer referrals. An example of the type of cases we work with is the case in which the government attempted to force a family to accept chemotherapy treatment for their child instead of allowing the parents to get a second opinion from out-of-state or international pediatric experts, and the government using child protection laws to enforce their medical decision-making. In this type of case, there are strong opinions about the protection of parental rights, as opposed to the state stepping in to recommend what it thinks is best for the child. Other cases involved holistic practitioners who had their offices raided and were jailed for not having a conventional medical license when there was no evidence of harm and no misrepresentation of background or training. The legal issues of these cases are similar to those of the Saunders case. There were cases involving manufacturers whose facilities were raided and inventory taken without notice, without showing of harm to consumers, and cases in which small farmers were prevented from selling fresh milk from their farms to willing customers. With regard to the milk issue, NHFA got involved in the state of Minnesota to draft protective language for raw milk sales so that farmers could sell milk and bring it to their customers directly instead of having to follow Minnesota's requirement that the sale take place on the farm. That law has not yet passed. There was a case where a family was denied the removal of an electrical frequency pulsing meter installed by the city to monitor utility usage even though the meter was causing their son to have seizures. We've reviewed cases in which health care employees were fired for choosing not to receive a flu shot before coming to work, even when past flu shots had given them adverse reactions. There are legislative bills that deny the right of parents to have their children in day care or public school because they choose to decline government-recommended vaccines.

Polarization is apparent when cases go public and one may observe the diverse remarks of citizens. These divergent views are increasingly affecting families, friends, and communities at large. My hope is that, rather than staying entrenched in positions, each of us will begin to aggressively participate in the conversation about health freedom and seek ways to listen to and converse with each other reasonably about our differences, our fears, and our hopes.

The stories and voices of people choosing to walk the health freedom trail are unique in that many have found themselves, sometimes reluctantly and only by necessity, in the conversation about their own basic freedoms, often while struggling to make their own decisions on their journeys toward health and healing. Their stories are the foundations upon which the health freedom movement has evolved.

United States Health Freedom Congress

NHFC was aware that many areas of health care were in need of health freedom protection and that many organizations and leaders were working in nonprofits around the country on particular issues to protect health freedoms. People were working to protect organic food standards, the right to decline vaccines, the right to make truthful claims about dietary supplements, and the right to be free from fluoridated water supplies and mercury toxicity in dental amalgams—and so much more. In 2003 NHFC discussed the need to bring together leaders in the health freedom movement to meet each other in person and discuss overarching issues for American health seekers. We wanted to work together with others to articulate health freedom expectations. NHFC decided to hold its first leaders conference in 2003, in Rochester, Minnesota. The launch conference was an inspiring experience. The leaders who gathered were of one mind and one heart. It was such a success that we decided to have another one the following year. These wonderful in-person leadership gatherings continue to be a highlight of our work. Since 2003 NHFC has hosted twelve national health freedom leadership conferences.[1]

As the conferences grew, NHFC began to add more structure to them. In 2006 the gathering included voting members with international health freedom leaders being invited. It was called the 2006 International World Health Freedom Assembly. At the World Assembly, we sat in the round and discussed, drafted, and voted on an International Declaration of Health

Freedom[2] (see appendix B). By 2012 the annual gathering had become a central gathering for US leaders and was named the United States Health Freedom Congress. The 2012 congress convened in Schaumburg, Illinois. That year we discussed and passed fifteen resolutions submitted by voting members on behalf of health freedom[3] (see appendix C).

As of this writing, the most recent congress was held in 2018 in St. Paul, Minnesota. The US Health Freedom Congress continues to bring together trusted leaders in the health freedom movement with NHFC's stated goals for the congress as follows:

- To experience an egalitarian gathering of autonomous and diverse leaders, where leaders communicate face-to-face in a large round congress-style format;
- To increase collaboration and inspire each other to unity and solidarity;
- To identify top health freedom issues and topics that are impacting health freedom;
- To find areas of common ground and pass resolutions;
- To work together to identify strategies for enhanced health freedom; and
- To celebrate the health freedom movement and give awards honoring successful leaders.[4]

State Action Needed for Health Freedom

Since its inception, NHFA, the lobbying organization, has fielded calls from all over the country from citizens requesting assistance with becoming active in reforming laws and public policies that are infringing on health freedom. Calls come for many different reasons.

Individuals call when they realize that they need to take action and change the laws of their state. NHFA has worked with citizens to assess the health freedom issues and respond. We research the laws. We help groups organize in their state to change laws. We send out education and action alerts to our subscribers to give citizens opportunities to write directly to their legislators. And we offer to be on-site when needed to testify or give presentations that help health freedom move forward.

Our efforts have given us opportunities to support efforts to protect the right of practitioners to practice their vocations, to protect parental rights to decline vaccines for their children who are attending schools or day cares, to assist in informing citizens about the dangers of genetically modified or engineered food, and to help protect access to organic pesticide-free foods.

The evolution of technology has brought about many new health freedom issues. The potential for infringements on personal freedoms is complex and diverse. For example, we address citizen concerns when they learn about the impact to human health and the effect on human DNA from the broadcasting of high-frequency electromagnetic frequency microwave radiation into the environment, including the most recent 5G antenna installations and broadcasting. We also address the long-term societal impact the engineering of biologics, including viruses, which we now have the capability to do. Most recently, we have spoken about the impact of computer internet applications designed for tracking people and tracing what goes on between them, and what goes on between people and their health care providers and other data-collecting entities. These evolutions in technology require citizen vigilance, research, and understanding when it comes to health freedom. NHFA is committed to protecting health freedom in the face of this evolution.

Federal and International Health Freedom

Over the years, as NHFA and NHFC expertise grew, we became active in responding not only to state issues but also to federal and international issues affecting health freedom.

Codex

In 2003 and 2004 we became aware that the United Nations Codex Alimentarius Commission was working on setting upper limits of dosage for dietary supplements being shipped between countries. The Codex

Alimentarius Commission, also known as CAC, is the central part of the Joint FAO/WHO Food Standards Programme and was established by FAO (Food and Agricultural Organization) and WHO (World Health Organization) to protect consumer health and promote fair practices in food trade.[5] Codex has 170 country member nations that set international safety standards for trading of food products between countries, which they have decided includes food supplements such as vitamins and minerals.

In delving into the international legal issues, we realized that this process could jeopardize the ability of people around the world from, for example, getting more than 10 mg of vitamin C in a capsule because their country would be treating vitamins like drugs, considering large doses of vitamins to be dangerous. We here in the United States were grateful for the consumer-driven passage of the United States 1994 Dietary Supplement Health and Education Act, which protects our dietary supplements from being regulated as drugs. The United States makes sure that vitamins are regulated as food with a presumption of their being generally regarded as safe and allows for large dosages in the United States.

In June of 2004 NHFC made a decision to send me and board member Linda Peterson to the annual seven-day Codex Commission meeting in Geneva, Switzerland, to support the voices of consumers who wanted their access to high dosages of vitamins protected. Linda and I also wanted to bring back firsthand information about the progress of the Codex meetings. It was a deep learning experience. When we arrived, I expected that there would be many citizens from all around the world participating in and observing the meeting. But to my surprise, there were three levels of attendees, and I and Linda were the only persons in the third level.

First, there were the official representatives from each country who had special seating placement and microphones just as legislators in Congress have. Then there was another level of attendees who were representing nonprofit nongovernmental organizations (NGOs) from around the world who had special Codex NGO status and seating and could only speak when called upon. Then there was balcony seating for observers such as I with headphones available with seven languages to listen to the discussions. I and Linda were the only observers to the Codex meeting all week.

I listened carefully and took a massive amount of notes. Many standards for the transportation of food between countries and food safety standards were discussed, and many reports were given by special expert committees on different food safety issues. I especially remember, for example, the debate regarding whether or not countries must require labeling of infant formula products to include information about the benefits of breastfeeding, which was part of a labeling resolution of the World Health Organization. The country of India was strong in their request to include this on all labeling of infant formula. I was surprised and disheartened to see resistance from many countries on that issue. The WHO resolution on infant formula in part stated as follows:

> 9.2 Manufacturers and distributors of infant formula should ensure that each container as a clear, conspicuous, and easily readable and understandable message printed on it, or on a label which cannot readily become separated from it, in an appropriate language, which includes all the following points: (a) the words *Important Notice* or their equivalent; (b) a statement of the superiority of breastfeeding; (c) a statement that the product should be used only on the advice of a health worker as to the need for its use and the proper method of use; (d) instructions for appropriate preparation, and a warning against the health hazards of inappropriate preparation.[6]

The standards for vitamin dosage came up as a topic in the meeting. But after only a short debate, it was sent back to a working committee and was not endorsed in its final stages that year. So we were very interested in reporting to our subscribers and looking ahead to the next meeting, which would be two years later. Upon our return, because consumers had not been present at the meetings and I was wanting all people to know what was happening at international meetings, I developed a consumer educational paper on Codex and made it available on our website. Annual international Codex meetings are lengthy and complex. To prepare for the next meeting, we connected with other health freedom organizations in the United States. We all agreed to go to the next Codex meeting in Rome, Italy. This was in 2005. National Health Federation is the lead NGO health freedom organization representing consumers at Codex.[7] They have made great strides in participating in discussions at Codex and voicing the sentiments of regular citizens. We joined them there in Italy to support their work.

We also did follow-up and wrote and distributed lengthy memorandums and shorter handouts to explain to consumers the issues being worked on at Codex.[8] Sadly, Codex did end up passing rules to limit dosages for the international marketing of vitamins. Arriving at those dosage amounts is the ongoing work of Codex.

Complementary and Alternative Medicine

In 2007 we learned that the FDA had issued a draft guidance document commenting on the ways that they planned on dealing with practitioners who were using natural health care products in their practices. Since we had been working with state laws and believed that state laws and not federal laws applied to vocational practices, we drafted formal comments on the FDA's draft guidance entitled "Guidance for Industry on Complementary and Alternative Medicine Products and Their Regulation by the Food and Drug Administration"[9] and gave them to the FDA. We opposed the FDA's attempt to have jurisdiction over holistic practitioners and their use of natural products in their complementary and alternative healing practices. We articulated the jurisdiction issues between state practitioner laws and state jurisdictions, and federal product and drug laws and federal jurisdiction for the FDA. The FDA attempted to call products "complementary and alternative health care products" if they were used by a holistic practitioner, a term which has never been defined in law. They insisted that since the products would be used by healing practitioners, the products may become "drugs" by definition because they were used for healing. And practitioners could be investigated by the FDA for using drugs that were not approved by the FDA. We sent strong comments to the FDA. Our summary in part stated the following:

> If the FDA sees a perceived need to clarify its jurisdiction as to which products are subject to regulation as a biological product, cosmetic, drug, device, or food (including food additives and dietary supplements), under the Act or the PHS Act, then it should do so in a forthright manner without focus on one particular group or another and without confusion as to infringement of state laws and regulations of health care systems, domains, practices, and practitioners. In the alternative, if the document continues to be developed, NHFA hopes that the FDA will seriously consider its comments and those of our colleagues

in the field of health care and health freedom, and revise the documents accordingly.

Thankfully the draft guidance did not move to final form.[10]

New Dietary Ingredients

In November 2011 we learned that the FDA had issued a draft guidance that would greatly affect the breadth of the Dietary Supplement Act and all the dietary supplements available to consumers. We drafted and gave formal comments to the FDA on their "Draft Guidance for Industry; Dietary Supplements: New Dietary Ingredient Notifications and Related Issues; Availability." NHFA opposed the FDA's attempt to prohibit the production and sale of dietary supplements that contain new dietary ingredients. The FDA was attempting to challenge the meaning of "new dietary ingredient" and take away the presumption of safety and place the burden of proof of safety on the manufacturers. NHFA held that there was a presumption of safety for new dietary ingredients that were in compliance with the food and new dietary ingredient regulations spelled out in the Dietary Supplement Health and Education Act. As of the writing of this book, the draft guidance has not moved forward to final form.

Communicable Disease

In September of 2016, NHFA learned that the CDC (Centers for Disease Control and Prevention) had issued a notice of proposed rulemaking regarding measures they would take to control communicable diseases. Their proposed rules included in part:

- Increased reporting requirements of ill persons by airline and vessel operators.
- Providing for persons to voluntarily enter into an agreement with the federal government when detained or apprehended regarding compliance with the federal quarantine order.*

---

* NHFA believed that this would create mass confusion and misrepresentation during a time of crisis. It could be viewed as a way to give the federal government documentation

- An inclusion of a definition of the term *noninvasive*, attempting to give the impression that the CDC was concerned about personal liberty, but in proposing clarification of the bounds of the CDC's authority regarding what they may do to a person's body, the new definition of "medical examination" stated that the CDC could order laboratory testing under certain conditions.*
- The ability to detain an individual for seventy-two hours or even more without a federal order.†

We drafted formal comments and gave them to the Department of Health and Human Services' Centers for Disease Control and Prevention requesting the withdrawal of the CDC's notice of proposed rulemaking entitled "Control of Communicable Disease."[11] NHFA held that the proposal had profound infringements on personal liberties in terms of increased citizen observation measures, lack of direct informed consent in agreements to comply with orders, detaining citizens for seventy-two hours without any orders, and the implementation of electronic monitoring of personal information and data. The proposed rule was eventually amended and passed taking into consideration some, but not all, of our opposing comments.

Homeopathic Remedies

In March 2018, NHFA learned that the FDA had issued a draft guidance that would drastically jeopardize the availability of a number of important homeopathic remedies. Guidance documents are policy guides for

---

and assurance that a detained person planned to carry out the health measures with which the federal government wanted them to comply with even if that person decided that they did not wish to comply, and as a way to check up on them as they were in the process of quarantine, isolation, or conditional release.

* NHFA held that forced laboratory testing, without the option of declining or quarantine instead, was entirely unacceptable and an invasive measure.

† NHFA held that detaining an individual for up to seventy-two hours without a federal order of quarantine, isolation, and conditional release is completely unacceptable. It is one thing to step off a plane and be questioned for thirty minutes or two hours to assess whether you or any person on the plane has been determined to be in a communicable stage of a quarantinable communicable disease. It is yet another thing to be held in limbo overnight, and up to three overnights, waiting to see if you will be served a federal order of quarantine.

71

what to expect from the FDA but are not actual law. Still, they are very influential in that they allow one to know how the FDA will function in a particular situation. We drafted and gave formal comments to the FDA on their draft guidance document entitled "Drug Products Labeled as Homeopathic: Guidance for FDA Staff and Industry."[12] NHFA opposed the draft guidance because it would repeal a current guidance document that had provided some guidance and limited protection for the manufacture and sale of homeopathic products since 1984. However, for years, even with a protective policy document in place, there was confusion regarding homeopathic remedies because homeopathic remedies were defined legally as drugs according to the definition of *drug* and thus were under the jurisdiction of drug regulations, not considered food and not included in the Dietary Supplement Act. NHFA, which has worked to educate citizens on the legal status of homeopathic remedies, in response to the restrictive proposed guidance, drafted and distributed to consumers and practitioners model federal legislation that would change and clarify the law so that homeopathic remedies would forever be legally generally regarded as safe even if they were to remain bound by the definition of *drug*. At the writing of this book, the historic protective 1984 guidance has been repealed, but no new protective guidance has been put in place. Health freedom advocates are working to continue to give their comments to the FDA. NHFA continues to voice a need for a change in the actual law.

The Breadth of Health Freedom

NHFC continues to educate about health freedom issues. NHFA continues to support taking action for health freedom. Both NHFC and NHFA support the following:

- the right of all healers to practice their vocations
- the organic food movement
- opposing genetically modified foods and the destruction of natural agricultural health, land, and environment
- the right of all persons to make their own health care decisions
- support of parental rights to decide what is best for their children
- the right to decline vaccines or other treatments

- food sovereignty and protection of access to natural resources, raw milk, and local food supplies
- the need for responsible technological development, free from harm to the health of humans, animals, plants, and Mother Earth
- access to all healing substances that are generally regarded as safe, such as homeopathic remedies, dietary supplements, and a host of other healing products
- continued vigilance to protect the personal liberty and health freedoms of people.

Our hope for health freedom is that together we can evolve into the universe we envision: a healthy nation with empowered people making informed health care decisions.

Chapter 4

Health Freedom — A Fundamental Right

> We hold these truths to be self-evident: that all men are created
> equal, that they are endowed by their Creator with certain
> inalienable rights, among these are life, liberty, and the pursuit
> of happiness, that to secure these rights governments are
> instituted among men.[1]

In the founding of our country there was intense debate about the role of
government in people's lives. The harsh history of personal sufferings under
British rule was spelled out boldly in the Declaration of Independence.[2]
The very reason for establishing a new form of government was to create
a government that would not lead to the oppression of individual people;
equal opportunity for life, liberty, and the pursuit of happiness for everyone
was the goal. In the last quarter of the eighteenth century, there was no
country in the world that governed with separated and divided powers
providing checks and balances on the exercise of authority by those who
governed.

This vision of protecting the freedom of each individual and providing
checks and balances on the authority of those who governed were defining
characteristics of a new community. Out of debate came the articulation
of the founding premise that freedom is not a privilege given to people by
governments or royal families; freedom arises out of a person's birth and
existence and their participation in life's experiences and conversations
among other humans.

A constitution was drawn up describing three branches of governmental powers: the legislative powers, the executive powers, and the judicial powers. The Constitution would be the law of the land. After the Constitution was passed, the founders added ten amendments to the Constitution entitled the Bill of Rights.[3] These additions address specific individual rights. They included a protectionary amendment, the Ninth, reminding everyone that all other inherent freedoms not listed were not to be infringed upon.

> Amendment IX
>
> The enumeration in the Constitution, of certain rights, shall not be construed to deny or disparage others retained by the people.[4]

A personal freedom that was not enumerated in the Bill of Rights was health freedom. Sadly, this freedom is now at the core of much upheaval and suffering in our country.

Elm Tree Bark

During the Revolutionary War, there was a battle after which the colonial forces were weakened. The snow and cold were treacherous, and there was no food for the troops. The men were starving, and another battle was forthcoming. The general was visited by local Native Americans wanting to offer support. The general told them his men were starving. They looked puzzled and asked how the men could be starving when they were surrounded by such a wealth of nutrients. The general was surprised to learn that the elm trees surrounding his encampment were made up of bark that was many times more nutritious than oatmeal. He proceeded to feed the men until they were strengthened; when they moved into battle, they succeeded. "George Washington and his troops are believed to have subsisted for several days on gruel made from slippery elm bark during the cold winter at Valley Forge, Pennsylvania. A poultice made from the inner bark was a field dressing for gunshot wounds during the Revolutionary War."[5]

The freedom of the general to gain health and survival information from others, and the freedom to access the bark of the elm trees in order to help his men survive, was a freedom taken for granted at that time.

However, in today's world, that story may have unfolded differently. In today's world someone might have put the Native Americans in jail for practicing medicine without a license when they claimed that the bark of an elm tree could help the troops survive. Or the general might have been disciplined by the military for telling his troops that elm bark could make them well. Or a local doctor supporting the efforts to use elm bark might be disciplined because it is advice outside the conventional medical standard of care for severe starvation symptoms. Or possibly, the elm bark might be banned from use at all because it was used for prevention and cure of illness and thus considered a drug that was not approved. Troops would not have had the freedom to eat the bark even if they would have wanted to in order to save their own lives.

I am happy to report that slippery elm bark is easily accessible in grocery stores and pharmacies in the United States today as a food. Since many foods are now regulated and sold as concentrated foods called dietary supplements, slippery elm bark remains accessible in that form as well, thanks to the work of health freedom advocates who protected dietary supplement foods in the passing of the 1994 Dietary Supplement Health and Education Act.[6]

Important health freedom conversations have been ongoing in the United States since the founding of our country. And it is only by way of these living freedom conversations that slippery elm bark and other nutrients are protected and accessible to health seekers today.

It is believed by many that health freedom was held by the founders of this country to be so basic that they could not imagine a day when it would be restricted or denied by government regulations or corporate monopolies. They could not visualize technology, intellectual property, and medical monopolies, which have now become a dominant element of American society, affecting our freedom. They could not foresee how these "advances" might dictate or determine the health experiences, treatments, or choices of an individual.

But there was one founding father, physician Benjamin Rush, who was concerned about health freedom. He is often quoted as promoting the inclusion of health freedom in the Bill of Rights. I offer the following original quotation from his lecture at the University of Pennsylvania on November 3, 1801, during which he enumerated twenty-four causes which had retarded the progress of medicine:

> 21st. The interference of governments in prohibiting the use of certain remedies and enforcing the use of others by law. The effects of this mistaken policy have been as hurtful to medicine, as a similar practice with respect to opinions, has been to the Christian religion.

> 22d. Conferring exclusive privileges upon bodies of physicians, and forbidding men, of equal talents and knowledge, under severe penalties, from practicing medicine within certain districts of cities and countries. Such institutions, however sanctioned by ancient charters and names, are the bastilles of our science.[7]

The founders of our country were well aware of the potential for abuse of power by governments and by power structures that affected the lives of citizens. As a physician, Rush was especially aware and vocal about the effect of power structures on the healing arts.

The founding fathers considered health freedom the most basic freedom. They knew that in order to protect one's own health and life, one needed to use all the other freedoms enumerated (and not enumerated) in the Constitution because all freedoms are necessary when a person is deciding how to live and survive.

Over the years, our courts have affirmed this very basic view of personal liberty and health freedom. In the famous 1990 Cruzan case, about whether an incompetent person retains the right to have her life support maintained, the court began with some historical background:

> Before the turn of the century, this Court observed that "[n] o right is held more sacred, or is more carefully guarded, by the common law, than the right of every individual to the

possession and control of his own person, free from all restraint or interference of others, unless by clear and unquestionable authority of law." Union Pacific R. Co. v. Botsford, 141 U.S. 250, 251 (1891). This notion of bodily integrity has been embodied in the requirement that informed consent is generally required for medical treatment. Justice Cardozo, while on the Court of Appeals of New York, aptly described this doctrine: "Every human being of adult years and sound mind has a right to determine what shall be done with his own body." ... Schloendorff v. Society of New York Hospital, 211 N. Y. 125, 129–130, 105 N. E. 92, 93 (1914).[8]

The Cruzan case protected the right of the State of Missouri to have Cruzan's hydration and nutrition maintained. The state was unwilling to accept the "substituted judgment" of a close family member who wanted to stop the hydration and nutrition, in the absence of substantial proof that that is what the patient would have wanted.[9]

US Government and US Citizens Freedom Conversation

As the founding fathers predicted, the conversation about individual rights and the role of government in the lives of individuals would be challenged. The fact that some rights are enumerated in the Bill of Rights and some are not forced the freedom conversation to continue throughout the years, and courts necessarily needed to continue to ask two questions about freedoms:

1) Should the government acknowledge and protect only the rights enumerated in the Constitution, which they presume are "fundamental" rights, or are there other rights based on general principles of liberty and justice that are fundamental and deserve protection?

2) If a right is enumerated, and fundamental or otherwise acknowledged as fundamental, or if a right is acknowledged but not considered so fundamental as to warrant as high a standard of protection as a fundamental right, how strongly and with what standards should the government work to protect these different rights?

Individuals have conversed at length with their governments about their rights, including their right to make their own health decisions and the role of the government to protect these health rights. They have done this with their legislators, designing laws that protect their health freedoms, and through court challenges. The arena of constitutional law is complex and covers a wide territory of subjects and challenges to protect personal freedoms. This area of law has grown according to the changes in culture, understandings and expectations of personal freedoms, and contributions of modern science. We look to our Supreme Court's guidance on medical freedom as it grapples with the many complex constitutional issues that arise in the exploding world of health and biotechnological advances.

The following quotations have always ignited my continued hope for the future of the protection of health freedom. Supreme Court justices work hard to discuss and debate on how to rule on important health-related cases. Important words from the Supreme Court are often not only from the primary opinion but also from dissenting justices as they grapple with important issues and lay out foundational principles that will affect the future understanding of freedom. The back-and-forth conversations of Supreme Court justices have moved our country forward in many areas of understanding, helping us understand the breadth and depth of responsibility we have for the grand vision of freedom and liberty in our country. The following historic words speak to our country's conversation of health freedom:

> Freedom from unwanted medical attention is unquestionably among those principles "so rooted in the traditions and conscious of our people as to be ranked as fundamental."[10]

> The right to be free from medical attention without consent, to determine what shall be done with one's own body, is deeply rooted in this Nation's traditions, as the majority acknowledges.[11]

> This right has long been "firmly entrenched in American torte law" and is securely grounded in the earliest common law.[12]

> Anglo-American law starts with the premise of thorough-going self-determination. It follows that each man is considered to be master of his own body, and he may, if he be of sound mind,

expressly prohibit the performance of life-saving surgery or other medical treatment.[13]

It is "a well-established rule of general law ... that it is the patient, not the physician, who ultimately decides if treatment— any treatment—is to be given at all. ... The rule has never been qualified in its application by either the nature or purpose of the treatment, or to gravity of the consequences of acceding to or foregoing it."[14]

The foregoing cases suggest that specific guarantees in the Bill of Rights have penumbras, formed by emanations from those guarantees that help give them life and substance.[15]

The United States clearly recognizes, struggles with, and works to protect the right to make one's own health decisions and secure one's health freedom. It does so just as we recognize and protect many other personal rights such as freedom of speech, freedom of religion, and freedom of association.

One could ask, then, how can a government infringe upon health freedom. How is it that a state can outlaw healers who are not posing harm? How is it that our government can outlaw remedies that are generally regarded as safe, and thereby make it impossible for citizens to access them? Or, one might ask, how is it that the government allows for the use of toxins in community spaces? Or how can a state require injections of vaccinations before school entrance against parental medical decisions?

Living Freedom

In a harmonious community, there dwells a group consciousness that animates the community persona while holding sacred and responsible the individual sovereign life experience to reign supreme.

Images of powerful great eagles soaring high and free come to many Americans when we hear the word *freedom*. History lets us know that the experience of living without personal freedom is excruciating. But beyond individual freedom is the additional broader aspect of freedom that encompasses freedom for family, community, and environment.

The freedom of a community to shape its own destiny is similar in many ways to an individual's freedom of self-determination. But communities are unique in that the community must always be aware of the individuals within it. The community must remain aware of the will of the individuals within it to make their own decisions. In the best of worlds, a community would shape its own persona and norms and would also be vigilant, protecting ways to hold sacred the individual's sovereign human life experience.

The founders of our country had to grapple with this more complex outlook on freedom. Their thinking on the balance of individual liberties with the will of communities became the foundation of our country's constitutional architecture. In order to fulfill both personal visions of freedom and the visions of our communities to live in harmony, a plan was designed that attempted to accommodate freedom overall. It was understood that a decision made by one human on the basis of their individual freedom generally would affect other humans. Our desire for community necessarily forced us into consideration of how we, in our great diversity, would organize ourselves and go about living peaceably with each other in community without infringing on personal freedoms.

This grand quest required a visionary organizational architecture that would avoid the trampling upon of individual freedoms and liberty by a new government. Ideas came forward by our founders for a representative discerning government that would serve the people and would have the duty to participate in constant dialogue and discuss ideas with citizens, groups, and colonies. Ideas came forth of providing systems for arbitration or judicial orders to settle disputes. Thus emerged the shaping of a representative government, with checks and balances on power, and a judiciary that would be able to uphold the Constitution and prevent a dominant power or majority from trampling on individual human rights. As the architectural plans of the Constitution unfolded, the founders, I assume, envisioned the protection of liberty and freedom, knowing that freedom would require perpetual ongoing communication and decision-making by the people to promote community harmony while protecting fundamental individual freedoms.

Freedom Is a Conversation

The needs of this complex view of freedom and my life's work with health freedom advocacy has brought me to the conclusion that freedom is not something just to be "had." Rather, freedom is necessarily an active experience, an ongoing conversation. Freedom requires a constant and ongoing conversation about life issues in the context of oneself and others and in the context of one's own community and environment.

The founders of the United States were in the midst of intense conversations, with passion and discernment, resonance and conflicts, friendships and rivalries, all part of being in the mix of what they wanted to define as a "whole." This was a grand freedom conversation—a living, breathing revolutionary body of great visions.

Freedom cannot be defined or experienced outside the context of an ongoing conversation in the living, changing universe because we are living, growing, evolving human beings. We are interdependent on one another and our environment, and we are forever changing. It is the freedom conversation that calls us to experience life in its fullest sense.

The freedom conversation is not for sleeping people. Freedom is for a people awake and engaged! The amazing design of our country allows for people to continually and fully participate with each other in communities and in government and be purposefully in the conversation of freedom.

My health practitioner colleague sent me the following note following a conversation we had about understanding freedom as living conversation:

> The tensegrity structure I have in my office demonstrates how tension in one part of the body causes stress throughout the system; it shows how one stress can result in symptoms forming in locations far away from the original injury. The model is made of wooden dowels and stretchy elastic cords so

I can demonstrate how the system performs under stress, since
the muscles and bones in our bodies are actually a tensegrity
structure.

Ah yes, *tensegrity* provides a wonderful analogy. That stretchy elastic
cord is like the carrier of the freedom conversation, always looking for
balance. It takes a strong will to choose to participate in freedom, that
elastic cord among us, to continually engage in important conversations
with individuals and communities seeking freedom and harmony. It takes
a strong elasticity to maintain flexibility, and it takes work to discern
solutions for the good of the individual and the good of the whole. It takes
a strong commitment and connection to listen to and hear the tension
between the parts and the whole to find the harmony.

If the elastic cord of the commitment to freedom is not present, then it is
all for nothing. If it is strong and flexible and completely open to finding
balance, then freedom will prevail and blockages will dissipate.

Health Freedom in the Context of Other Freedoms

Some say that one personal freedom is not more important than another
because each is part of the human experience and they are all interdependent
on each other and interface with each other constantly. If freedom of speech
is suppressed, then we cannot access the information we need to exercise
our health freedom decision-making. If freedom of religion is suppressed,
then we cannot make life-and-death decisions that resonate with our belief
system. If freedom of association is suppressed, then we cannot network
with like-minded people to explore the human experience and find health
solutions that match our preferences and needs. If health freedom is
suppressed, then someone else might dictate our path to wellness or death.

Whether one freedom is more important than another, when a person
exercises her health freedom to its full extent, she necessarily touches
upon and requires full cooperation regarding many, if not all, of the other
personal freedoms and liberties. My colleague Clinton Miller used to say
that if you don't have health freedom, you don't have life, and then you
don't have the need for any other freedom.

The Future

As we relate to each other individually and as we relate to each other in the context of the human family and our environment, we have the opportunity to maintain the health of the community and the freedom of the community while holding sacred our individual cultures, spirits, and intentions.

We have many profound assurances in US law that health freedom is the law of the land. One would think that such fundamental freedoms could never be abrogated. But looking closely throughout our beloved country, one sees that the seemingly impossible has happened: we are on the brink of the extinction of the most fundamental and survival freedom of all—health freedom.

The conversation of freedom requires alert individuals who know that they are free and who seek health on their own behalf and on behalf of their loved ones. The conversation of freedom requires that individuals be in active conversation with each other, with their communities, and with their government. Americans need to take back the personal authority that they have delegated to others and activate once again that grand freedom that they have always had but that today lies dormant. It is happening. We are waking up and participating in the health freedom conversation.

Chapter 5

The Eight Principles of Health Freedom

Principles arise from the stories of people. As our survival as a human family is being challenged and even jeopardized, it is apparent that health freedom needs to be understood as *the greatest freedom of all.*

The stories of Americans have motivated me to articulate and write down basic principles of health freedom. I will be discussing each of these principles in depth in the chapters that follow.

The following are principles that have been lost in the midst of an industrialized society. They have reemerged as stories come forward of people struggling to be heard, to be protected, and to have their health needs and decisions honored.

These principles are tools that can help the human family, hopefully for generations to come, in its search for freedom, health, and harmony. They can provide guidance while we are in a polarized debate about health freedom topics, encouraging us to listen carefully and consider the long-term breadth and impact of health freedom.

Pressing questions are being explored. What do Americans and people all over the world want when it comes to health care and personal liberty? What is it that people expect when they get sick, from other humans, from the community at large, from health care provider systems, and from their own government? What expectations do people have about their personal freedom as it relates to health care decisions?

Guiding Principles Responding to an Awakening

The good news is that there is an awakening of people who have a desire for health freedom and support in their healing journeys. There is a sense of urgency among many for greater health and assurance of survival, amid the confusion and chaos in society.

As a first step, the United States needs to move forward and ensure that health freedom and personal liberty is protected at all costs, just as our country has vigorously defended freedom of speech, freedom of religion, and many other freedoms. Governments and corporations have had an increasing role in our health, our health choices, and our liberties. It is now apparent that if people want to be in charge of their health decisions, their health outcomes, and ultimately their survival, then health freedom needs to be understood as *the greatest freedom of all*.

As a second step, in order to enlighten us in our understanding of this grand freedom, we need to learn about basic fundamental principles that are emerging from the stories of people from this time in history— principles born out of the evolution of individuals demanding that they get their health needs met, while retaining their bodily sovereignty and responsibility for their own health and health choices, all this in the context of an industrialized society.

Principles in Action

The principles of health freedom can be used in many ways. They can be used as a starting point for a health freedom conversation. They can be used to initiate action to protect health freedom. They can be used as underpinnings and justification for the making of laws. They can be read to inspire judicial discernment in challenging health freedom legal cases. They can even be challenged and amended as we evolve as a people in our technological world.

I believe that laws and customs must be carefully reviewed, revised, and even repealed if necessary, and new ones created, to reflect the continual development, evolution, and spiritual maturation of a people.

You and Me

Stories of everyday people like you and me are the foundation of the principles of health freedom. For individuals, the principles can assist in coping with the complexity of today's world, living within the parameters of one's own circle of life, and living by the other principles that one believes in. For communities, the principles can inspire active enlightened individuals to participate in complex conversations about health and survival while protecting the sacred sovereignty and liberty of individuals. Hopefully the principles will help us find a way to survive in an industrialized society and, at the same time, preserve our human rights and liberties.

Principles of Health Freedom

Principle 1: Freedom to Be Let Alone

Individuals and members of the human family have the inherent fundamental right of self-determination, to be let alone to survive on their own terms and in their own manner.

Principle 2: Freedom to Act

Individuals and members of the human family hold the fundamental right and freedom to act on their own behalf and as they choose to secure health and survival.

Principle 3: Freedom to Access

For freedom of choice to be implemented or meaningful, individuals and members of the human family hold the fundamental right and freedom to access their choices, whomever and whatever they deem necessary or prefer for their own health and survival.

Principle 4: *Responsibility to Do No Harm*

To maintain the health and survival of individuals, members of the human family, and the community as a whole, have the responsibility to do no harm.

Principle 5: *Responsibility of Tolerance*

Because of the diverse nature of the human experience, members of the human family have the responsibility to show tolerance to the extent of avoiding hostile acts toward diverse health and survival options and toward those who choose those options.

Principle 6: *General Responsibility of Corporations*

Corporations have the potential of significantly affecting the health and survival of the human family and thus have the responsibility and duty to be trustworthy entities safeguarding health freedom rights and responsibilities.

Principle 7: *Special Responsibilities of Corporations*

In light of the special legal nature of corporate entities and their potential systemic impact on the health and survival of the human family, corporations have the following five responsibilities:

Principle 7-1

To honor and preserve the sovereign nature of individuals and the sovereignty of the United States, and to avoid any negative impact on the sovereignty of other nation-states as applies to health and survival.

Principle 7-2

To honor and preserve American financial and cultural diversity and multicultural systems that are abiding by and upholding US law, and to avoid negative impact on the financial or cultural status of other nation-states as applies to health and survival.

Principle 7-3

To avoid creating or being monopolies with large ownership of resources and allowing that status to dictate or dominate cultures, public policies, regulations, or laws that affect health and survival.

Principle 7-4

To avoid the dominant control of natural resources and the suppression of access to natural resources, and not to cause potentially harmful modifications or destruction of natural resources.

Principle 7-5

To avoid promotion of products, protocols, policies, regulations, or laws that would encourage unlimited dependence on corporations and institutions or that would discourage, prohibit, or otherwise negatively affect the ability or will of humans and local communities to survive and prosper without the existence of the corporation or institution.

Principle 8: *Responsibility of Government*

Government has the responsibility and duty to protect health freedom and to make no law or public policy abridging health freedom or its fundamental principles.

(See appendix D: Principles of Health Freedom.)

I will expand upon these principles in the following chapters. These principles emerge from diverse scenarios of how health freedoms have been infringed upon and what solutions might be helpful to protect the basic human right of people to make decisions for their own well-being. There are direct infringements, for example, where a person is not allowed to make a choice that meets his needs, such as an employee who prefers to decline a vaccine but has an employer who requires the vaccine for employment. Then there are indirect infringements, for example, a person who wishes to have water in his home that is fluoride-free but who lives in a municipality that mandates fluoridation of the water. The principles of health freedom may help to guide us as we actively participate in the freedom conversation surrounding health decisions.

Chapter 6

Health Freedom Principle 1 —
Freedom to Be Let Alone

Principle 1: Freedom to Be Let Alone

Individuals and members of the human family have the inherent
fundamental right of self-determination, to be let alone to
survive on their own terms and in their own manner.

Self-Determination

The foundational principle of self-determination is the bedrock of personal
liberty. It ensures that our bodies are safe and secure unto ourselves and that
we decide what we want to experience regarding our health and survival.
We manage our bodies, minds, and spirits all day long, from knowing how
much sleep to get to knowing what kinds of foods to eat. When we get sick
or are physically or mentally challenged, it may require a more focused
decision-making mode. It is our right and our job to make decisions for
our own bodies, minds, and spirits if we want to maintain our health and
survival.

Ordinarily we use measures at home to help ourselves be well. Or we may
use health practitioners or other options in our community. If it is a serious
health issue, we may even spend time in a home of another family member
or friends, or a clinic, hospital, rehabilitation center, or some other care
place. When others become involved in assisting us, we are challenged to
continue to discern what we ourselves want and which recommendations

outside ourselves we would like to use or experience. When we do not feel good, this is especially challenging. Principle number one is to remind us that we have the right and the freedom to say yes and no according to our own wishes.

An extreme example of this is a patient in an intensive care situation who may not wish to have invasive testing and treatments and who wishes to be let alone. Or they may want to use options that are not recommended by conventional medical professionals. In some situations, the person may even intentionally wish to be let alone to die. But family and medical staff may want to insist upon particular measures or treatments, including in some circumstances to take lifesaving measures to bring the person back to health. In these situations, it is important for the patient to know their rights and to have them honored at all times, and for the family and health care providers to know the boundaries of the person's desire for intervention. Relationships and emotions run high in these situations. Living will laws have been passed to help in assisting patients, families, and health care providers to prepare for this type of situation.*

There are decisive examples in the history of our country where the principle of self-determination has been put to the test and has called us to understand the depth of the meaning of personal liberty. In the already cited famous 1990 Cruzan case, about whether an incompetent person retains the right to have her life support maintained, the court began with some historical background:

> Before the turn of the century, this Court observed that "[n]o right is held more sacred, or is more carefully guarded, by the common law, than the right of every individual to the possession and control of his own person, free from all restraint or interference of others, unless by clear and unquestionable authority of law." Union Pacific R. Co. v. Botsford, 141 U.S. 250, 251 (1891). This notion of bodily integrity has been embodied in the requirement that informed consent is generally required for medical treatment. Justice Cardozo, while on the Court of Appeals of New York, aptly described this doctrine:

---

* Living wills are documents prepared ahead of time that describe the wishes of a person in the event that they need help in health care decision-making and that give guidance to family and health care workers to assist them during an illness.

"Every human being of adult years and sound mind has a right to determine what shall be done with his own body." ... Schloendorff v. Society of New York Hospital, 211 N. Y. 125, 129–130, 105 N. E. 92, 93 (1914).[1]

The Cruzan case protected the right in the state of Missouri to have Cruzan's hydration and nutrition maintained by holding that the due process clause does not require a state to accept the "substituted judgment" of close family members in the absence of substantial proof that their views reflect the patient's.

Consequences for Saying No

The freedom of self-determination to be let alone in the United States is now, more than ever, being put in the crosshairs of public debate. As technology advances, there are more and more ways that citizens are directly offered aids in securing health that may have potential negative side effects, such as pharmaceutical drugs and vaccines, and more and more ways that our bodies are being negatively affected by measures that are being taken on behalf of the entire community, such as fluoridation of water, use of dangerous insecticides on common walkways, and utility meters that broadcast electromagnetic microwave radiation. What happens if a person wants to say no to something that they deem harmful? People are finding that they may experience painful consequences if they attempt to exercise their fundamental constitutional right of self-determination to avoid a health care measure or treatment in order to protect their own bodies from what they may perceive as harmful. How does one decide to survive on one's own terms and in one's own personal manner in these situations?

Health measures that are directly offered to people and that people respond to with a yes or a no are presenting challenges when a person chooses to decline. For example:

- A nurse at Christ Hospital Health Network in Cincinnati, Ohio, lost her job in 2017 because she was not willing to receive a flu vaccine mandated by her employer.[2]

93

- The parents of Danny Hauser, a thirteen-year-old boy, were legally challenged with the loss of custody of their son when they wished to stop painful chemotherapy treatments for him and use alternative cancer treatments.[3]
- The parents of children in California had their parental rights infringed upon in 2015 when Senate Bill 277 passed and they could no longer have their children attend day cares, or public or private schools, if the children did not receive, on schedule, the more than sixty-nine doses of vaccines recommended by the State of California.[4]

Saying no to these direct requests for treatment, which I call "the crossing of the skin barrier," had severe consequences. Often the enforcers of these types of liberty infringements argue that what they are doing is being mandated in the name of public health. To protect their liberties, themselves, and their families, citizens have had to take legal or legislative action.

For example, regarding employee vaccination, a number of states have now introduced special legislation to protect the right of employees to decline vaccines. The following Minnesota and Louisiana bills are examples:

- Minnesota Senate Bill SF 3109, introduced February 2020, which would prohibit an employer from disciplining or discharging an employee who refuses an immunization if they provided a statement that they have not been immunized because of conscientiously held beliefs; and
- Louisiana House Bill 642, introduced February 2020, which states that employees cannot be required to present evidence of immunity or have a vaccine if they provide a written dissent objecting to the vaccine.

Also for example, regarding families who wish to use complementary and alternative health care measures, more than half the states have now passed laws that allow licensed medical doctors to practice complementary and alternative medicine, unconventional medicine, integrative medicine, or holistic medicine. For example, Florida's law regarding complementary and alternative health care treatments begins with a strong legislative intent:

456.41   Complementary or alternative health care treatments.—

(1)   LEGISLATIVE INTENT.—It is the intent of the Legislature that citizens be able to make informed choices for any type of health care they deem to be an effective option for treating human disease, pain, injury, deformity, or other physical or mental condition. It is the intent of the Legislature that citizens be able to choose from all health care options, including the prevailing or conventional treatment methods as well as other treatments designed to complement or substitute for the prevailing or conventional treatment methods. It is the intent of the Legislature that health care practitioners be able to offer complementary or alternative health care treatments with the same requirements, provisions, and liabilities as those associated with the prevailing or conventional treatment methods.[5]

Regarding the right of parents to decide whether their child will receive a vaccine, numerous state citizen groups are vigorously working to preserve their right to decline vaccines for their children. According to the National Council of State Legislator:

All 50 states have legislation requiring specified vaccines for students. Although exemptions vary from state to state, all school immunization laws grant exemptions to children for medical reasons. There are 45 states and Washington D.C. that grant religious exemptions for people who have religious objections to immunizations. Currently, 15 states allow philosophical exemptions for those who object to immunizations because of personal, moral or other beliefs.

The foregoing data show a number of states where a parent can decline a vaccine for their child student, but many bills have been introduced in states to repeal these vaccine exemptions. It has been a constant struggle by parents to protect their rights. In addition, for example in California, there have been no exemptions for the childhood vaccine schedule for religious or personal belief reasons since 2015, when the exemption was repealed by very contentious legislation. So many parents have been forced to homeschool their children or move out of California in order to protect their health care decision-making for their children and still have access to education and day cares.

In addition to these direct challenges, people are being negatively affected in ways originating from the overall advancement of a technological society. Many Americans are unaware of these impacts and often are not given a choice as to whether they will say yes or no to the measure affecting them. These challenges are also affecting our freedom to be let alone.

Americans and the natural environment are negatively affected daily by water and air pollution and by hazardous waste. These dangers infringe on our freedoms because most often they do not require our consent and we are not given the ability to say yes or no in a straightforward, uncomplicated manner. Aggressive citizen activism and political advocacy is needed to affect public health policies that impact large numbers of people. And this is often an uphill battle. The Environmental Protection Agency works continually to advance civil and criminal cases to enforce laws to protect the environment and the health of consumers. The list of their legal actions is public information, available on their website.[6]

In addition to air and water, the land and soil that foods are grown in is negatively affected daily by chemicals and pesticides used in industrial agricultural practices. Many people are attempting to say yes or no to these dangers with their purchasing preferences, buying safe organic food or making choices about protective land stewardship. But it is often not easy. On June 24, 2020, Monsanto-Bayer settled a lawsuit for ten billion dollars brought by people suffering from cancer because of their exposure to Roundup. Roundup's dangerous glyphosate is now found in the soil, on foods, and in water supplies, and countries are beginning to ban it.[7] Victims in the lawsuit commented, "Bayer admitted no guilt, will continue to sell Roundup, and refused to label it as carcinogenic. People will continue to get cancer from it."[8] The Organic Consumers Association is a leading organization helping citizens navigate and participate in these health freedom issues.[9]

Our planet of Earth, including air, water, and land, is now being affected by human expansion into space and the advanced uses of technology. Arthur Firstenberg of Cell Phone Task Force warns that people across the globe are now, without consent, being affected by the launching of satellites in the ionosphere.[10] The ionosphere is a source of high voltage that controls the global electric circuit, which in turn provides the energy for life.[11] He reports that in May 2020, SpaceX filed an application with the Federal Communications Commission "for 30,000 'next-generation' ('Gen2') satellites."[12] Firstenberg warns that the ionosphere "provides us energy for life, and information that organizes our bodies. If you pollute this circuit with billions of digital pulsations, you will destroy all life."[13] The impact of digital technology, including our exposure to cell phones, to computers, and now to dangerous close-range antennas broadcasting levels of fifth-generation (5G) radiation, is of great concern. The human race is in a dilemma: enjoying the expansion of communication opportunities provided by technology and, at the same time, not completing due diligence on the potential long-term impact of that technology on the health of the human species. Deciding whether to say yes or no to this technology is a complex challenge. Finding ways to have the technology and still protect human health will be our great challenge.

In our daily attempts to be let alone to control our own health, our own lives, and our own destiny, we look to the laws of our country that offer protection of our personal liberty. As Americans, we look to our existing state and federal constitutions and our existing state laws to determine how an individual's rights are protected or whether they have been infringed upon.

State constitutions affirm the civil and religious rights of the people. State constitutions also set forth the reason for and role of governments. For example, Minnesota's government was instituted "for the security, benefit, and protection of the people, in whom all political power is inherent."[14] In addition to a constitution, state laws are passed by legislatures. These laws are specific and are passed based on constitutional principles. They provide people with guidance and give governments the ability to enforce laws for particular topics. For example, a state public health law that recommends vaccines also, in most states, includes language that ensures the right of parents to choose whether to have their children receive government-recommended vaccines. As Americans, we are called to continually be in the conversation of freedom in order to preserve our inalienable rights and to honor principle 1, stating that individuals and members of the human family have the inherent fundamental right of self-determination, to be let alone to survive on their own terms and in their own manner.

The Health Emergency Constitutional Frontier

But what about freedom during emergencies? The year 2020 has given Americans the opportunity to experience how laws affect them when government officials believe that there is a health emergency. We have learned that when there is a special emergency, there is a set of special state laws, passed by each state, that provide guidance and give special powers to the state governor and legislatures. Legislatures have to be very careful when passing laws delegating powers to the governor in emergencies so that whatever the governor does is constitutional and protective of constitutional rights. In most states, these governor power laws are called national security emergencies or peacetime emergency laws. In Minnesota, *emergency* means an unforeseen combination of circumstances that calls for immediate action to prevent a disaster from developing or occurring.[15] When a governor declares a national security or peacetime emergency, these special laws are triggered, and in most states, any orders and rules produced by the governor during the emergency, as long as they have followed the state law passed by their legislature regarding gubernatorial power, have the full force and effect of law.

But even if the governor has special powers to make orders with the effect of law, the orders must still be constitutional. Since health freedom rights are fundamental rights, they are primarily protected by the Constitution, and any infringement of them presents a constitutional law question. When talking about state infringements on an individual's fundamental rights during a declared emergency, the constitutional analysis would remain the same as it is in peacetime: the interests of the individual (to fully exercise their liberty right) must be balanced against the interest of the state (to protect the public's health by containing or eliminating the threat). Constitutional analysis is complex, based on decades of court opinions and legal arguments and thresholds in order to arrive at proper interpretations in each factual and legal circumstance.

Emergency Power Acts

State emergency power laws have been enacted in many states and are extremely important and sometimes controversial because orders and rules are produced by the governor during an emergency and governors are members of the executive branch of government, not the legislature. Although the governor's orders must be constitutional and often have time limitations and eventual oversight by legislative bodies, in most states they have the full force and effect of law.

I became keenly aware of emergency power laws and the importance of the delegation of authority to governors in 2002, when I was asked by a friend to review a bill (SF 2669) introduced in the Minnesota Legislature to expand the power of the governor in times of emergency. At the time I was unaware of such laws. As I reviewed the introduced bill, I was alarmed. It literally said that if my doctor did not do what they were told by the governor in an emergency, it would be a crime. Here is the paragraph in the bill that was introduced in the Minnesota Legislature on February 1, 2002, that caused my alarm. The bill was attempting to make it a misdemeanor for a physician to refuse to perform a medical examination or testing ordered by the governor:

> Subd. 2. [Health care providers; penalty.] During a national security or peacetime emergency declared due to a public health emergency, the commissioner of health may require a physician or other health care provider personnel, according to the individual's scope of practice, to perform a medical examination or testing under subdivision 1. Refusal to perform a medical examination or testing under this subdivision is a misdemeanor and may be reported by the commissioner of health to the individual's respective licensing board.[16]

Thank goodness that this paragraph did not pass in the Minnesota Legislature! I gathered my health freedom advocate friends together, and we discussed the entire lengthy bill. There were many provisions in the bill that were not acceptable to citizens. We worked hard with other interested citizen groups to defeat and amend various provisions of the bill.

Most importantly, our group drafted protective language for citizens in times of emergency. The following is the right-to-refuse law that we drafted and passed in Minnesota:

12.39 INDIVIDUAL TREATMENT; NOTICE, REFUSAL, CONSEQUENCE.

Subdivision 1. Refusal of treatment. Notwithstanding laws, rules, or orders made or promulgated in response to a national security emergency or peacetime emergency, individuals have a fundamental right to refuse medical treatment, testing, physical or mental examination, vaccination, participation in experimental procedures and protocols, collection of specimens, and preventive treatment programs. An individual who has been directed by the commissioner of health to submit to medical procedures and protocols because the individual is infected with or reasonably believed by the commissioner of health to be infected with or exposed to a toxic agent that can be transferred to another individual or a communicable disease, and the agent or communicable disease is the basis for which the national security emergency or peacetime emergency was declared, and who refuses to submit to them may be ordered by the commissioner to be placed in isolation or quarantine according to parameters set forth in sections 144.419 and 144.4195.

Subd. 2. Information given. Before performing examinations, testing, treatment, or vaccination of an individual under subdivision 1, a health care provider shall notify the individual of the right to refuse the examination, testing, treatment, or vaccination, and the consequences, including isolation or quarantine, upon refusal.

(See appendix E: Minnesota Statute 12.39.)

This refusal-of-treatment language that passed protects a citizen's right to refuse medical treatment, testing, physical or mental examination, vaccination, participation in experimental procedures and protocols, collection of specimens, and preventive treatment programs during emergencies.

The foundational shift that this 2002 bill regarding emergencies represented was a shift to expand the power of the governor to deal with health emergencies. For example, before 2002, the Minnesota governor could not declare an emergency unless it was a national security emergency or a peacetime emergency. A peacetime emergency may be declared only "when an act of nature, a technological failure or malfunction, a terrorist incident, an industrial accident, a hazardous materials accident, or a civil disturbance endangers life and property." But the bill expanded that power to add in times of "a public health emergency," with the legislature's definition of "public health emergency" being as follows:

> Subd. 9a. [PUBLIC HEALTH EMERGENCY.] "Public health emergency" means an occurrence or imminent threat of an illness or health condition in Minnesota:
>
> (1) where there is evidence to believe the illness or health condition is caused by any of the following:
>
> > (i) bioterrorism; or
> > (ii) the appearance of a new or novel or previously controlled or eradicated airborne infectious agent or airborne biological toxin; and
>
> (2) the illness or health condition poses a high probability of any of the following harms:
>
> > (i) a large number of deaths in the affected population;
> > (ii) a large number of serious or long-term disabilities in the affected population; or
> > (iii) widespread exposure to an airborne infectious or airborne toxic agent that poses a significant risk of substantial future harm to a large number of people in the affected population.[17]

After the bill passed, many people were concerned about this new law because "public health emergency" was defined very broadly. Three years later, the legislature passed a law to delete the phrase *public health emergencies* from the legal language list of national and peacetime emergencies.

Minnesota's Emergency Powers Act was the effort of just one of many states that attempted to pass what was at the time called the MEHPA. MEHPA stands for Model State Emergency Health Powers Act. At the time, the ACLU stated that MEHPA had been drafted as "model legislation to increase state powers to respond to bioterrorism or other outbreaks of disease that the Centers for Disease Control and others want the states to pass into law. Although such legislation is needed, the current draft of the Model Act unfortunately is written in a way that doesn't adequately protect citizens against the misuse of the tremendous powers that it would grant in an emergency."[18]

Coronavirus Response and Personal Freedom

In March of 2020, in the flurry of activity to respond to what was being called a novel virus crisis, government officials encouraged leaders to dust off those emergency powers acts that had been passed after 2001. Governors began to declare emergencies and write governor's executive orders that took the effect of law.

Citizens, shocked at what they personally had been asked to do, came to our organization with many questions. Citizens were concerned that they had been asked to stay in their homes and not go to school or their places of work, get tested for a virus, and wear masks. The most basic question was "Can governments do *anything* that it thinks it needs to in order to cope with the emergency?" The sad news in many states is that the state has passed a version of the Model State Emergency Health Powers Act or another act to provide guidance for health emergencies. In a number of states, the language states that a state can take measures as are necessary to ascertain the nature of the disease and prevent its spread. Even though it is questionable whether these laws are constitutional, they were passed and are now being looked to during this crisis. Hopefully the current crisis will be an opportunity to have legal challenges go forward regarding these laws and to gain some sense of the parameters of their constitutionality.

In particular, I recently had the opportunity to review California's health emergency laws. The laws are very broad and give health officials expansive power to do what is necessary to cope with emergencies. For example is California Statute Health and Safety Code Section 120140:

> Upon being informed by a health officer of any contagious, infectious, or communicable disease the department [California

State Department of Health Services] may take measures as are
necessary to ascertain the nature of the disease and prevent its
spread. To that end, the department may, if it considers it proper,
take possession or control of the body of any living person, or
the corpse of any deceased person.[19]

Many California citizens, along with many other citizens across the
country, are questioning the authority of the government to infringe on
their constitutional rights and personal liberties, including the right of
the government to request that citizens stay in their homes, avoid travel,
refrain from going to work, wear masks in public, avoid contact with other
humans, and much more. These drastic measures are so new that citizens
are confused as to what their rights are.

An organization in California called the California Health Coalition
Advocacy (CHCA) recently requested my help in drafting a bill that would
clarify and protect California citizens' rights during health emergencies.
The bill, if passed, would protect the citizen's right to refuse medical
treatments or procedures; testing; physical or mental examination;
vaccination; experimental procedures and protocols; collection of
specimens; participation in tracking or tracing programs; the wearing
of masks; the maintaining of measured distance from other humans and
animals that is not otherwise unlawful; and the involuntary sharing of
personal data or medical information.[20]

National Health Freedom Action then made a decision to draft model
right-to-refuse legislation (see appendix F) for all states to consider going
forward as a template to protect personal bodily autonomy during health
emergencies. The language is based on the concept that the right of people
to make their own medical decisions as to how they want to promote their
own health and survival is at the heart of American values and personal
liberty. The protection of personal autonomy, health choice, and basic
human fundamental rights of self-determination is what is at stake as we
move into the future of our country.

2020 Constitutional Challenges to Governor Orders

Governor orders are presenting unique opportunities to test our nation as to how far a government can go to mandate personal behavior. The 2020 crisis constitutional challenges will contribute to the evolution of law and society as we evolve in our technical world.

For example, the Supreme Court of Wisconsin overturned its governor's stay-at-home order with judicial comments reflecting that expansive governor orders cannot go beyond the constitutional inalienable rights of citizens, even in the case of declared emergencies. "It is especially in times of emergency that we must protect the rights of the people, lest we establish a dangerous precedent empowering less benevolent government officials in the future to oppress the people in the name of exigency."[21]

In Florida, citizens filed a legal challenge against Palm Beach County opposing its mask mandate. The case was heard on July 21, 2020, and parties are awaiting judicial review. The case cited Florida's constitution, reading, "Every natural person has the right to be let alone and free from government intrusion in to the person's private life" (Fla. Const. art. I, § 23).

The following is a citation of case law:

> Florida's Right of Privacy also includes the right to liberty. (State v. J.P., 907 So. 2d 1101, 1115 9 Fla. 2004 holding that the Florida constitutional right to privacy includes the right to liberty and self-determination). An integral component of self-determination is the right to make choices pertaining to one's health and to determine what shall be done with one's own body. In re Guardianship of Browning 568 So. 2d 4, 9–12 (Fla. 1990) ("Recognizing that one has the inherent right to make choices about medical treatment, we necessarily conclude that this right encompasses all medical choices").

In Minnesota, the Upper Midwest Law Center announced its federal lawsuit on behalf of multiple Minnesota churches and small business owners and a request for a temporary restraining order to suspend enforcement of Governor Walz's continuing shutdown of religious services.[22]

Freedom to Be Let Alone in an Evolving World

As our country and the world evolves, people must hold fast to the natural and legal concept that there are fundamental inalienable rights inherent to the human experience and that there is a need for our laws to protect the integrity and sacredness of those rights. If citizens are not vigilant in protecting these sacred rights, we could lose them to entities that seek control. I have confidence that individuals and local communities can work together to find ways to survive and thrive without sacrificing those inalienable rights of life, liberty, and the pursuit of happiness and without running afoul of constitutional protection—even in an emergency.

Chapter 7

Health Freedom Principle 2 —
Freedom to Act

Principle 2: Freedom to Act

Individuals and members of the human family hold the
fundamental right and freedom to act on their own behalf and
as they choose to secure health and survival.

The actions that people take to maintain their health and survival require
a plethora of basic freedoms to act, including freedom of speech, freedom
to move about and associate freely, and freedom to perceive, believe, heal,
and pray freely. There are many ways to act to maintain health and survive
on this beautiful planet. There are as many ways to survive as there are
people and cultures. Survival is a completely unique experience for each
person. From the moment of birth, people strive to stay alive and live in
the world surrounding them.

All peoples find ways to keep themselves and their young ones warm
in cold climates and cool in hot ones. They find ways to get water in
dry climates and nutrients in frozen climates. They find shelter from
tornadoes and stability from earthquakes. Humans have learned that
Mother Nature cannot be dismissed. They have learned to understand her
and work with her to ensure survival. There are indigenous cultures that
have a seven-generation perspective on survival, that is, making sure that
their survival activities ensure survival for the next seven generations.
Responding successfully to environments over a period of years brings

shared knowledge, habits, and cultural traditions to help people more assuredly meet the quest for survival.

Survival is no simple task. Left alone, a human does not generally thrive or survive. It is paradoxical that we are socially dependent and yet strive for individual independence. We take pride in independence and expect to have a personal say in our destinies. But we need others to collaborate with us to ensure our basic survival needs.

Trust

Our need to act to survive often demands that we trust others. Cultures develop hierarchies of trust regarding survival within relationships, families, local communities, larger communities, and the world. Since others help us survive, the essential question becomes, "Whom can I trust who will help me to survive?" This is a foundational question for any person. As we seek people to trust in, we find that people function in the context of their own survival tradition, environment, cultural values, beliefs, and relationships with others, among a host of other factors that affect their lives.

If you were to ask twenty different people from twenty different backgrounds the question "Who are the ten people you would consult if your health or survival were in jeopardy?" most likely you would get twenty different answers. First responses might be "my mother," "my partner," "my father," "my grandmother," "my grandfather," "my uncle," "my aunt," "my children," "my family," "my good friend," "my neighbor," "my teacher," "my mentor," "the pastor," "the medicine man or medicine woman," "the curandero," "the midwife," or "the village elder."

Trusting persons whom we do not know is more challenging. In the complex world in which we live, we are often called to trust "strangers" who are part of a larger circle of life based on the outcomes of modern civilization and technology. We might be asked to trust "outsiders" such as shopkeepers, school educators, government leaders, specialists, retailers, and specially educated professionals. We may want to trust information sources, such as media, literature, and now the internet. The industrialization of our country and its resources puts us in a position of needing to trust people whom we do not know for our food and water, the air that we breathe, our fuel and energy sources, and much more.

Chain of Trust

How do we trust those we do not know? That is the essential question of many people in today's modern world. It appears that we develop a "chain of trust." This chain includes systems of people who learn, verify, and share information, and systems of laws and infrastructures that promote and track trust relationships. Through understanding of and access to a wide range of information, data, and people with knowledge bases, the trust chain helps us decide whom and what to trust to survive.

There is a broad range of opinions about whom and what to trust in our society, including those who believe it is best to trust only those within their community's reach, advocating that small communities should remain self-sustaining in light of their natural surroundings and limit their dependence on outside sources as much as possible. Then there are those who wish to see a complete globalization of information and resources. Within the globalization camp, there are those who warn against the role that governments and multinational corporations play in the chain of trust. These people say that government officials might be affected by financial pressure or gain from their supporters and therefore may not be trusted. They say that corporate motivates might be based on profit or power and therefore their products or information are not to be trusted unless heavily regulated on behalf of the welfare of the people.

Whether or not it is wise to trust information from outside an immediate circle of known contacts, or to trust global contacts, humans have attempted to expand their survival trust systems to go far beyond the local. Communities have become dependent on local, state, federal, and global resources, products, people, and information for their survival. In the arena of health care, the issue of trust is paramount.

Today, people are examining the trust chain regarding health and survival that has been built around them, and they are asking important questions about trustworthiness and long-term survival.

Health Is More than Survival

Once basic survival needs have been secured, people and cultures all over the world act to develop and practice techniques for preventing pain and suffering and increasing a sense of wellness, health, and vitality. When we are pain-free, we work toward building our physical health and vitality. With good health and robust energy, we can enjoy the activities that satisfy our endless desire for a rich, full life. Beyond these efforts, humans seek the complete experience of the joy of being human. People look for meaning and joy. Life beckons humans to explore how to live, how to relate to other humans, how to understand the purpose of life, how to view death, and even how to die. Humans enjoy rituals and traditions to express individual and shared ideas and belief systems, joys, and sorrows. Humans look to each other and to their cultures and traditions for cues on not only how to survive but also how to experience being human. There are millions of practices around the world that work to bring meaning and holistic health to the experience of life.

The Experience of Healing

The term *healing* is a dynamic term that puts its arms around almost all the elements of health, including survival, freedom from pain, search for vitality, and the experience of finding meaning in our lives. It provides us with a verb that we recognize: *healing*. We know healing when we experience it.

I once participated in a national healing council that included more than twenty renowned healers from many different backgrounds in the healing arts. It was suggested that we begin our council work together by defining the term *healing*. After we put our pens to the paper, the days went by, the weeks and months went by, and the long and expansive email communications flew by discussing what healing actually was. Although

109

we worked long and hard, we never did arrive at a unanimous agreement on the definition of healing.

Is healing a treatment provided by another? Is healing an individual's search for harmony with the Source of all life? Is healing a catharsis of some kind, a movement from one state of being to another? Is it freedom from a disease diagnosed by a conventional medical professional? Is healing the cessation of suffering? Is it the arrival at a place acceptable to the health-seeking person?

Although the word *healing* is difficult to limit to a simple definition, the actuality of healing embodies a universal concept and an integral part of our life experience. All people know when they need healing and when they have been healed, whether in a big way or a small way. Whether it be from a mother's kiss on the finger, a rescue mission on a mountaintop, or the release of grief after a loved one passes on, everyone knows when they experience healing.

Some people equate medicine with healing. For thousands of years, the terms *medicine* and *healing* were somewhat interchangeable. But the two words have grown to be conceptually worlds apart. The origins of medicine were close to the concept of healing. Those who helped others heal were labeled medica, medicine man, priest, philosophia, shaman, grandmother healer, or herbalist. Those healers often had a broad understanding of illness that encompassed a person's unique situation, including physical, emotional, spiritual, cultural, and moral status. Their medicine treatments included healing traditions that recognized any of a wide array of reasons for a person's illness; their medicines were based on a diverse use of natural substances, treatments, and rituals to assist a person and his family to return to full health.

Medicine, however, has evolved away from its original broad-based meaning and embodiment of healing. The past one hundred years of evolution in healing happened with extreme speed partly because of the fact that it was based on an entire set of new material criteria that were not available to the world before this time. Conventional medicine that incorporates pharmaceutical drugs, medical devices, and medical procedures evolved hand in hand with material discoveries in technology, physics, chemistry, engineering, biochemistry, biology, and more. Conventional medicine now incorporates new methods every day. The options coming forth keep practitioners busy learning and practicing the new methods based on technology and pharmaceuticals. It is important to note that this modern medicine evolved in close relationship with commercial and legal responses to the discoveries in material and conventional medicine.

A Return to Healing

The beauty of humans is that they not only seek to survive but also move toward the light when things look bleak. When circumstances present problems, they seek new solutions. People are recognizing that conventional medicine alone does not always address their desire to live a healthy life, to prevent discomfort, or to enjoy greater vitality. There is a beginning of a return to broader healing options; people are adding supplemental treatments to their conventional medical protocols and finding themselves searching for a more holistic experience of healing. People are returning to these roots in order to survive.

Freedom to Act

Given the diversity of survival practices across the country and globe, and given the wide breadth of practices individuals and cultures use to promote their health and well-being, the second principle of health freedom is of the utmost importance.

Americans have a fundamental constitutional right to act on their own behalf to have health. But we have arrived at a conundrum in our country because of the dominance of the modern medical model of health care. The quick evolution of modern society into a culture that is medically monocultural or monopolistic in its approach to health and healing makes it very difficult and sometimes impossible to go outside the dominant system of health care. People find that options include only things based on modern technology and pharmaceutical solutions. People also know there are grave consequences, physically, emotionally, socially, and financially, if they wish to take action outside that framework. In addition, since members of the culture are continually discouraged from going outside the system, eventually, over decades, people have lost the realization that there are other options and that they have the right to act in other ways. In fact, many have begun to completely defer to and depend on this system as part of their chain of trust to advise them on how to act for survival.

Exercising the freedom to act to gain health may be more doable in a different legal climate. It may be more possible within a culture that is pluralistic in its approach to healing and medicine, providing the individual with the greatest number of healing options and couched in an environment of honored freedoms, supportive of a person's individual choices in healing. This would avoid any indirect infringement on a person's ability to act on her own behalf and to survive on her own terms and in her own manner.

The Action of Speech in Health Care

Speech is a powerful action when it comes to health. It is also a fundamental right of all Americans. We recognize it whether it is through voice and sound, signs, or symbols. Americans count on the protection of free speech. We are offended by the concept of banning free speech.

Yet in the health care arena, a large portion of health care speech has been banned for most and may only be voiced by certain individuals, such as licensed medical professionals or by manufacturers who create special labels for approved medical products, drugs, and devices. For example, although medical diagnoses are often arrived at through exams and testing, only state-licensed medical professionals may diagnose a medical disease based on their conversations with a patient. And a manufacturer or seller of a dietary supplement, including vitamins or minerals, may not make a health claim about a supplement they are selling, or its ability to prevent, cure, or treat a disease, unless it is one of the very rare health claims approved by the FDA. That type of speech is still prohibited speech, even if the statement is truthful and the product has no potential for harm and is generally regarded as safe.

Americans seem to be more tolerant of bans on speech in health care because of their trust in the conventional medical model. On the other hand, many Americans do not know that their manufactures and practitioners are abiding by laws that prohibit them from saying what they know. And oftentimes, if a person is reprimanded for health speech, possibly on his own website, he is shocked to find that he does not have the right to say anything he wants even if it is true.

Our digital world of internet and social media adds another layer of opportunity but also potential conflict around freedom of speech in health care. For example, corporate owners of media outlets are in a unique position to proactively censor the content of their subscribers. In October of 2019, Congressman Posey questioned Mark Zuckerberg, founder and CEO of Facebook, in a congressional hearing, about vaccine safety information censorship. Congressman Posey was concerned that people posting about the dangers of vaccines were being intentionally censored. Zuckerberg stated, "We don't go out of our way to make sure that our group recommendation systems try to show people or encourage people to join those groups. We discourage that."[1] When Congressman Posey asked how they discourage that, Zuckerberg explained how the discouragement was done within their system.[2]

Another recent example of free speech discouragement in health care nationwide is the FTC's (Federal Trade Commission) actions. Since March 2020, the FTC has put out warning letters to 250 companies for unsubstantiated claims that their products could help consumers with prevention or treatment of coronavirus.

The Federal Trade Commission announced it has sent letters warning thirty more marketers nationwide to stop making unsubstantiated claims that their products and therapies can treat or prevent COVID-19, the disease caused by the novel coronavirus. This is the seventh set of warning letters the FTC has announced as part of its ongoing efforts to protect consumers from health-related COVID-19 scams. In all, the commission has sent similar letters to 250 companies and individuals.[3]

> Most of the letters announced today target "treatments" the FTC
> has warned companies about previously, including intravenous
> (IV) Vitamin C and D infusions, supposed stem cell therapy,
> vitamin injections, essential oils, and CBD products. Other
> letters sent recently challenged claims that infrared heat, oral

peroxide gel, and oxygen therapy can treat or cure COVID-19. However, currently there is no scientific evidence that these, or any, products or services can treat or cure the disease.[4]

You may note that many of the holistic approaches that the FTC has highlighted in its warnings are therapies that many holistic medical professionals utilize to support the immune system of their patients, whether they have COVID-19 or not. One could argue that instead of censoring options for consumers, as long as the entity offering the service is up front and truthful with the consumer about the knowledge they have about the product or protocol, and as long as they are providing protocols or products that are legally generally regarded as safe and available to the public, then the consumer should be able to make their own decisions and have access to that information.

Over the years I have heard arguments that attempt to justify the banning of free speech. These arguments include such things as "Speech should be less protected and more able to be regulated by the government when it is part of a commercial transaction or advertisement to protect vulnerable consumers"; "Speech can be regulated if it has to do with telling people about cures or diagnosing because state-licensed medical doctors and drug companies with approved drugs are the only ones that know about cures or diagnosing"; "Speech on health product labels that include health claims, even if those claims are true, should be censored by the government to protect consumers"; and "Government-approved schools and exams are the only legitimate foundation to evaluate whether to infringe on the free speech of a health care professional."

The arguments in support of the protection of free speech are many and are grounded in the concept of truth and whether the speech is misleading. If commercial speech is truthful and not misleading, many advocates think that it should be protected, even though it is in a commerce situation. For example, if someone was selling vitamin C and the label on the bottle was limited by laws regarding labeling restrictions on dietary supplements, but the person selling the product had further information regarding the use of vitamin C in health care, that additional truthful speech beyond the labeling should be protected free speech. And, for example, if a health care practitioner practicing her vocation as, for example, a traditional naturopath and she has a conversation about healing methods that is truthful and not misleading, then that speech should be protected. Some would say that if government regulates freedom of speech by giving a special group of people a privilege to speak based on whether they graduated from a government-approved school or have taken a government-approved exam, then that is tantamount to having set up a medical police state.

What is the solution here? Do people want the government to be involved in the regulation of free speech when it comes to health care? What should professional practice laws, product laws, or the myriad of health care laws look like that have been set up to regulate the health care system regarding free speech?*

The information explosion, including information technology and internet and digital information access, has permanently changed the course of history and the ways that people obtain and sort information, including health care information. Americans are venturing forth to find their own health answers. Freedom of speech is essential in evolving health care.

The Act of Moving about and Associating Freely in Health Care

The act of moving about freely to take action on behalf of one's own health is squarely in the crosshairs now because of the many governors issuing orders in response to declared emergencies commanding citizens to stay

---

* NHFA supports truthful speech, and laws and legislative initiatives that support access and protection of truthful speech that is not misleading or harmful. We work to pass safe harbor practitioner exemption laws that protect the freedom of speech and the practices of homeopaths, herbalists, traditional naturopaths, and many more who daily converse with health seekers. We support supplement companies that work to write proper labeling for their products that avoid diagnostic language and describe to consumers the benefits of their products in light of the normal structure and function of the body, thinking this is helpful. We contribute information to educational materials, videos, and webinars and support the establishment of holistic health and nutrition centers and places dedicated to helping people with prevention measures to maintain their health.

in their homes and not go to clinics or hospitals for medical care. Some of these orders have fines and criminal penalties for violation.

In peacetime, I have noticed that if the citizens do not show up to defend their liberties at legislatures, then laws can pass and liberties are lost, delegating more police power to the government. For example, in response to the 2009 pandemic H1N1, Massachusetts passed a bill, Senate No. 2028, that is now current law that gave their agency commissioner, in response to the governor's declaration of an emergency, broad police power authority for the future of Massachusetts, as follows:

> Section 2A. Upon declaration by the governor that an emergency exists which is detrimental to the public health, the commissioner may, with the approval of the governor and the public health council, during such period of emergency, take such action and incur such liabilities as he may deem necessary to assure the maintenance of public health and the prevention of disease.
>
> The commissioner, with the approval of the public health council, may establish procedures to be followed during such emergency to insure the continuation of essential public health services and the enforcement of the same.[5]

The current laws in every state defining the powers that have been given by the legislature to the governor and the executive branch of government to be used in emergencies are important laws worth scrutinizing. Those laws should be reviewed to see if they are constitutional or if they provide an overly broad delegation of power to the governors that does not protect the inalienable rights of citizens.

Perceive, Believe, Heal, and Pray Freely

Life perceptions, philosophies, and general belief systems of individuals are the bedrock on which most people base their decisions to act. Many people have general belief systems that also resonate with their spiritual beliefs; they may choose to follow a religion. In the United States, freedom of religion is a foundational cornerstone of the liberties we claim as fundamental. It is our inherent God-given right to believe anything we want and claim any religion or spiritual belief. But our religion in and of itself does not allow us to outright break criminal laws that are in place for the rest of the culture.

Regarding our freedom to act in regard to our health, we ask: Do we want to have healers with various perceptions, beliefs, philosophies, and ways of approaching illness or wellness practicing under the threat of criminal charges, and do we want to keep them out of society if they are using practices or substances that are not endorsed by the dominant, conventional, government-approved medical community? Do we want to quash a person's beliefs and healing journey that allows them to have their own life perspectives on healing and to receive the assistance of healers that resonate with their beliefs and desires?

Laws have been passed that support the monopolization of conventional drugs and surgery-based medicine and disallowing healing practices of other natures. But new laws are coming forward that protect many forms of healing. For example: Colorado now protects many healing practices such as the following:

- practices using reflexology, auricular therapy, and meridian therapies that affect the reflexes of the body;
- practices using touch, words, and directed movements to deepen a person's awareness of movement patterns in their body, such as the Feldenkrais method, the Trager approach, and body-mind centering;
- practices using touch or healing touch to affect the human energy systems, such as Reiki, shiatsu, and meridians;
- structural integration practices such as Rolfing and Hellerwork; and
- the process of muscle activation techniques.[6]

But a negative law that was passed in Texas affected all the bodyworkers and energy healers in Texas and the consumers who utilize their services. The new law demands that all healer practitioners go to government-endorsed massage schools and become licensed massage therapists before they practice their healing trades. In order to be licensed, a person in Texas has to go to a particular school for massage, for a particular length of time, and pass an exam as a massage therapist. This new law was great for the schools but bad for practitioners and consumers alike. Many consumers lost access to their preferred healers. This is how the Texas law reads:

> (c) A person may not for compensation perform or offer to perform any service with a purported health benefit that involves physical contact with a client unless the person:
>
> (1) holds an appropriate license issued under this chapter; or
>
> (2) is licensed or authorized under other law to perform the service.[7]

Whether we are talking about an energy healer or the substance that a healer uses to relieve symptoms, we find that many laws have been made in the United States that infringe on our access to health care and healing modalities that are based on belief systems and perceptions differing from those of conventional medicine. There are thousands of traditions that are gentle, noninvasive, and based on life perceptions throughout the world. And now that we are in the global age, all these perceptions are being melded together, and many perceptions are being experienced by new people.

How can we protect our freedom to perceive the world through our very own eyes and to experience the healing that we need when we need it? How can we bridle the government's attempt to architect laws that only cater to special interest groups? It seems like a bizarre question, but it's very real when we live in a legal environment of laws that appear to prohibit access to practitioners and products that are supposedly based on perceptions that are not considered true by the dominant system. I guess it leads us back to that eternal question of "What is truth?" Can we live in a society where we honor each other's perceptions of truth? The information and technology explosion has enabled information sharing between people, communities, states, countries, and nations, which has rocked our foundations of truth. We are in evolutionary times with many new facts and experiences being shared quickly with many people. Assimilation of information is taking place at rapid speeds, and sometimes it seems as if truth is a fluid concept. The role of the government must always be scrutinized to make sure that it is not suppressing information unnecessarily and that is it forever protecting a person's fundamental right to perceive the universe as she or he wishes.

Practice the Healing Arts

In many stories of infringement upon health freedoms, there is an underlying theme that includes infringement on the overall right to practice the healing arts. The regulation of occupations has instigated what we call turf wars between various types of practitioners, all clamoring to convince the government that their approach is best and should be endorsed by the state and that healers who specialize in other forms should be denied the right to practice.

Burden of Proof Upside Down

The most disturbing element of this regulation trend is the turning upside down of the legal concept of burden of proof. In a free society, the burden of proof of harm always remains on the government before the government can restrict things that negatively affect fundamental rights or block access to resources that are generally regarded as safe. The burden should never rest on the public to prove safety before it can do a healing act such as a person recommending foods, a grandmother giving chicken soup, an individual performing gentle healing techniques, or someone providing natural health care practices that involve the integration of mind, body, and spirit in order to produce a life lived in harmony.

If some act is "inherently dangerous," such as performing surgery or giving toxic substances, then the burden switches and is then placed on the people wanting to perform the act to demonstrate the safety of the procedure before being able to perform the act.

In today's world, the burden of proof often is upside down. Not only have dangerous practices been allowed, endorsed, and regulated without sufficient proof by the government of their safety, but also practices that pose no risk of harm to the public have been prohibited by law, scorned, or otherwise eliminated by governments because they are not first proven safe by the holistic people. In a free society this is considered a misplaced burden of proof. Dangerous practices should always have the burden of proof on practitioners or manufacturers to show if and how the practices can be performed in a safe manner. But practices generally regarded as safe that have historical records of safety,* such as naturopathy, homeopathy, and herbalism, should be protected—and if regulation is considered, it must require the government to provide proof of harm before prohibiting these practices.

Least Restrictive Regulations

When fundamental liberties are at stake or could be negatively affected, government always needs to heed the constitutional parameters, be watchful, and regulate only in the least restrictive means possible to achieve an end, including not regulating at all. A number of laws are now being passed to remove unnecessary restrictions.† The goal is to remove the damaging public policy that has disempowered the people and encouraged them to believe that there are many paths to healing and that they are capable of making health care decisions, and encouraging people to participate in the broad range of health care options that are accessible to them.

---

* Safety of homeopathy.
† 2019 Maine LD 364, Act to Establish the Right to Practice Complementary and Alternative Health Care Act; 2015 Nevada A.B. 295, the Healing Arts Bill for Wellness Services; 2013 Colorado Senate Bill 13-215—Colorado Natural Health Consumer Protection Act; 2009 New Mexico, the Unlicensed Health Care Practice Act; 2008 Arizona Revised Statutes Sections 32-2911 Amended; 2005 Louisiana Revised Statutes 20-37 VI-B; 2003 Rhode Island Statute 23-74—Unlicensed Health Care Practices; 2001 California SB 577—California Complementary and Alternative Health Care Practitioners; 1999 Minn. Stat. 146A—Minnesota Freedom of Access to Complementary and Alternative Health Care Practitioners; 1994 Oklahoma Statute 59-480 (Oklahoma Parameters for Jurisdiction of Physician Licensing Act)—Oklahoma Allopathic and Surgical Licensure and Supervision Act.; 1976 Idaho 54-1804 (Idaho Exemptions to the Medical Practice Act)—Unlicensed Practice. Penalties, and Remedies Relating to Unlicensed Practice.

Chapter 8

Health Freedom Principle 3 — Freedom to Access

Principle 3: Freedom to Access

For freedom of choice to be implemented or meaningful, individuals and members of the human family hold the fundamental right and freedom to access their choices, whomever and whatever they deem necessary or prefer for their own health and survival.

Underpinnings of Access

Informing citizens that they have access to a comprehensive health care system that can meet their every need and that they can choose their own care plan, but having that health care system not include ninety-eight out of the hundred healing options available around the world, really isn't freedom of access. Freedom of access is about what is available and accessible.

Principle 1 is about being "let alone," and principle 2 is about freedom to act. Both those principles are grounded in a person's vision and desires for their health and the health of others. But freedom to access is about what it takes to make that vision a reality. It is about opportunities available. It is about providing health seekers access to whatever they need to make their visions come true. Whether it is the opportunity to be in an environment that allows them to direct their own decision-making when they are in a health crisis, the opportunity to work for an employer who respects their health decisions, or the opportunity to send children to educational and day-care programs that respect their decisions regarding the use of vaccines, access is about a clear path to one's health wishes.

Access is a complex question in today's world. How can we ensure access to clean air, clean water, and foods that are safe to eat without pesticides or genetic modifications? How can we ensure the sustainability of the earth for our future? How can we ensure access to practitioners and products of our choice, even those that are not government endorsed? How can we ensure that public policies and laws take into consideration health freedom? These are the questions that access presents us with.

The United States has developed laws and public policies that limit our health care options to a narrow domain of government-endorsed professionals, products, and sources of information. We are given broad access to corporate-owned or -controlled conventional medical practitioners, treatments, and drugs; device-based medicine; and air, water, and natural resources that have been negatively affected by corporations. This has been done over a period of many years, by lawmakers, at the request of special interest groups desiring exclusive rights to provide health care services or to gain exclusive product patents and markets, in the name of evolving science. A complex system of mostly uncontested health care laws has been passed. And citizen access has everything to do with these laws.

The Impact of Licensing Laws on Access

Professional licensing laws are one of the most prominent sets of laws that has contributed to infringements on freedom to access. I attribute this to the fact that these laws affect people in their very own communities, in their personal lives, and in their relationship with their family doctor. When licensing laws were applied over time, they shaped the culture in terms of whom to trust regarding health care. The passage of licensing laws has affected belief systems, communities, and decisions related to chains of trust. Historically, people had an informal system of establishing their chains of trust for whom to reach out to in times of need. For example, people reached out to local midwives, herb doctors, and trusted community healers. But licensing laws, put in place by surgeons and physicians in the early 1900s, changed all of that. To ensure that people would know whom to trust in their communities and whom they could trust to help them in a crisis, legislatures passed laws that provided the public with practitioners who could deal with medical emergencies. However, these laws eliminated many practitioners and were not grounded in protecting freedom. These laws have acted to both establish a chain of trust with a particular group and limit access to many other desirable options.

Licensing laws are the most restrictive form of professional regulation in existence because they prohibit citizens who do not have the license from performing certain actions. They were designed to give a particular group of persons the privilege to do dangerous acts under certain circumstances, for example, physicians doing surgery. The laws ban anyone in the community from doing a particular act unless they have a license. The laws also remove particular titles from the public domain and reserve them for a special group of people, such as the term *doctor*. These laws set up a privilege system where the state grants a certain group of people the privilege to do certain things. Of course, as we saw in the Farmer Saunders case earlier, the definition of the practice of medicine within these laws was overly broad and included all of healing, thus making all of healing illegal. The law infringed on the healing practices of many practitioners, such as midwives, nurses, and traditional herb doctors—and many more.

To accomplish licensure, state legislatures set up state agencies called occupational boards that license and regulate individual professions. In most states, a physician may obtain a license from the board only if they attend the government-endorsed school listed in the law and complete all the educational requirements and exams required by the law. The professional laws include reasons and grounds for disciplinary actions, often including the requirement that physicians abide by a particular minimum standard of care. And standard of care is generally reflected in the dominant medical community. The board is authorized to enforce these laws with the support of the state attorney general's office. The state medical boards are often made up of physicians with a token consumer member.

I first got involved in the issue of access to holistic physicians when I was approached by a group of consumers who were angry that their physician, who had been providing them with successful chelation treatments, had

---

been investigated and was no longer allowed to practice because he had gone outside the standard of care for conventional medicine. My thought at the time was, *How would any physician be able to do a new or innovative treatment without getting investigated for going outside an acceptable standard of care?* I soon learned that oftentimes, physicians doing new approaches or even old approaches that are less invasive and more holistic, such as the use of homeopathy, the use of nutritional supplements instead of drug therapy, or the use of detoxification with chelation agents, were being investigated for not practicing under the existing standards of care. And then eventually, when enough of them were doing the same thing and their practices became a new standard of care for a minority of physicians, the enforcement measures were fewer. This seemed so very sad to me that good, brilliant, educated doctors who had happy, willing, informed patients with no showing of harm were being censored and lost their professional licenses because they were going outside a particular conventional standard.

To this day, one of the most critical areas of care being affected by this dilemma is the area of cancer treatments. Oftentimes cancer patients are given the option of surgery, radiation, or chemotherapies and are discouraged from using any other type of cancer treatments. Physicians and other practitioners and clinics who utilize innovative cancer treatments are investigated and marginalized. Former New York State legislator Daniel Haley documented these injustices in his book *Politics in Healing: The Suppression and Manipulation of American Medicine.*[1] Haley explores the suppression of twelve well-documented cancer treatments and the politics of their marginalization. The power of medical boards to enforce the conventional standard of care based on chemotherapy, surgery, and radiation treatments and to discredit innovation or holistic practices in cancer is still prevalent in the United States today.

Sometimes the standard of care issue dovetails with public policy agendas. Take for example the issue of the use of vaccines. Individuals, oftentimes after consultation with their own physicians, may choose not to utilize vaccine treatments. But government officials may want to promote the use of vaccines on a broad scale. And medical boards may want to support the government's overall public policy and investigate doctors who do not comply. Does this mean that the standard of care is set by government officials and is taken away from the medical community?

A current example of a medical board's involvement in public policy and the suppression of options for consumers is the physician investigation cases in California. Many California parents of vulnerable children have lost their access to their primary physicians who were providing them with guidance regarding the use of vaccines. In 2015 a new California law was passed banning parents from being able to use day cares or public or private schools for their children unless their child received all government-recommended vaccines or else had a medical exemption, including the reason for declining, signed by a physician. Since that law passed, a number of California-licensed physicians have been investigated by the Medical Board of California for providing medical exemptions to parents for their vulnerable children. These cases fall squarely into the question of standard-of-care issues and who is in charge of standard of care.

Generally, standards of care are reflected by members of the professional medical community overall and include scientific evidence, research, academia, expert clinicians, and much more. Determining what a physician should have done in a particular situation and with a certain set of circumstances and what would have been the applicable standard of care can be a complex question of fact and testimony. Juries struggle with this concept of expectations. There is a presumption that physicians abide by a minimally expected standard of care. But they can be disciplined. For example, in Minnesota a physician may be disciplined for "conduct that departs from or fails to conform to the minimal standards of acceptable and prevailing medical practice in which case proof of actual injury need not be established."[2]

In California the new law had specific language to protect medical exemptions given by licensed physician and surgeons prior to January 2021 in cases where "the physical condition of the child is such, or medical circumstances relating to the child are such, that immunization is not considered safe, indicating the specific nature and probable duration of the medical condition or circumstances, including, but not limited to, family medical history, for which the physician and surgeon does not recommend immunization."[3]

But the long-term intent of the legislature stated in California law is to provide a means for the eventual achievement of total immunization of appropriate age groups against diphtheria, hepatitis b, *Haemophilus influenzae* type b, measles, mumps, pertussis (whooping cough), poliomyelitis, rubella, tetanus, varicella (chickenpox), and any other disease deemed appropriate to vaccinate against by the department, taking into consideration the recommendations of the Advisory Committee on Immunization Practices of the United States Department of Health and Human Services, the American Academy of Pediatrics, and the American Academy of Family Physicians.[4]

The question is, Will consumers maintain their access to the physician of their choice even if their physician provides a recommendation that does not agree with a governmental public policy? Will physicians, the medical community, and those active in the profession of healing be able to protect their patient or client relationships and apply standards of care that they view as best for their individual patients? Physicians are in the best position to discern what is best for a patient given their close relationship with the facts of their patient's health care situation and the extensive and ongoing education and knowledge they gain over their years of practice. Medical doctors are constantly challenged to discern and study how advances in technology may either help or harm their patients in today's medical world. Will governments attempt to impose their public policy agendas on physicians and patients and attempt to have governmental agencies set standards of care in medicine? Will governments see physicians as implementers of their public policy agendas?

Over the years I have followed many heart-wrenching cases of good physicians, dentists, and nurses who have lost their licenses for providing innovative care to satisfied patients. Thankfully, laws are being reformed gradually. There are more than twenty-five states now that have begun to protect some physicians who use complementary, alternative, integrative, holistic, and other practices for their patients. The laws were not comprehensive or similar in each state. So, in response to the need, in 2006 I drafted a Model Act for Expanded Care for Licensed Physicians. The Minnesota Natural Health Legal Reform Project worked to get it introduced into the Minnesota Legislature. It was HF 3213 in the Eighty-Eighth Legislative Session (2006–2007) (see appendix G). However, the bill did not pass. It is encouraging that many patients are gradually beginning to seek out and have access to holistic practitioners of all kinds.

There are many areas of infringements on freedom of access in today's world. There are laws prohibiting access to raw whole milk from certified organic farms, access to chemical-free bike trails, access to water meters that aren't sending out electromagnetic frequency impulses, access to practitioners practicing innovative healing treatments, access to products with healing potential, and much more.

All licensing laws should include exemptions to ensure that all vocations that pose no imminent risk of harm to the public be practiced and be freely accessible to health seekers. Licensing laws should reflect our constitutional underpinnings of liberty and freedom, which would not allow the government to be a gatekeeper of health freedom and access.

Chapter 9

Health Freedom Principle 4 —
Responsibility to Do No Harm

Principle 4: Responsibility to Do No Harm

To maintain the health and survival of individuals, members of
the human family, and the community as a whole, individuals
and members of the human family have the responsibility to
do no harm.

Justification to do harm to ourselves or someone else is part of life's hard
discernments. When we get in a jam, it sometimes calls for harsh measures.
Veering off the road and into a ditch to avoid a more dangerous automobile
accident is an automatic response to being in danger and wishing to be
safe. In today's health care world, we proactively make these types of
decisions every day. We may decide to get a tooth pulled to be free from a
more extensive infection. A practitioner may recommend we take a drug
with dangerous side effects in order to prevent early death. A mother may
decide to have a cesarean surgical birth to prevent harm to herself and her
child. The advancement of technology and medical science has given us
many options to consider in managing our health, many of which have
elements of harm.

Justification to do harm goes beyond medical science. As technology
advances in terms of the environment, agriculture, and communication
systems, public policies are discussed and implemented that may cause
harm but that are launched for what some pose to be the greater good.
Harm can come from the allowance of air and water pollution at toxic levels

in order to allow manufacturers to produce their products, the allowance of pesticides and chemicals in soil to allow for greater yields of food and crops, and the allowance of microwave radiation in the air in order to make available communication options for all people.

Principle 4 is to remind us that we have a responsibility to do no harm if at all possible. When justification to do harm becomes normalized, humans run the risk of doing so much harm that it could weaken human health or cause the extinction of the human family.

Principle 4 encourages us to ask basic questions: Can we save our tooth with a gentle homeopathic remedy? Can we prevent death by using a holistic approach to our health challenges? Can we lower the cesarean rate of births from 32 percent to below 10 percent, where it used to be, with fewer mortalities by approaching childbirth in a different manner? Can manufacturers make products with more limited pollution? Can we produce the food we need without using methods that pose a danger to humans and the earth? Can we use fiber-optic cables or some other communication system instead of loading the atmosphere with microwave radiation? Can we prohibit the encirclement of the earth in space with garbage and unnecessary materials that might affect our planet?

Modern Medical Harm—Chemotherapy

Chemotherapy and radiation are well-known to have severe dangerous side effects, yet these methods are often used by people who have a form of cancer. They are used because early scientific research evidence indicated that chemotherapy and radiation had certain percentages of success over time for particular types of cancers. The various types of chemotherapy and radiation are often the only measures modern medicine has available for patients. Doctors often have no other standard of care treatments to use. They do not have enough research articles to depend on that would otherwise describe another or alternative standard of care to save the lives of their patients. This is certainly a dilemma for both doctors and patients.

There are many alternative cancer options and clinics outside the United States. One of the reasons that there are no helpful studies available to doctors in the United States comparing conventional chemotherapy treatments to alternative treatments is that under the ethical guidelines for cancer research, it is considered medically unethical in a clinical trial not to give a cancer patient a standard treatment of chemotherapy knowing that historically it had a certain percentage of success. Researchers are not able to give a member of a research trial a substance that is an alternative treatment with no proven effectiveness and then give other members of the trial the chemotherapy standard of care with known effectiveness ratings—even if the effectiveness ratings of standard treatment are small percentages with dangerous side effects. Placebos are rarely used in cancer treatment clinical trials.[1] They are used when there is no standard treatment.[2] Or, they may be used in a clinical trial that compares standard treatment plus a placebo with standard treatment plus a new treatment.[3] Blocking comparative or placebo-type research maintains the status quo and the use of dangerous chemotherapy. And innovative cancer treatments continue to be marginalized.

Modern Medical Harm—Vaccines

There are numerous vaccines on the market today. Vaccines have many known and potentially permanent dangerous side effects, including death.[4] Each vaccine is different in its purpose and its level of risk. Vaccines are generally offered to healthy persons in order to prevent illness or death from a future potential disease. Before a person receives a vaccine, they are generally not experiencing an immediate risk of loss of life. But because of the wish for prevention and because of the known side effects, healthy people want to weigh the risks and ask a lot of questions as to the purpose of the vaccine before they receive it.

Since the early 1900s governments have passed laws recommending vaccines in certain circumstances, such as school attendance, to prevent illness and deaths from particular diseases such as measles. But in response to these recommendations, because of the medical risks, and on behalf of personal medical privacy and personal liberty interests and parental rights, states have also passed laws providing legal exemptions for obtaining vaccines based on religious or personal beliefs or medical circumstances. The authority of a government to recommend to the general population a health measure with known dangerous side effects is a controversial issue and an ongoing fundamental health freedom issue.

Principle 4, "Do no harm," is pivotal in the vaccine conversation. Vaccine advocates tend to marginalize concerns of vaccine harm in order to promote their recommended health measure. A government employee responsible for public health measures becomes passionate about meeting goals of prevention and sometimes does not acknowledge the presence of toxic substances in vaccines or hear the concerns of persons who experience adverse events or the death of a loved one. Other vaccine advocates ask that parents be willing to accept the risk to their child on behalf of protecting the larger community from illness. Other advocates might even deny that vaccines pose serious health risks. Honoring parental decision-making or respecting the methods of parents using natural methods to boost the immune health of their children in order to protect their natural broad-based immunity is often marginalized. Leaders need to examine this dynamic in greater depth. It is important that the politics of vaccines and vaccine-promotion agendas not overshadow health freedom principle 4: "Do no harm."

The physician group Physicians for Informed Consent,[5] whose mission is to deliver data on infectious diseases and vaccines and to unite doctors, scientists, health care professionals, attorneys, and families who support voluntary vaccination, is an example of a leading resource in the conversation of principle 4. Tapping into the wealth of knowledge that organizations such as this one possess could go a long way toward creating an understanding of the benefits and risks of vaccines.

It is common knowledge that there are numerous noninvasive, safe ways to bolster a person's immune system to prevent disease. And physicians are well aware of the benefits of contracting childhood diseases that play an important role in the immunological development of youth. Understanding natural forms of immunity and being cautious about weakening the overall health and immunity of a population by narrowly targeted interventions needs to be considered.

Modern Medical Harm—Iatrogenic

A number of years ago, Caroline Dean, MD, ND, and Trueman Tuck, rights advocate, wrote a book entitled *Death by Modern Medicine*. In it they referenced a startling paper written in the fall of 2003 titled "Death by Medicine." The paper reported that almost 784,000 Americans are killed annually because of medical interventions. The term for death caused by medicine is *iatrogenesis*. The paper reported that iatrogenic deaths are more common than heart disease or cancer, yet iatrogenic death has no official designation in death tables. Instead the deaths are counted as heart deaths or cancer accordingly. Dr. Dean, who was able to review more than a dozen peer-reviewed medical journals and government health publications and provide an accounting of the iatrogenic deaths, including prescribed medications given in hospitals, surgical errors, unnecessary hospitalization, outpatient mishaps, infections, bedsores, and malnutrition, verified that 783,936 deaths were caused by medical intervention in one year. This information was a bellwether report urging the evaluation overall of a health care system based on modern technology.

More recently, in 2016, I read this: "Analyzing medical death rate data over an eight-year period, Johns Hopkins patient safety experts have calculated that more than 250,000 deaths per year are due to medical error in the United States. Their figure, published May 3 in the *BMJ*, surpasses the US Centers for Disease Control and Prevention's (CDC's) third leading cause of death—respiratory disease, which kills close to 150,000 people per year."[6]

Reforms and improvements are necessary on many levels to make our health care system safe for participants. Learning how to take advantage and implement modern technology in our world, at the same time making sure that we do no harm, is a principle we all need to consider.

Do No Harm—the Hippocratic Oath

The Hippocratic oath, an ethical code attributed to the ancient Greek physician Hippocrates, has been adopted as a conduct guide by the medical profession throughout the ages and is still used in the graduation ceremonies of many medical schools.[7] In the oath, the physician pledges to prescribe only beneficial treatments according to their abilities and judgment; to refrain from causing harm or hurt; and to live an exemplary personal and professional life.[8] The text of the Hippocratic oath (c. 400 BC), translated from the Greek by Francis Adams (1849), is considered a classical version and differs from contemporary versions, which are reviewed and revised frequently to fit with changes in modern medical practice.[9] The classical version is lengthy and includes statements such as "I will follow that system of regimen which, according to my ability and judgment, I consider for the benefit of my patients, and abstain from whatever is deleterious and mischievous. I will give no deadly medicine to anyone if asked, nor suggest any such counsel; and in like manner I will not give to a woman a pessary to produce abortion."[10]

Many people have asked me over the years why the Hippocratic oath is not being followed by doctors in our modern times. I believe that there are many doctors working to implement the Hippocratic oath to do no harm. The advancement of technology and pharmaceutical and surgical measures presents many challenges and has provided us with extensive opportunities to evaluate whether and when we need to make a choice to do no harm. The burgeoning holistic and integrative health care movement is a way that we can explore arriving at health without doing harm. Finding ways to avoid harmful and high-risk drugs, surgeries, and health measures and, at the same time, being able to attain health and well-being is the hope of the future. The Hippocratic oath is a tool, a guideline. I think we would do well to apply it not only to human health but also to animals and Mother Earth. Our responsibility to do no harm will be essential in protecting the life and longevity of planet Earth.

Chapter 10

Health Freedom Principle 5 —
Responsibility of Tolerance

Principle 5: Responsibility of Tolerance

Because of the diverse nature of the human experience, members of the human family have the responsibility to show tolerance to the extent of avoiding hostile acts toward diverse health and survival options and toward those who choose those options.

Figuring out where to draw the line for tolerance is like honing in on a moving target, depending on your frame of reference and depending on the stakes if a person decides not to tolerate. Most people want others to show them maximum tolerance so that they can do, say, hear, and experience whatever they want, whenever they want. But all people have different beliefs and preferences. "You can smoke as long as you are not in my space" or "You can smoke as long as I can smoke with you." "You can be my patient as long as you do what I recommend" or "You can be my patient, and we will work together to get you well."

The first foundational question to ask when being called to tolerate something is whether it is generally tolerable to humanity. The International Declaration of Health Freedom attempted to articulate health freedom expectations.[1] Americans in general look to their constitutional inalienable rights of life, liberty, and the pursuit of happiness and a whole host of laws in existence that protect human rights as they apply to health. We live in a country where we expect protection of human rights in the health care setting. If these rights are being infringed upon, we resist the infringements and seek recourse in our courts and legislatures. We do not have tolerance for infringements of human rights in health care.

Limited Tolerance

Tolerance in health care choice has become an issue in the United States due to the nature of the overall dominant health care system. For example, because of a belief in and dependence on conventional pharmaceutical-based medicine, a family member might have a hard time respecting another family member's wishes if that family member decides to decline a conventional physician's recommendations and do something alternative. Or a physician may become frustrated with a patient who does not comply with their recommendations. Court systems sometimes even challenge parents who use alternatives and decline medications for their children, suggesting that the parents were neglectful. Tolerance is so very important to sort through when a person's life or health is at stake. What does it take to be tolerant of someone's wishes when human life is at stake if the person does not prefer to utilize expected procedures? This question has been discussed and argued throughout time, always amid great controversy, and always in the context of cultural values, economic interests, and social norms.

I once monitored a legal case where a child had been diagnosed with cancer and the parents were doing their best to make decisions for their child. They had agreed to a chemotherapy regimen for their child. But when the child had a very bad reaction and ended up in the ICU and almost died after the first dose, the parents chose to get a second opinion. They decided to go overseas, to Switzerland, to a special pediatric cancer hospital for care. The original US physician was angry that the parents had discontinued treatment and reported the parents to child protection to try to get the child back. The legal stress on the family was extreme. The physician in the international country protected the parents' wishes and would not release the child back to the United States because the child was receiving a recommended special lower dose of chemotherapy appropriate for children. In this case, there was much pain and suffering because of the high stress of the situation and the urgency under which all parties were acting. The need for tolerance and respect was sorely needed. With tolerance, possibly this could have been handled in a much different manner.

Diane Miller, JD

Recipe for Tolerance

Health freedom struggles encompass many situations where human constitutional rights are potentially infringed upon, and tolerance is greatly needed to cope with pain and suffering. The complexity of the responsibility of tolerance in any given situation calls us to be discerning in our approach.

Knowledge of who is primarily responsible is essential in supporting tolerance in health freedom issues. When life and death is at stake, we ask, "Whose life is it?" and "Who is responsible for this life?" In the United States we honor a person's fundamental right to make their own health care decisions. This right is well-documented in case law. Under this law, competent persons may say no to any medical treatments and lifesaving measures anytime they wish.

In the United States we even go so far as to protect the preferences of a person who is incapable of making decisions by allowing family members the ability to become legal living decision makers for those who are not competent to make health care decisions or for those who do not wish to make those decisions. Sometimes there are multiple interested parties in a person's life, such as the case where the state and the parents or family are both interested in protecting vulnerable adults and children. And finally, parents have the fundamental right to make health care decisions for their children. Knowing who is responsible for the health of a person gives us a starting point in order to develop a tolerant approach to problem-solving.

Honoring the primary responsible person's decisions and standing down once it is determined who is responsible is an important ingredient of tolerance. This can be a very challenging thing to do.

In 2020, this very basic human right to have our health care decisions protected and honored is being threatened as some suggest that people should be forced or coerced to take a vaccine. Health freedom advocates disagree. We must ask, whose life is it? Does the state have an overriding interest in my life, one that is greater than my own interest in my own life? When a state claims to have more interest in a life than the person himself or herself and is prepared to override constitutional fundamental rights

136

established under a republic form of democracy guided by a constitution, then I believe we are in major trouble as a free nation. Honoring a person's fundamental right to make their own health care decisions is essential to the liberty principles upon which our country was founded. Protecting freedom is a challenge when fear is rampant, but health freedom advocates are reminding citizens of the United States of this most precious protected inalienable fundamental right of self-determination.

Creating new ways to proceed in creating harmony and tolerance is challenging, but it is important we do this so that we can implement the vision of what things would be like in an ideal world. Seeing if we can put something together piecemeal and come to some solution that protects our constitutional rights and that is a win-win for everyone demands participation in the freedom conversation. The temptation to believe that there is only one way to remain healthy, heal, and survive, and that this one way is exclusively to rely on the dominant US biomedical health system, needs to be released. With tolerance, we can protect our health freedoms and promote dialogue about all forms and factors of health and all methods of gaining health, protecting health, and affecting health.

Chapter 11

Health Freedom Principles 6 and 7 — Responsibility of Corporations

Principle 6: General Responsibility of Corporations

Corporations have the potential of significantly affecting the health and survival of the human family and thus have the responsibility and duty to be trustworthy entities safeguarding health freedom rights and responsibilities.

Principle 7: Special Responsibilities of Corporations

In light of the special legal nature of corporate entities and their potential systemic impact on the health and survival of the human family, corporations have the following five responsibilities:

Principle 7-1

To honor and preserve the sovereign nature of individuals and the sovereignty of the United States and to avoid any negative impact on the sovereignty of other nation-states as it applies to health and survival.

Principle 7-2

To honor and preserve American financial and cultural diversity and multicultural systems that are abiding by and upholding US law, and avoid negative impact on

the financial or cultural status of other nation-states as
it applies to health and survival.

Principle 7-3

To avoid creating or being monopolies with large
ownership of resources and allowing that status
to dictate or dominate cultures, public policies,
regulations, or laws that affect health and survival.

Principle 7-4

To avoid the dominant control of natural resources
and the suppression of access to natural resources,
and not to cause potentially harmful modifications or
destruction of natural resources.

Principle 7-5

To avoid promotion of products, protocols, policies,
regulations, or laws that would encourage unlimited
dependence on corporations and institutions or that
would discourage, prohibit, or otherwise negatively
affect the ability or will of humans and local
communities to survive and prosper without the
existence of the corporation or institution.

Corporations: Nonhuman Entities that Live Forever

Humans who are alive have fundamental human rights; they live and
experience the dynamic of life amid the freedom conversation. But there
are entities that have been created under law and by contract that have
"life," that can live forever, and that have many of the same rights as human
persons; we call these entities corporations. Shouldn't there be a *concern*
because nonhuman contractual legal entities cannot experience the human
spirit, light, and intention of life necessary to be in the conversation of
freedom in order protect the good of individuals, the good of the whole,
and the survival of a people?

Some corporations that have been sued for wrongdoing have demonstrated that they do not abide by a moral code or care for the welfare of individual health or the communities out of which they arise. I give you examples below. The most dangerous aspect of these unhuman legal entities is that many of them have a core goal of financial profit, rather than a core responsibility to ensure the welfare of their community or individual rights of survival. A corporation has the ability to live a very long time with an agenda that could run counter to the well-being of the people it serves.

We are starting to hold corporations accountable for the well-being of humans, but if this effort is not done more aggressively, some corporations may endanger the lives of millions or possibly destroy the human family as we know it. An example of this is when a corporate entity markets what it knows to be a potentially dangerous product that could cause injuries or death and, before taking it market, anticipates the possibility of lawsuits for when harm is incurred—and then budgets for legal fees accordingly. When potential lawsuits are budgeted, profits remain intact.

Roundup

Take, for example, the Monsanto Corporation (now owned by Bayer), its production of the weed killer Roundup, and the negative impact that Roundup has had on human health.

In March 2015, the World Health Organization's International Agency for Research on Cancer classified glyphosate, the active ingredient in Monsanto's Roundup and other weed killers, as "probably carcinogenic to humans."[1] Yet, Monsanto continued to sell the product to people worldwide. We now know that farmers, farm workers, landscapers, and gardeners who have used Roundup or other glyphosate products are at risk for developing non-Hodgkin's lymphoma and other forms of cancer. Consumers across the United States who have been diagnosed with cancer caused by Roundup or glyphosate herbicide exposure are making the decision to file a Roundup lawsuit.[2]

In 2018, *Dewayne Johnson v. Monsanto Company* was the first Roundup cancer lawsuit to proceed to trial. The lawsuit alleged that exposure to

Monsanto's Roundup weed killer and its active ingredient, glyphosate, caused Northern California resident Dewayne "Lee" Johnson to develop non-Hodgkin's lymphoma (NHL).[3]

In August 2018, the jury unanimously found that the company's Ranger Pro and Roundup products presented a "substantial danger" to consumers, and that Monsanto knew or should have known of potential risks and failed to warn consumers such as Dewayne "Lee" Johnson.[4] The jury ordered Monsanto Co. to pay $289.2 million. The judge upheld the jury's verdict but reduced the punitive damages award, bringing the total award to $78.5 million.[5]

Bayer, maintaining that there was no valid evidence of cancer causation associated with Monsanto's herbicides, said it believed it would win on appeal. But in April 2019, US district judge Vince Chhabria ordered Bayer[6] to begin mediation talks aimed at potentially settling the sprawling mass of lawsuits that includes roughly thirteen thousand four hundred plaintiffs in the United States alone. All the plaintiffs or their family members are cancer victims, and all allege Monsanto engaged in a range of deceptive tactics to hide the risks of its herbicides, including manipulating the scientific record with ghostwritten studies, colluding with regulators, and using outside individuals and organizations to promote the safety of its products while making sure they falsely appeared to be acting independently of the company.[7]

US Right to Know, July 6, 2020, updated consumers about the Roundup trials, saying: "Last month, Bayer said it had reached agreements to settle the majority of lawsuits currently filed and had crafted a plan for handling cases that likely would be filed in the future. To handle the current litigation Bayer said it will pay up to $9.6 billion to resolve roughly 75 percent of the current claims and will continue working to settle the rest."[8] Several members of the lead law firms who won the three Roundup cancer trials oppose the proposed class action settlement plan, saying it would deprive future plaintiffs of their rights while enriching a handful of lawyers who have not previously been at the forefront of the Roundup litigation.[9] The plan requires the approval of Judge Chhabria, but the order, issued Monday July, 6, 2020, indicated he did not plan to grant approval. The judge said he would hold a hearing on July 24 on the motion for preliminary approval of the class action settlement. "Given the Court's current skepticism, it could be contrary to everyone's interest to delay the hearing on preliminary approval," he wrote in his order.[10] As of the publishing of *Health Freedom*, the Monsanto trials have progressed and the US Right to Know website provides updates.

Vaccines

Vaccines provide another example of the dangers of the lack of accountability of corporations in terms of human health. Childhood school-recommended vaccines are a group of products manufactured, marketed, and sold by some of the largest corporations in the world and used by millions of Americans. Yet these vaccines are known to have side effects like other medicines do, including severe injury or death.[11] The profits from these vaccines are astronomical, yet, unlike with glyphosate Roundup and every other manufactured product in the United States, those claiming injury from a childhood school-recommended vaccine cannot sue a vaccine manufacturer without first filing a claim with the US Court of Federal Claims under the National Vaccine Injury Compensation Program (NVICP) of 1988. If a claim is denied, or if the claim is approved and the claimant rejects the compensation, only then may the claimant file a civil lawsuit.

In 1982, before the special claims court was set up, important attention was brought to the issue of vaccine safety when a courageous woman, Barbara Loe Fisher, told her story and joined with other parents of vaccine-injured children in founding the nonprofit charity known today as the National Vaccine Information Center (NVIC). NVIC had the goal of preventing vaccine injuries and deaths through public education and securing safety reforms and informed consent protections in the vaccination system. In 1980 Barbara Loe Fisher's life was affected by a vaccine. Her healthy, precocious two-and-a-half-year-old son suffered a convulsion, went into shock, and lost consciousness within a few hours after his fourth DPT shot. He was left with minimal brain damage that took the form of multiple learning disabilities and attention deficit disorder, which confined him to a special education classroom for twelve years.[12] Barbara Loe Fisher recounts her experience and that of more than one hundred other parents of vaccine-injured children in her 1985 book *DPT: A Shot in the Dark* (Harcourt Brace Jovanovich), which she coauthored with Harris Coulter, PhD. The book was the first major well-documented critique of the United States' mass vaccination system, calling for safety reforms and the human right to informed consent to vaccination.[13] Currently NVIC is a leading voice in efforts to increase public education about vaccines and the safety of vaccines.

How did it come to pass that a vaccine-injured claimant was not able to sue in civil court? In the 1980s, the federal Center for Disease Control (CDC) recommended that children going to school should have vaccines for polio, measles, mumps, rubella, diphtheria, tetanus, and whooping cough. States passed laws to recommend the same but honored the parents' right to decline the vaccines.

In December of 1984, one of two remaining American manufacturers of the whooping cough vaccine said it was withdrawing from manufacturing the vaccine rather than paying sharply higher rates for liability insurance, premiums, and deductibles.[14] The number of lawsuits against manufacturers of all vaccines had risen sharply. The whooping cough vaccine had caused a relatively higher rate of side effects than others, including brain damage and death.[15] The withdrawal of that company because of its fear of lawsuits meant that each vaccine for childhood diseases was then produced by a single manufacturer. Dr. Martin Smith, a vice president of the American Academy of Pediatrics, said reliance on a single manufacturer would portend shortages because "it gives us no cushion of safety whatever" in case the plant has to shut down for any reason or in case batches of vaccine are rejected by federal regulators.[16]

Many of the lawsuits involving vaccine injuries had focused on whooping cough vaccine. At that time, medical experts said that it was possible for a vaccine to cause a reaction in an otherwise healthy child, even if such vaccine was made according to federal standards and properly administered by the doctor.[17] The development stimulated a drive to set up a federally sponsored system of compensation for children harmed by vaccines.

On November 14, 1986, under Senate Bill 1744 of the Ninety-Ninth Congress, Congress passed the National Childhood Vaccine Injury

Act (NCVIA) to shield drug companies and doctors from civil product liability and malpractice lawsuits for injuries and deaths caused by federal- and state-recommended vaccines.[18] The law, which acknowledged that vaccines can cause injuries and death, created a federal Vaccine Injury Compensation Program (VICP). Provisions in the original law allowed vaccine-injured petitioners to file a lawsuit in civil court only if (1) federal compensation was denied; (2) the compensation award was not acceptable to the petitioner; or (3) after either (1) or (2) a civil suit is brought and it can be proven that the manufacture was liable under one or more conditions spelled out in the law where a manufacturer could be liable, for example, if the vaccine was not properly prepared and was not accompanied by proper directions and warnings.[19] However, in 2011, a US Supreme Court ruling effectively gave drug companies complete product liability protection, even when there was evidence that the vaccine was defectively designed.[20]

According to the August 1, 2020, National Vaccine Injury Compensation Program Data Report, from October 1, 1988 through August 1, 2020, 4.4 billion dollars in federal compensation has been paid to children and adults who have been injured or died from recommended vaccines. Out of the 20,798 injury petitions filed, more than 6 percent were filed for deaths. And 11,637 of the petitions were dismissed and the alleged victims denied compensation.[21] The workings and the reasons for what some say are unfair dismissals of claims by the court are spelled out in detail in author of Wayne Rohde's books, entitled *The Vaccine Court: The Dark Truth of America's Vaccine Injury Compensation Program.*[22] It is estimated that only between 1 percent and 10 percent of all serious health problems, hospitalizations, injuries, and deaths that occur after vaccinations given to children or adults are ever reported to the federal Vaccine Adverse Events Reporting System (VAERS).[23]

Since 1986, when twelve vaccines were recommended for children, the number of recommended vaccines for schoolchildren has increased with the CDC now recommending fifty-four shots for sixteen diseases with seventy antigens in the vaccines.[24] In addition, there is a strong effort by the conventional medical and pharmaceutical lobby and community to take away the parental right to decline vaccines for their children if they want their children go to day care or schools. Taking away the right of parents to send their children to school if the children do not receive a vaccine is a medical freedom issue and is a clear example of how corporate and government powers can affect freedoms.

Vaccine Safety and Efficacy Responsibility

The Centers for Disease Control holds that vaccines are a great success story. But there are numerous medical professionals who disagree. One such professional is Dr. Christine Northrup, who has prepared a well-documented list indicating why she would not recommend getting a flu shot.[25]

For purposes of this chapter, I will focus on the use of vaccines as they affect health freedoms. Vaccines present a real health freedom problem when a dominant group begins to attempt to force or coerce another group to make a particular health decision. For those who do not embrace the dominant CDC view of vaccines, they find themselves looking for other options, and if their options are not protected, they look to the Constitution for protection of their health care decision-making rights. The legal exemptions to government-imposed vaccine requirements for schoolchildren that are based on medical, religious, or conscientiously held beliefs or on personal beliefs are grounded in fundamental constitutional rights: the right of self-determination and bodily autonomy, medical freedom and the right to consent, and parental rights.

In 2018 an important development unfolded as citizen leaders concerned about vaccine injuries noted that a clause in the National Childhood Vaccine Injury Act of 1986 compelled the Department of Health and Human Services (DHHS) to take responsibility for improving vaccine safety and efficacy, charging the agency with constant monitoring and improving of adverse event reporting.[26] The Mandate for Safer Childhood Vaccines clause also tasked DHHS with providing a report on improvements made in those areas to Congress every two years.[27] Finding no reports, an organization called ICAN (Informed Consent Action Network) sued DHHS to obtain the reports. The result of the lawsuit was that the DHHS said they did not locate any records of biennial reports to Congress detailing the improvements in vaccine safety.[28]

When you step back and consider that millions of doses of vaccines are being given to healthy children without any liability responsibility on the part of the corporation and without any oversight or reporting by the federal agency initiating the program, you discover that if all adverse reactions were reported for the thousands of children who have been disabled or have died from vaccine reactions annually* without adequate legal recourse, it would call for a health freedom conversation.

Corporation-Owned Information and Media Outlets

The health of citizens is affected by information and media outlets. Products manufactured by corporations that consumers use and depend upon include more than home, agricultural, and health products. They also include information products such as media and literary products. The advancements of technology include multiple forms of communication. The invention of the printing press in 1400 changed the world and has affected the human experience. The ability to communicate the written word across geographic miles changed the nature of communication in general.

Books and libraries became staples of communities worldwide. The invention of photography changed the visual world, where paintings were no longer the only method of capturing the moment. Advances allowed for people to tell their stories in intimate realistic detail and distribute them to others easily. The remarkable invention of moving drawings and photographs over decades evolved into motion pictures, the ultimate in storytelling.

My father was an avid fan of new inventions. My claim to fame is that he was the first one in our county to purchase a television. It happened to be on the day I was born in 1949! One of my mother's claims to fame was

---

* There have been 22,685 claims filed since 1988, 6 percent of these for deaths. The Grant Final Report for Electronic Support for Public Health—Vaccine Adverse Event Reporting System (ESP:VAERS) stated that "fewer than 1 percent of vaccine adverse events are reported." In the period of January–September 2020, 1,191 adverse event claims were made.

winning a contest on *Queen for a Day* on the TV. They sent her a new set of china, which she dearly cherished over the years.

In my lifetime we have gone from that little rounded walnut wood-framed TV to smart TVs large enough to fill your living room and with a plethora of content available to watch and listen to. In addition to information coming directly to you through a device, we now have the ability to have devices communicate with each other, along with the internet, smartphones, and more, all offering instant communication and access to information of any kind.

Going back to the chain-of-trust issue, how do people decide what to listen to and what to trust when making health care decisions? The struggle to acquire visibility in such an arena is intense. Bertrand Russell, in his controversial 1953 book entitled *The Impact of Science on Society*, expounded on the political importance of mass psychology and the growth of modern methods of propaganda. He even stated, "It may be hoped that in time anybody will be able to persuade anybody of anything if he can catch the patient young and is provided by the State with money and equipment. This subject will make great strides when it is taken up by scientists under a scientific dictatorship."[29]

The climb to visibility in the media world has reached the money threshold. In June of 2016, Kate Vinton, as part of the Forbes Wealth Team, wrote: "Billionaires own part or all of several of America's influential national newspapers, including the *Washington Post*, the *Wall Street Journal* and the *New York Times*, in addition to magazines, local papers and online publications. Several other billionaires, including Comcast CEO Brian Roberts and Liberty Media Chairman John Malone, own or control cable TV networks that are powerful but not primarily news focused."[30]

In addition to owning media outlets, billionaires and corporations are participating in and affecting politics and public policy. Wealth allows entities to buy visibility, and then they can impart their political and public policy preferences to millions of people all at once. This phenomenon impacts the culture at large. For example, a regular citizen comes home from work, has supper, and turns on the TV to get the latest news. Not many citizens doing this would think of the news as a paid advertisement or a promotion of a political strategy or belief system. More and more, citizens are being called to go back to their internal conversation as to whom to trust. Health freedom leaders encourage Americans to consider the source of the information they depend on and to seek many avenues of information in addition to the large media outlets when making decisions concerning their health and well-being.

Corporate Accountability

In the case of Roundup, the judicial system has come to the rescue of victims of harm. Indeed, the judicial system is turning out to be the protector of the health of the people. Monsanto and Bayer could spend huge sums of money promoting their products to the agricultural community and lobbying federal and local governments to protect their interests, but the courts can hear all the evidence and hold them accountable.

In the case of school-recommended vaccines, it is difficult or nearly impossible for a victim to obtain relief. The manufacturers spend huge sums of money promoting their products to the medical and health insurance industry and lobbying federal and local governments to protect their interests, and the federal vaccine compensation plan, with its weak federal administrative protocols and lack of accountability reporting, does not protect the legal interest of victims. Manufacturers are completely shielded from liability and responsibility to the human family.

In the case of trusted sources of information regarding health care issues, new alternative sources of information are growing, and citizens are challenged to do more of their own research and establish their own chain of trust that reflects their own values in terms of how to maintain their own health. With the existence of the World Wide Web, life has changed for many, and information is more accessible. For example, many schools, institutes, and practitioners of holistic or unconventional health care are now able to share their information online with consumers, and consumers are educating themselves about many aspects of their own health. They are also evaluating which sources of information they want to trust for their health concerns.

Understanding the power of advertising, propaganda, and potential conflicts of interest is essential in the health freedom conversation. Citizens need to be awake and aware in a free society and are encouraged to think for themselves when it comes to their own health and the health of their family members to help promote the longevity of liberty within the culture.

Health Seekers and Corporations

Large corporations providing products to massive numbers of consumers can easily affect the welfare of the human family. The danger of an unscrupulous corporation marketing potentially dangerous information or products that regular people use for their health or ingest on a daily basis is very real. For example, media outlets run hundreds of ads for pharmaceutical drugs each day, with happy, healthy people in the ads, promising great results and downplaying the potential side effects of the drugs. Corporate food chains run colorful enticing ads on large media outlets about their food products, including foods that may not promote health if eaten on a regular basis, without educating consumers of the risks. It is of paramount importance to hold corporations up to the standard of all the health freedom principles and to hold them legally liable when entire populations are negatively affected by behavior.

Principle 1, the freedom to be let alone, can be honored by a corporation that honors the right of people to avoid being exposed to products that they don't personally choose to be exposed to. Principle 2, the freedom to act, can be honored by corporations by giving consumers adequate truthful information about products so that they may be informed and act on their own behalf. Principle 3, freedom to access, is coveted by corporations because it allows them to provide their products to willing consumers who want access to them. Principle 4, to do no harm, is the challenging principle in today's world. When a product accomplishes a particular task appreciated by some but leaves in its wake a path of destruction or misinformation for individuals and communities, then the corporation is challenged to either do the right thing or be held liable if it chooses profits over health and welfare.

Health seekers are affected by corporate products in many ways. In fact, consumers have become dependent on many products. In some instances, consumers have the opportunity to choose whether to utilize the product or not. In such situations, truthful information and truthful advertising about products is paramount. In other instances, products are inserted into the environment without the consent of consumers, such as chemicals on public walkways or microwave radiation in the air emitted by telecommunication companies. Corporations count on consumers to want their products and to use them. In today's world, health seekers eagerly seek products that reflect the overall evolution in the use of technology. Regular people are often willing to extend their survival chain of trust to corporations without questioning the details of products in order to gain access to the products they want, even though the corporations producing the products may not be promoting the health of an individual or community. For health freedom to be fully realized, corporations and health seekers need to be awake and aware and be held to the high standard of the principles of health freedom.

As people become more aware of the need for corporate responsibility, they are asking the question "Am I too late?" The founders of our country may not have adequately foreseen the impact of advanced technology—and its resulting corporate wealth—on the human family, but they provided us with the architecture of a government capable of protecting our life, our liberty, and the pursuit of happiness. They provided us with a vehicle to have the freedom conversation. And that we must do now for the survival and good of all.

Chapter 12

Health Freedom Principle 8 — Responsibility of Government

Principle 8: Responsibility of Government

Government has the responsibility and duty to protect health freedom and to make no law or public policy abridging health freedom or its fundamental principles.

The United States is a country based on laws. Rather than looking to a monarch or other leaders to give us privileges to act, we honor our inherent inalienable rights as humans to act on our own behalf. We see the government as providing a service to us, to protect our life, our liberty, and the pursuit of happiness. We look to the architecture of our Constitution and the laws that have been established under it for guidance in terms of the way in which our government should function.

The United States is now at a crossroads, delving deeply into the question of what Americans expect of their government. The polarization of opinions is presenting an enormous opportunity to assess the laws and affirm the principles upon which our country was founded. Applying our founding principles in a technologically advancing society will be our greatest challenge.

Health freedom is being affected by the overall issue of freedom in our country. Our health laws and our healing culture are being scrutinized by health seekers who want their health freedoms protected. Our health laws and our healing culture may need to change to protect our health freedom as we face changes in the world.

Culture and Law

Law, in its purest form, rises out of people's stories and their deepest desire as a community to survive. Law not only is designed for individuals but also addresses the desire of all members of a community. The roots of law are often found by observing the cultural norms and visions of a people. The relationship between cultural norms and law is extremely important. To understand any law, it is helpful to understand a people's cultural norms.

Cultural norms are often encouraged rather than enforced, and they often change. They develop organically and morph with the ebb and flow of internal and external conversations and interactions that affect a group. When you travel the world over, you will quickly find an ornate tapestry of complex and richly beautiful cultures. Laws, on the other hand, usually exist to empower a designated authority to enforce particular behaviors, values, or activities. Laws seem to be born when cultural pressures or coercive measures lead to the formalizing and systematic enforcement of a value among the people.

Laws and cultural norms are not identical, but they share a strong common bond: both naturally resist change. Often, a response to a push for a legal change is "That's the law!" The same is true of a push for change within a culture: "That's the way we do things around here!"

Resistance to change may seem like a negative characteristic, but this resistance to change is what most people like about laws and customs. People want to know the rules so that they can set up their chains of trust and depend on a way of life and social harmony. People seek trusting relationships to promote their own peaceful states of mind and the peace of the community. Laws and customs that are unchanging and dependable provide foundations for trusting relationships. Laws and customs bring many humans peace of mind and give them orderly expectations for their everyday world.

For example, my father, recovering from hip surgery and approaching his ninetieth birthday, asked me, after having had a week of serious complications, if he needed to stay in the hospital. Could he return home to recover or else to prepare to pass peacefully in his own home? He wanted to know what his rights were. I assured him that adults in our country can always refuse medical treatment at any time and that if he wanted to, he could leave, even if that decision was contrary to the recommendation of his doctors. His face lit up and he felt noticeably better knowing he had a choice in the matter. I was glad that I had been able to speak those words to him and that I lived in a country that had laws that would protect his rights to live out his own destiny. The roots of the laws that were protecting my father's inalienable right to live and die in peace and with his own choices were reflected in the beautiful caring hospital environment and the medical staff's approach to health care. Those cultural attitudes and norms were most likely the basis for the establishment of the laws that protected my father's rights.

Balancing the resistance to change with the normal and natural need for change is challenging. Lawmakers are expected to honor existing laws and hold fast to the rationales for them. On the other hand, lawmakers are expected to listen to urgent new developments, the needs of the people, and reasons why a change in the law would be good. Lawmakers are in the often challenging position of making new laws for a diverse community and amending old laws that no longer accomplish what they were originally legislated to accomplish. They must continually evaluate new information and trends and keep up with an evolving world.

Can you imagine the struggle going on with our founding fathers, who valued the laws of their homeland yet recognized that change of those laws was needed? Thomas Jefferson's words displayed on panel four of the Jefferson Memorial say it well:

> I am not an advocate for frequent changes in laws and constitutions, but laws and institutions must go hand in hand with the progress of the human mind. As that becomes more developed, more enlightened, as new discoveries are made, new truths discovered and manners and opinions change, with the change of circumstances, institutions must advance also to keep pace with the times. We might as well require a man to wear

> still the coat which fitted him when a boy as civilized society
> to remain ever under the regimen of their barbarous ancestors.[1]

The Challenge of Growth of Government

The architecture of the US Constitution provides checks and balances to protect against abuses of power and to protect freedom. This was accomplished by providing three branches of government: the legislative branch, the executive branch, and the judicial branch. I have touched upon each of these branches in various ways throughout *Health Freedom*, including examples of state legislation that affects health freedom, examples of state executive orders that affect health freedom, and legal cases that have articulated health freedom principles.

But an issue of great concern overall in our country today is the growth of government itself and the lack of proper checks and balances to protect constitutionality. Since the 1930s, Congress has passed laws delegating legislative powers to agencies led by unelected officials to deal with certain areas of concern. The delegation of governmental powers to agencies and nonelected bureaucrats was originally challenged in the courts as unconstitutional, but as attorney Jonathan Emord spells out in his book *The Rise of Tyranny*:

> Today there is no matter of any economic or political import that is not regulated by a federal agency or commission. There is also almost no such matter to which the Congress acts unilaterally, rather than by simply affording more power to act to agencies and commissions. The law-making power while vested in an elected Congress by the Constitution is in fact routinely exercised by the appointed heads of the regulatory agencies and commissions. Neither the Congress nor the courts impose an effective check. We have created the very union of legislative, executive, and judicial powers that the founders defined as tyranny.[2]

Today Congress has delegated power to the executive branch of federal government, including the establishment of a total of 398 agencies, commissions, and organizations. A number of these have the power to make rules according to an administrative rulemaking process, and they adjudicate cases by the use of special administrative courts. The heads of the fifteen main agencies of the federal government are also members of the president's cabinet. They include the following:

- US Department of Agriculture
- US Department of Commerce
- US Department of Defense
- US Department of Education
- US Department of Energy
- US Department of Health and Human Services
- US Department of Homeland Security
- US Department of Housing and Urban Development
- US Department of Justice
- US Department of Labor
- US Department of State
- US Department of the Interior
- US Department of the Treasury
- US Department of Transportation
- US Department of Veterans Affairs.[3]

The existence of agencies may be beneficial to assist with the overwhelming details of how to manage the needs of people. But health freedom advocates have experienced the downside of agency power when agency unelected officials set policy and rules that clash with the will of the people.

Agency Impact on Vaccine Law

For example, the Centers for Disease Control (CDC), part of the Public Health Service within the federal Department of Health and Human Services, recommends multiple vaccines for school-aged children without advocating for parental rights or promoting liberty or freedom concepts. State legislators look to this agency for guidance on how to draft laws that reflect the will of the agency. State agencies also look to federal agency recommendations for guidance. For example, in 2015 California legislators passed a law that took away the right of California parents to send their children to private or public day cares or schools if they did not have their children receive recommended vaccines. The law stated in part:

> 120325. In enacting this chapter, ... it is the intent of the Legislature to provide:
>
> (a) A means for the eventual achievement of total immunization of appropriate age groups against the following childhood diseases:
>
> > (1) Diphtheria.
> > (2) Hepatitis B.
> > (3) *Haemophilus influenzae* type b.
> > (4) Measles.
> > (5) Mumps.
> > (6) Pertussis (whooping cough).
> > (7) Poliomyelitis.
> > (8) Rubella.
> > (9) Tetanus.
> > (10) Varicella (chickenpox).
> > (11) Any other disease deemed appropriate by the department, taking into consideration the recommendations of the Advisory Committee on Immunization Practices of the United States Department of Health and Human Services, the American Academy of Pediatrics, and the American Academy of Family Physicians.

This law is a stunning example of a state legislature passing a law that completely endorses a governmental agency's particular opinion and health care paradigm and then attempts to force that view on all citizens by coercion. I think that prohibiting access to government resources for not participating in a dominant government-endorsed health recommendation plan completely infringes on parental constitutional rights and health care decision-making rights.

Some might say that a person who does not agree with the government's recommendations for health should not be entitled to government resources. But that view does not reflect the basic underpinnings of our Constitution and the architecture of our government. We are not only a democracy that utilizes the concept of majority; we are also a republic with a representative government and a constitution. The Constitution is the law of the land and often is relied upon by people who hold minority views to protect human rights. The importance of government to protect the rights of citizens to make their own health and survival decisions as they see fit is paramount in this time when governments and corporations attempt to work together to promote a paradigm that they wish to see implemented.

Agency Power to Declare Corporate Liability Shield in an Emergency

In 2005, Congress passed the Public Readiness and Emergency Preparedness Act (PREP Act), which delegated authority to the Secretary of Health and Human Services to declare a legal liability shield during an emergency to certain individuals and entities (covered persons).[4] The liability protection in the PREP Act is liability protection against any claim of loss caused by, arising out of, relating to, or resulting from the manufacture, distribution, administration, or use of medical countermeasures (covered countermeasures), except for claims involving "willful misconduct" as defined in the PREP Act.[5] The Act would provide a shield from liability for the use of an emergency "countermeasure," which could include, for example, the use of a ventilator that caused a death or the use of a mask that caused a person to experience lethal hypoxia (low oxygen levels).

If you are injured, a new agency program was set up and is available to you, the CICP (Countermeasure Injury Compensation Program).[6] Injured persons attempting to get relief will be required to provide "compelling, reliable, valid, medical and scientific evidence" of injury. In order to win a case, the burden of proof will be on the injured person, not the government, as follows:

> The causal connection between the countermeasure and the serious physical injury must be supported by compelling, reliable, valid, medical and scientific evidence in order for the individual to be considered for compensation.[7]

The presence and impact of agencies and their officials, organizations, and recommendations is completely prevalent in the lawmaking process today. Almost every state legislative hearing that I have attended in the past twenty years has had agency leaders testifying at the hearings. Agencies carry a lot of weight with lawmakers, as lawmakers look to them for their expertise and protocols to cope with public concerns, or for justification for passing bills that the lawmaker deems important. Holding agencies accountable, prohibiting financial conflicts of interest, demanding truth and transparency, and requiring agencies to promote constitutional principles and health freedom principles all will be needed. If this is not done, tyranny will prevail.

Where Is Government Headed?

Can Americans trust their government to protect liberty and, in good faith, be in the conversation of freedom? Can they trust government to protect health freedom? Our government, a government of the people, for the people, and by the people, has accomplished amazing things since 1776. Will we continue to build a legacy of liberty?

Governments are increasingly responsible for laws that negatively affect health freedom and laws that may negatively affect the survival of all humans. It will take the undoing or amending of some current US laws and public policies to protect health freedom.

Americans are questioning whether governments still have the power to govern or whether they have become simply puppet structures implementing the wishes of large policy and financial interests. Some are even asking whether nationalism is becoming obsolete given the globalization of resources and society. Addressing the expansion of government, technology, corporations, and wealth in general, and their impact on governments, will be essential to the future of our nation.

The Road to Health Freedom

More than fifty years ago, my sister often sang a song with me that I dearly loved when we were in college. It went like this: "It's a long, long road to freedom, a winding steep and tall, but when you walk in love with the wind on your wings and cover the earth with the songs you sing, the miles fly by."[8]

True freedom is not only about the physical world. Freedom is about the human experience, about spirit, light, and intention. Freedom is about people, about relationships, about dreams and visions. The leaders who are being called forth now to challenge and explore the depths of the meaning of freedom are providing a service to all of us who will decide our destiny on the road to freedom. Citizens, lawmakers, and communities will be profoundly rewarded when they enter into meaningful dialogue and arrive at solutions that reflect freedom and the vision of a harmonious future.

Consider these expectations for lawmakers, executives, judges, veterans, employees, servants, and all of us faithful citizens:

- The ability to discern the path of the preservation of liberty and freedom ahead.
- The humility to seek the truth and act upon it.
- The strength to resist financial interests that could obliterate independent thinking.
- The compassion to hear and understand the stories of the people.
- The courage to stand for freedom.
- The creativity and innovativeness to develop successful solutions.
- The willingness to communicate, collaborate, and decrease polarizations.
- The openness to listen, tolerate, and look beyond.
- The wisdom to navigate the path of a free people.

Our hope for the future is in the fact that our government is made up of people. People in the United States have the ability to participate in the freedom conversation. Any undermining of the political process or the integrity of the election system of a representative government, or in any way prohibiting the voice of the people to be heard, would undermine our

159

country and our health freedom. People have the ability to experience the spirit, the light, and the intention of life. Our Constitution is designed to enable citizens to participate at all times in the freedom conversation.

It is apparent: we are in uncharted waters. May we all pull together and navigate this evolutionary process successfully and bring our ship into safe harbor.

Chapter 13

A People at Risk

Why did we come to this country if we are going to be regulated out of our own health and our own health choices? Our immune systems are being compromised by environmental hazards and our lifestyle, and we are not allowed to access the things that will help us survive.

The Foundation of Fear

Whether the loss of freedom happens quickly or slowly, fear is often at the root of oppression or suppression. We all know fear. Fear can be our saving grace to catapult us to actions that lead us to safe harbors, or it can be our nemesis by holding us in silence. Fear is often the gatekeeper of our inner voices and the determiner of whether we live freely.

Health freedom is withering on a vine of messaging that is based on fear. These messages include the idea that you will die without a particular drug; there is no cure for cancer, diabetes, or heart disease; you won't know what is going on without watching the news; you will die if you do not obey your doctor's recommendations; your child will die if they don't receive fifty-nine doses of vaccines; you will die if you don't obey your governor's order and stay away from your neighbors and wear a mask in public; it is dangerous to give birth outside a hospital; your county will not have enough food if it doesn't accept industrialized farming techniques; and without 5G antennas, you will not be able to use your technological devices. This fear messaging that promotes suppression of health freedom is happening even in the midst of an evolution of an enlightened world community.

Americans do not naturally stand down when they are afraid or during the silencing of personal liberties, but when silencing happens by erosion over generations of messaging based on fear and encouragement of dependency, people gradually lose sight of the original vision of freedom, and then relinquishment of personal authority takes place. Over time, an understanding of personal freedom decreases, and finally people are passive, dependent, and silent when it comes to health. Concepts of health freedom are washed away.

Foundation of Denial

Many of the fear messages are now being explored, researched, and reevaluated by Americans who are looking at expanded options for health and well-being. But if a person remains in fear, believing they cannot arrive at health in any other way, they might move into denial. Denial is a side effect of the progression of fear. If fear is prolonged or not acknowledged and alleviated, then the one who is fearful often picks up the tool of denial to arrive at "Everything is OK." Denial is more problematic even than fear. A person or a community in denial is convinced that there is no reason to be afraid and that there is no problem. A person in denial will seldom address original fears or change a course of behavior or conviction, even in some cases to save their own life or the life of a loved one. Denial is a survival technique. Unlike fear, denial does not generally help us eliminate the original threat that caused us to have fear.

When denial is passed from generation to generation, the original fear or problem moves further and further away from awareness. A mode of denial handed down from a previous generation becomes the new truth for the new generation. The new generation thinks of it as truth, even if they may die of a lethal situation or message while believing that truth.

In the United States, silencing health freedom has been a gradual process with bad health outcomes made to look normal. Take, for example, the fact that the National Cancer Institute projection for 2018 was that an estimated

1,735,350 new cases of cancer would be diagnosed in the United States and 609,640 people would die from the disease.[1] Six in ten Americans live with at least one chronic disease, including heart disease, stroke, cancer, or diabetes.[2] These and other chronic diseases were reported as the leading causes of death and disability in the United States as of January 2020.[3] However, many people believe that there is no definitive reason and no possible cure for these ailments. These statistics are what are motivating some to step out of the box of the dominant medical and research culture and look to other sources of information and successes. Take for example former congressman Berkley Bedell's work at the National Foundation for Alternative Medicine, publishing information about successful cancer treatments from other countries on his website for Americans to read.

If we are in denial, we don't miss health freedom because we don't perceive a need to exercise it. We have been trained to delegate personal decision-making authority and assessment of our own bodies and lifestyles to a system of medical, environmental, and agricultural scientific experts delegated to perform the paid task of keeping us alive and healthy. We entrust these experts with our health, life, quality of life, and safety based on our learned trust in technological advances and the accomplishments of the employees working in these systems.

What this acceptable delegation of personal self-assessment and authority looks like in real time is that anything outside of accepting advice from a conventional medical health care provider or an environmental or agricultural professional is thought of by many as dangerous or irresponsible. Today, not only have many of us become submissive about looking beyond conventional approaches to our own health care decision-making, but also some people experience serious anxiety at the mere thought of asserting themselves in opposition to the recommendation of conventional practitioners.

If one does finally muster up the courage to discuss one's own health perspectives and goes so far as to request innovative methods to explore and enhance health, that person is often shamed, ridiculed, and intimidated, by either family members or health care practitioners, or discouraged from suggesting alternatives outside of what the conventional systems recommend or provide. And of course in the medical field, anything outside the conventional system of drug-and surgery-based medicine is generally not covered by insurance programs. This leaves us financially dependent and financially coerced into staying within the dependency-promoting system.

The US health care system flourishes on popular denial. It flourishes on Americans' trusting that their medical conditions are not caused by environment, consumption, or lifestyle and that there are quick answers to medical conditions. Many of us believe the words of technology experts: *We know best, and we know what is good for you.* Tragic loss of life of those who have accepted the narrow system of conventional health care is considered the best that could have been done and, somehow, "normal." This deep sense of denial and the actual real-time ability to accept these unnecessary tragedies as normal, I believe, is putting us in jeopardy of becoming a slowly dying nation and extinct as a people.

A People at Risk

A people at risk is a people who accept the claims of those who promote dangerous medical products and practices and who continue to advertise and promote to the general public through media campaigns the use of dangerous products and treatments despite the knowledge of their life-threatening side effects, and despite the knowledge that thousands of United States citizens die each year from iatrogenic medical error deaths.

A people at risk is a people living in a country that is falling in rank on the international comparative charts assessing successful performance of health systems, according to the World Health Organization.[4] These are a people with a greater probability of dying from a cardiovascular disease, cancer, diabetes, or chronic respiratory disease in the United States than people living in forty other countries,[5] a people whose probability of their children's surviving after childbirth is lower than that of forty other countries,[6] and whose probability of a child's surviving past the age of five is lower than that of forty-three other countries.[7] Additionally, a people at risk is a people dying of unintentional poisoning, the percentage of which is higher in the United States than in one hundred nine other countries.[8] Denial of these facts is the domain of a people at risk.

A people at risk is a people with daily health habits that are not conducive to health and who do not oppose those habits, including people who eat, drink, and live with carcinogens and who do not demand the halt of the use of carcinogens in their food supply, water supply, and soil. It is a people who daily consume genetically modified foods, proven to destroy the neurological systems of research animals and that lack long-term studies on human populations.[9] Genetically modified ingredients exist in up to 70 percent of all processed foods,[10] yet many people are not demanding that those GMOs be banned or labeled so they can choose to consume them or not.

Breaking Out of Denial

We are expected to follow our cultural training and beliefs when we are working to improve our quality of life and ensure our survival. But if we are dying at the hands of a lethal system and we are not willing to entertain the possibility that the system might not be supporting our health, or if we are not willing to help change that system, then we are putting ourselves in ongoing danger.

We the people would do better to break out of denial, rise, and question the medical and health circumstances at hand. If we do not, and if we remain in a state of complacent denial, then I fear that we will become, one by one, weaker and die as a people. It is my belief that a health care system that promotes human dependency will collapse from its misplaced burden of responsibility on the culture of technology.

The voice of the health freedom movement not only seeks to preserve the option of experiencing a relaxing massage to alleviate stress but also seeks to intervene in a dangerous situation with the hope that we can survive on this earth. We have a nation on the brink of collapse from the illnesses of its individual citizens. Every day I live with the possibility that I am a citizen of a young nation experiencing a slow death before it has had the opportunity to fully develop its conscience. I find myself living in a nation in which the governmental, legal, corporate, and public policy framework regarding health has transformed us into dependents, actually causing the physical death of its people.

Reclaiming Health Freedom

If we want to shed our denial and take back personal authority, we have to face the reality of our own complex health situations. We will have to accept that the evolution of a technological world has affected our health and that our environment has health components that need immediate attention. We will have to actually live as though we are responsible for every aspect of our health and survival.

We will have to start evaluating the health impact of our behaviors and our culture on Mother Earth. We will have to evaluate the food that we eat and its impact on our health; we will have to evaluate the environmental toxins we are exposed to, the audio, visual, and technical environment that we participate in, and their impact on our health. We will have to consider the way in which we spend our time, our level of stress or joy, the relationships and communities that we have, the laws that we live by, and the world economic and cultural situations that drive all of the above.

Freedom is a *radical* concept. It places the responsibility of life, liberty, and happiness on the individual. There is no one else to blame, no one else to supply the ultimate answers, no one to share the work of discernment. We live and die by our own choices. Freedom is scary, painful, and hard work, but its glories cannot be matched.

Images of Truth

The heretofore unseen truth in the United States is slowly emerging. The images come from people living and telling their stories and following their hunches and intuitions. The images come from people trying to make sense of the devastation they are experiencing. As the images of truth make their way into the hearts and minds of a people who want to heal, those people become ready to act on their own behalf.

There are many examples of truth emerging all around us. Preventive, holistic, integrative approaches to health care are growing.[11] Laws are being passed to prevent the use of dangerous pesticides in agriculture and on public or school grounds, and to promote the placement of warning signs on toxic but beautiful green manicured lawns, golf courses, and plush grounds. Organic farming is growing. The voices of parents who have children with disabilities due to vaccines that pose serious neurological risks are being heard.[12] Protection of the rights of parents to make medical decisions for their children is being called for. Physicians are coming forward to report the large number of vaccine adverse events and are working to protect their patients' rights to more truthful information and complete informed consent. Government officials who are helping to approve new drugs that promise cures are being asked whether they have any financial conflict of interest with the drug company requesting approval.

A Nation Sparks a Movement

Our founders believed that to create a truly free world, the government would have to be premised on the belief that people *want* to be engaged in the living conversation of freedom and that, based on this thirst for freedom, they would together provide for the general welfare of all while honoring the sacredness of the individual. Thus, the Preamble to the Constitution of the United States reads as follows:

> We the People of the United States, in Order to form a more perfect Union, establish Justice, ensure domestic Tranquility, provide for the common defense, promote the general Welfare, and secure the Blessings of Liberty to ourselves and our Posterity, do ordain and establish this Constitution for the United States of America.[13]

Now the people's intention and their will to survive has sparked a movement, the health freedom movement. The health freedom movement attracts people who want the earth and the people on the earth to survive in health. These people are speaking the truth about the health and survival of our culture. They are working night and day to support, nurture, and save the people and the earth. I call them the health freedom advocates. They are fighting to protect the purity of our food supply, our air, water, and soil, and our outer space. They are working to protect the truthfulness of the information that we receive. They are working to provide more options for ailing family members and friends. Health freedom advocates are delving into the reasons why our survival is in jeopardy. Health freedom

167

advocates have stories that have led them to a place where they are willing to question the status quo of health. They are also the healers and health care practitioners who are willing to speak the truth.

Freedom advocates are the voice of the health freedom movement. They utilize communication systems of all kinds, including art, literature, media, music, storytelling, gatherings, and technology, to give truth, hope, and new information to the people. They are the ones who see the link between health care and the socioeconomic, spiritual, humanistic, and cultural practices of a people. They revere the pluralism of the people and work toward solutions that are beneficial to the health of all people and to the earth.

The Freedom Conversation

I have watched the freedom conversation take place over these years, sometimes with great success, arriving at amazing harmony, and sometimes breaking down completely, which is when picking up the pieces and rebuilding becomes necessary. No matter the outcome, the passion in these conversations that attempt to arrive at harmony brings forth *miracles*. Living, breathing people put their hopes and fears into these conversations, and amazing things happen. I am convinced that the freedom conversation, in and of itself, is part of the basic life force of the human experience. I believe that if we learn the importance of the freedom conversation, participate in it, and recognize the essence of this life force acting among us, we will survive and thrive as a people.

A question I have often asked myself is, how can true freedom exist without having informed people participating in the ongoing conversation of what that freedom would look like? My conclusion is that it cannot. During my work as a health freedom advocate, I often wrote about, visualized, and described freedom as a living light, a dynamic energy. One day I visited the Jefferson Memorial in Washington, DC. There I read what Thomas Jefferson wrote of enlightenment and freedom:

> Enlighten the people generally, and tyranny and oppressions
> of body and mind will vanish like evil spirits at the dawn of

day. (Thomas Jefferson to Pierre Samuel Du Pont de Nemours, April 24, 1816)[14]

I look to the diffusion of light and education as the resource to be relied on for ameliorating the condition, promoting the virtue, and advancing the happiness of man. (Thomas Jefferson to Cornelius C. Blatchly, October 21, 1822)[15]

I deeply appreciate Jefferson's thoughts about an enlightened people, the diffusion of light, and the promotion of virtue. The breadth of his vision and his commitment to understanding what it would take to make freedom a reality is remarkable.

As I struggled to understand the evolution of freedom, I began to think of the enlightened and educated people whom Jefferson spoke of. I view these people as acquiring more than brick-and-mortar education or having the experience of gathering knowledge. What is that something more? It is the fact that no matter what a person's station in life, a person can understand and embrace the fact that they are inherently free in their *humanness* and that they have the right and responsibility to be in the conversation of freedom. These enlightened people, hopefully people all over the world, are the people who contribute to true freedom through participation in the freedom conversation.

It is not information that makes our world go round. It is the positive intention to live freely and in harmony with oneself and others. We are born with the light and positive intention to live, but we do not thrive alone. With the light of intention to live in harmony with ourselves and with others, we are animated and self-directed. We are in conversation with ourselves and with others.

True freedom requires intention and openness to engagement in conversation on behalf of the whole and each of its parts. Freedom requires that people understand that they are inherently free in their humanness and that they have the right and responsibility to be in the conversation about freedom.

I find myself in the midst of a movement for change that is so compelling, so important, that I believe the outcome will affect our survival, the survival of our nation, and the survival of the planet.

Afterword

As *Health Freedom* is finishing production, the culmination of issues surrounding health freedom have come to a head around the world. The concept of freedom and personal liberty is being tested to the max. Fear of losing health and the quest for survival is being put forward as the basis for governments to curb and control personal freedoms and liberties. Methods of prevention and wellness that do not include vaccines or other products from the dominant drug model are not being promoted. Governments are not willing to curb the actions of entities that wreak havoc on the health of individuals and the whole, entities that introduce health challenges to the population with the introduction of toxins and other lethal agents and products in food, water, land, air, and the overall environment.

There are many ways that abuse of power is now playing out on our planet. It is the opportunity we have been approaching in our industrialized world. Will personal liberty and the law of the land withstand the exigency of a crisis—be it a pandemic or some other event that unleashes attempts by governments and large power entities to take control of individual liberties? Where do we draw the line, and what does it look like for a government to serve its people instead of control its people?

The conversations about freedom that are happening now are at the very heart of whether the vision of our country, with its government of the people, by the people, and for the people, will survive. Will our freedom to protect and maintain our own health and survival in the manner that we ourselves decide be protected? Or will governments attempt to decide for us how to live?

Health freedom is a freedom basic to our survival. Without it, we would be rendered dependent subjects being managed, controlled, and even exterminated as authorities see fit.

My hope is that by reading these single truths, you are inspired to activate the health freedom conversations happening in your own life and become part of a reawakening of truth, health, and freedom in our world.

List of Appendices

Appendix A: Minnesota Statute 146A

Appendix B: International Declaration of Health Freedom

Appendix C: 2012 US Health Freedom Congress Resolutions

Appendix D: Principles of Health Freedom

Appendix E: Minnesota Statute 12.39

Appendix F: NHFA Model Right to Refuse

Appendix G: Model Physician Expanded Practice Act, Introduced in Minnesota in 2006

Appendix A

Minnesota Statute 146A
Complementary and Alternative Health Care Practices

146A.01 Definitions.

Subdivision 1. **Terms.** As used in this chapter, the following terms have the meanings given them.

Subd. 2. **Commissioner.** "Commissioner" means the commissioner of health or the commissioner's designee.

Subd. 3. **Complementary and alternative health care client.** "Complementary and alternative health care client" means an individual who receives services from an unlicensed complementary and alternative health care practitioner.

Subd. 4. **Complementary and alternative health care practices.** (a) "Complementary and alternative health care practices" means the broad domain of complementary and alternative healing methods and treatments, including but not limited to: (1) acupressure; (2) anthroposophy; (3) aroma therapy; (4) Ayurveda; (5) cranial sacral therapy; (6) culturally traditional healing practices; (7) detoxification practices and therapies; (8) energetic healing; (9) polarity therapy; (10) folk practices; (11) healing practices utilizing food, food supplements, nutrients, and the physical forces of heat, cold, water, touch, and light; (12) Gerson therapy and colostrum therapy;

(13) healing touch; (14) herbology or herbalism; (15) homeopathy; (16) nondiagnostic iridology; (17) body work, massage, and massage therapy; (18) meditation; (19) mind–body healing practices; naturopathy; (21) noninvasive instrumentalities; and (22) traditional Oriental practices, such as Qi Gong energy healing.

(b) Complementary and alternative health care practices do not include surgery, x-ray radiation, administering or dispensing legend drugs and controlled substances, practices that invade the human body by puncture of the skin, setting fractures, the use of medical devices as defined in section 147A.01, any practice included in the practice of dentistry as defined in section 150A.05, subdivision 1, or the manipulation or adjustment of articulations of joints or the spine as described in section 146.23 or 148.01.

(c) Complementary and alternative health care practices do not include practices that are permitted under section 147.09, clause (11), or 148.271, clause (5).

(d) This chapter does not apply to, control, prevent, or restrict the practice, service, or activity of lawfully marketing or distributing food products, including dietary supplements as defined in the federal Dietary Supplement Health and Education Act, educating customers about such products, or explaining the uses of such products. Under Minnesota law, an unlicensed complementary and alternative health care practitioner may not provide a medical diagnosis or recommend discontinuance of medically prescribed treatments.

Subd. 5. **Office of unlicensed complementary and alternative health care practice or office.** "Office of Unlicensed Complementary and Alternative Health Care Practice" or "office" means the Office of Unlicensed Complementary and Alternative Health Care Practice established in section 146A.02.

Subd. 6. **Unlicensed complementary and alternative health care practitioner.** "Unlicensed complementary and alternative health care practitioner" means a person who:

(1) either:

(i) is not licensed or registered by a health-related licensing board or the commissioner of health; or

(ii) is licensed or registered by the commissioner of health or a health-related licensing board other than the Board of Medical Practice, the Board of Dentistry, the Board of Chiropractic Examiners, or the Board of Podiatric Medicine, but does not hold oneself out to the public as being licensed or registered by the commissioner or a health-related licensing board when engaging in complementary and alternative health care;

(2) has not had a license or registration issued by a health-related licensing board or the commissioner of health revoked or has not been disciplined in any manner at any time in the past, unless the right to engage in complementary and alternative health care practices has been established by order of the commissioner of health;

(3) is engaging in complementary and alternative health care practices; and

(4) is providing complementary and alternative health care services for remuneration or is holding oneself out to the public as a practitioner of complementary and alternative health care practices.

History: 2000 c 460 s 9; 2014 c 291 art 4 s 1

146A.02 Office of Unlicensed Complementary and Alternative Health Care Practice.

Subdivision 1. **Creation.** The Office of Unlicensed Complementary and Alternative Health Care Practice is created in the Department of Health to investigate complaints and take and enforce disciplinary actions against all unlicensed complementary and alternative health care practitioners for violations of prohibited conduct, as defined in section 146A.08. The office shall also serve as a clearinghouse on complementary and alternative health care practices and unlicensed complementary and alternative health care practitioners through the dissemination of objective information to consumers and through the development and performance of public education activities, including outreach, regarding the provision of complementary and alternative health care practices and unlicensed complementary and alternative health care practitioners who provide these services.

Subd. 2. **Rulemaking.** The commissioner shall adopt rules necessary to implement, administer, or enforce provisions of this chapter pursuant to chapter 14.

History: 2000 c 460 s 10

146A.025 Maltreatment of Minors.

Nothing in this chapter shall restrict the ability of a local welfare agency, local law enforcement agency, the commissioner of human services, or the state to take action regarding the maltreatment of minors under section 609.378 or 626.556. A parent who obtains complementary and alternative health care for the parent's minor child is not relieved of the duty to seek necessary medical care consistent with the requirements of sections 609.378 and 626.556. A complementary or alternative health care practitioner who is providing services to a child who is not receiving necessary medical care must make a report under section 626.556. A complementary or alternative health care provider is a mandated reporter under section 626.556, subdivision 3.

History: 2000 c 460 s 11

146A.03 Reporting Obligations.

Subdivision 1. **Permission to report.** A person who has knowledge of any conduct constituting grounds for disciplinary action relating to complementary and alternative health care practices under this chapter may report the violation to the office.

Subd. 2. **Institutions.** A state agency, political subdivision, agency of a local unit of government, private agency, hospital, clinic, prepaid medical plan, or other health care institution or organization located in this state shall report to the office any action taken by the agency, institution, or organization or any of its administrators or medical or other committees to revoke, suspend, restrict, or condition an unlicensed complementary and alternative health care practitioner's privilege to practice or treat complementary and alternative health care clients in the institution or, as part of the organization, any denial of privileges or any other disciplinary action for conduct that might constitute grounds for disciplinary action by the office under this chapter. The institution, organization, or governmental entity shall also report the resignation of any unlicensed complementary and alternative health care practitioners prior to the conclusion of any disciplinary action proceeding for conduct that might constitute grounds for disciplinary action under this chapter or prior to the commencement of formal charges but after the practitioner had knowledge that formal charges were contemplated or were being prepared.

Subd. 3. **Professional societies.** A state or local professional society for unlicensed complementary and alternative health care practitioners shall report to the office any termination, revocation, or suspension of membership or any other disciplinary action taken against an unlicensed complementary and alternative health care practitioner. If the society has received a complaint that might be grounds for discipline under this chapter against a member on which it has not taken any disciplinary action, the society shall report the complaint and the reason why it has not taken action on it or shall direct the complainant to the office.

Subd. 4. **Licensed professionals.** A licensed health professional shall report to the office personal knowledge of any conduct that the licensed health professional reasonably believes constitutes grounds for disciplinary action under this chapter by any unlicensed complementary and alternative health care practitioner, including conduct indicating that the individual may be incompetent or may be mentally or physically unable to engage safely in the provision of services. If the information was obtained in the course of a client relationship, the client is an unlicensed complementary and alternative health care practitioner, and the treating individual successfully counsels the other practitioner to limit or withdraw from practice to the extent required by the impairment, the office may deem this limitation of or withdrawal from practice to be sufficient disciplinary action.

Subd. 5. **Insurers.** Four times each year as prescribed by the commissioner, each insurer authorized to sell insurance described in section 60A.06, subdivision 1, clause (13), and providing professional liability insurance to unlicensed complementary and alternative health

179

care practitioners or the medical Joint Underwriting Association under chapter 62F shall submit to the office a report concerning the unlicensed complementary and alternative health care practitioners against whom malpractice settlements or awards have been made. The response must contain at least the following information:

(1) the total number of malpractice settlements or awards made;
(2) the date the malpractice settlements or awards were made;
(3) the allegations contained in the claim or complaint leading to the settlements or awards made;
(4) the dollar amount of each malpractice settlement or award;
(5) the regular address of the practice of the unlicensed complementary and alternative health care practitioner against whom an award was made or with whom a settlement was made; and
(6) the name of the unlicensed complementary and alternative health care practitioner against whom an award was made or with whom a settlement was made.

The insurance company shall, in addition to the above information, submit to the office any information, records, and files, including clients' charts and records, it possesses that tend to substantiate a charge that an unlicensed complementary and alternative health care practitioner may have engaged in conduct violating this chapter.

Subd. 6. **Courts.** The court administrator of district court or any other court of competent jurisdiction shall report to the office any judgment or other determination of the court that adjudges or includes a finding that an unlicensed complementary and alternative health care practitioner is mentally ill, mentally incompetent, guilty of a felony, guilty of a violation of federal or state narcotics laws or controlled substances act, or guilty of abuse or fraud under Medicare or Medicaid; or that appoints a guardian of the unlicensed complementary and alternative health care practitioner under sections 524.5-101 to 524.5-502 or commits an unlicensed complementary and alternative health care practitioner under chapter 253B.

Subd. 7. **Self-reporting.** An unlicensed complementary and alternative health care practitioner shall report to the office any personal action that would require that a report be filed with the office by any person, health care facility, business, or organization pursuant to subdivisions 2 to 5. The practitioner shall also report the revocation, suspension, restriction, limitation, or other disciplinary action against the practitioner's license, certificate, registration, or right of practice in another state or jurisdiction for offenses that would be subject to disciplinary action in this state and also report the filing of charges regarding the practitioner's license, certificate, registration, or right of practice in another state or jurisdiction.

Subd. 8. **Deadlines; forms.** Reports required by subdivisions 2 to 7 must be submitted not later than 30 days after the reporter learns of the occurrence of the reportable event or transaction. The office may provide forms for the submission of reports required by this section, may require that reports be submitted on the forms provided, and may adopt rules necessary to ensure prompt and accurate reporting.

History: 2000 c 460 s 12; 2004 c 146 art 3 s 47

146A.04 Immunity.

Subdivision 1. **Reporting.** Any person, other than the unlicensed complementary and alternative health care practitioner who committed the violation, health care facility, business, or organization is immune from civil liability or criminal prosecution for submitting a report to the office, for otherwise reporting to the office violations or alleged violations of this chapter, or for cooperating with an investigation of a report, except as provided in this subdivision. Any person who knowingly or recklessly makes a false report is liable in a civil suit for any damages suffered by the person or persons so reported and for any punitive damages set by the court or jury. An action requires clear and convincing evidence that the defendant made the statement with knowledge of falsity or with reckless disregard for its truth or falsity. The report or statement or any statement made in cooperation with an investigation or as part of a disciplinary proceeding is privileged except in an action brought under this subdivision.

Subd. 2. **Investigation.** The commissioner and employees of the Department of Health and other persons engaged in the investigation of violations and in the preparation, presentation, and management of and testimony pertaining to charges of violations of this chapter are immune from civil liability and criminal prosecution for any actions, transactions, or publications in the execution of, or relating to, their duties under this chapter.

History: 2000 c 460 s 13

146A.05 Disciplinary Record on Judicial Review.

Upon judicial review of any disciplinary action taken by the commissioner under this chapter, the reviewing court shall seal the portions of the administrative record that contain data on a complementary and alternative health care client or a complainant under section 146A.03, and shall not make those portions of the administrative record available to the public.

History: 2000 c 460 s 14

146A.06 Professional Cooperation; Unlicensed Practitioner.

Subdivision 1. **Cooperation.** An unlicensed complementary and alternative health care practitioner who is the subject of an investigation, or who is questioned in connection with an investigation, by or on behalf of the office, shall cooperate fully with the investigation. Cooperation includes responding fully and promptly to any question raised by or on behalf of the office relating to the subject of the investigation, whether tape recorded or not; providing copies of client records, as reasonably requested by the office, to assist the office in its investigation; and appearing at conferences or hearings scheduled by the commissioner. If the office does not have a written consent from a client permitting access to the client's records, the unlicensed complementary and alternative health care practitioner shall delete in the record any data that identifies the client before providing it to the office. If an unlicensed complementary and alternative health care practitioner refuses to give testimony or produce any documents, books, records, or correspondence on the basis of the fifth amendment to the Constitution of the United States, the commissioner may compel the unlicensed complementary and alternative health care practitioner to provide the testimony or information; however, the testimony or evidence may not be used against the practitioner in any criminal proceeding. Challenges to requests of the office may be brought before the appropriate agency or court.

Subd. 2. **Data.** (a) Data relating to investigations of complaints and disciplinary actions involving unlicensed complementary and alternative health care practitioners are governed by this subdivision and section 13.41 does not apply. Except as provided in section 13.39, subdivision 2, and paragraph (b), data relating to investigations of complaints and disciplinary actions involving unlicensed complementary and alternative health care practitioners are public data, regardless of the outcome of any investigation, action, or proceeding.

(b) The following data are private data on individuals, as defined in section 13.02:

(1) data on a complementary and alternative health care client;

(2) data on a complainant under section 146A.03; and

(3) data on the nature or content of unsubstantiated complaints when the information is not maintained in anticipation of legal action.

Subd. 3. **Exchanging information.** (a) The office shall establish internal operating procedures for:

(1) exchanging information with state boards; agencies, including the Office of Ombudsman for Mental Health and Developmental Disabilities; health-related and law enforcement facilities; departments responsible for licensing health-related occupations, facilities, and programs; and law enforcement personnel in this and other states; and

(2) coordinating investigations involving matters within the jurisdiction of more than one regulatory agency.

(b) The procedures for exchanging information must provide for the forwarding to the entities described in paragraph (a), clause (1), of information and evidence, including the results of investigations, that [is] relevant to matters within the regulatory jurisdiction of the organizations in paragraph (a). The data have the same classification in the hands of the agency receiving the data as they have in the hands of the agency providing the data.

(c) The office shall establish procedures for exchanging information with other states regarding disciplinary action against unlicensed complementary and alternative health care practitioners.

(d) The office shall forward to another governmental agency any complaints received by the office that do not relate to the office's jurisdiction but that relate to matters within the jurisdiction of the other governmental agency. The agency to which a complaint is forwarded shall advise the office of the disposition of the complaint. A complaint or other information received by another governmental agency relating to a statute or rule that the office is empowered to enforce must be forwarded to the office to be processed in accordance with this section.

(e) The office shall furnish to a person who made a complaint a description of the actions of the office relating to the complaint.

History: 2000 c 460 s 15; 2005 c 56 s 1

146A.065 Complementary and Alternative Health Care Practices by Licensed or Registered Health Care Practitioners.

(a) A health care practitioner licensed or registered by the commissioner or a health-related licensing board, who engages in complementary and alternative health care while practicing under the practitioner's license or registration, shall be regulated by and be under the jurisdiction of the applicable health-related licensing board with regard to the complementary and alternative health care practices.

(b) A health care practitioner licensed or registered by the commissioner or a health-related licensing board shall not be subject to disciplinary action solely on the basis of utilizing complementary and alternative health care practices as defined in section 146A.01, subdivision 4, paragraph (a), as a component of a patient's treatment, or for referring a patient to a complementary and alternative health care practitioner as defined in section 146A.01, subdivision 6.

(c) A health care practitioner licensed or registered by the commissioner or a health-related licensing board who utilizes complementary and alternative health care practices must provide patients receiving these services with a written copy of the complementary and alternative health care client bill of rights pursuant to section 146A.11.

(d) Nothing in this section shall be construed to prohibit or restrict the commissioner or a health-related licensing board from imposing disciplinary action for conduct that violates provisions of the applicable licensed or registered health care practitioner's practice act.

History: 2014 c 291 art 4 s 2

146A.07 Professional Accountability.

The office shall maintain and keep current a file containing the reports and complaints filed against unlicensed complementary and alternative health care practitioners within the commissioner's jurisdiction. Each complaint filed with the office must be investigated. If the files maintained by the office show that a malpractice settlement or award has been made against an unlicensed complementary and alternative health care practitioner, as reported by insurers under section 146A.03, subdivision 5, the commissioner may authorize a review of the practitioner's practice by the staff of the office.

History: 2000 c 460 s 16

146A.08 Prohibited Conduct.

Subdivision 1. **Prohibited conduct.** (a) The commissioner may impose disciplinary action as described in section 146A.09 against any unlicensed complementary and alternative health care practitioner. The following conduct is prohibited and is grounds for disciplinary action:

(b) Conviction of a crime, including a finding or verdict of guilt, an admission of guilt, or a no-contest plea, in any court in Minnesota or any other jurisdiction in the United States, reasonably related to engaging in complementary and alternative health care practices. Conviction, as used in this subdivision, includes a conviction of an offense which, if committed in this state, would be deemed a felony, gross misdemeanor, or misdemeanor, without regard to its designation elsewhere, or a criminal proceeding where a finding or verdict of guilty is made or returned but the adjudication of guilt is either withheld or not entered.

(c) Conviction of any crime against a person. For purposes of this chapter, a crime against a person means violations of the following: sections 609.185; 609.19; 609.195; 609.20; 609.205; 609.2112; 609.2113; 609.2114; 609.215; 609.221; 609.222; 609.223; 609.224; 609.2242; 609.23; 609.231; 609.2325; 609.233; 609.2335; 609.235; 609.24; 609.245; 609.25; 609.255; 609.26, subdivision 1, clause (1) or (2); 609.265; 609.342; 609.343; 609.344; 609.345; 609.365; 609.498, subdivision 1; 609.50, subdivision 1, clause (1); 609.561; 609.562; 609.595; and 609.72, subdivision 3; and Minnesota Statutes 2012, section 609.21.

(d) Failure to comply with the self-reporting requirements of section 146A.03, subdivision 7.

(e) Engaging in sexual contact with a complementary and alternative health care client, engaging in contact that may be reasonably interpreted by a client as sexual, engaging in any verbal behavior that is seductive or sexually demeaning to the client, or engaging in sexual exploitation of a client or former client.

(f) Advertising that is false, fraudulent, deceptive, or misleading.

(g) Conduct likely to deceive, defraud, or harm the public or demonstrating a willful or careless disregard for the health, welfare, or safety of a complementary and alternative health care client; or any other practice that may create danger to any client's life, health, or safety, in any of which cases, proof of actual injury need not be established.

(h) Adjudication as mentally incompetent or as a person who is dangerous to self or adjudication pursuant to chapter 253B as chemically dependent, mentally ill, developmentally disabled, mentally ill and dangerous to the public, or as a sexual psychopathic personality or sexually dangerous person.

(i) Inability to engage in complementary and alternative health care practices with reasonable safety to complementary and alternative health care clients.

(j) The habitual overindulgence in the use of or the dependence on intoxicating liquors.

(k) Improper or unauthorized personal or other use of any legend drugs as defined in chapter 151, any chemicals as defined in chapter 151, or any controlled substance as defined in chapter 152.

(l) Revealing a communication from, or relating to, a complementary and alternative health care client except when otherwise required or permitted by law.

(m) Failure to comply with a complementary and alternative health care client's request made under sections 144.291 to 144.298 or to furnish a complementary and alternative health care client record or report required by law.

(n) Splitting fees or promising to pay a portion of a fee to any other professional other than for services rendered by the other professional to the complementary and alternative health care client.

(o) Engaging in abusive or fraudulent billing practices, including violations of the federal Medicare and Medicaid laws or state medical assistance laws.

(p) Failure to make reports as required by section 146A.03 or cooperate with an investigation of the office.

(q) Obtaining money, property, or services from a complementary and alternative health care client, other than reasonable fees for services provided to the client, through the use of undue influence, harassment, duress, deception, or fraud.

(r) Failure to provide a complementary and alternative health care client with a copy of the client bill of rights or violation of any provision of the client bill of rights.

(s) Violating any order issued by the commissioner.

(t) Failure to comply with any provision of sections 146A.01 to 146A.11 and the rules adopted under those sections.

(u) Failure to comply with any additional disciplinary grounds established by the commissioner by rule.

(v) Revocation, suspension, restriction, limitation, or other disciplinary action against any health care license, certificate, registration, or right to practice of the unlicensed complementary and alternative health care practitioner in this or another state or jurisdiction for offenses that would be subject to disciplinary action in this state or failure to report to the office that charges regarding the practitioner's license, certificate, registration, or right of practice have been brought in this or another state or jurisdiction.

(w) Use of the title "doctor," "Dr.," or "physician" alone or in combination with any other words, letters, or insignia to describe the complementary and alternative health care practices the practitioner provides.

(x) Failure to provide a complementary and alternative health care client with a recommendation that the client see a health care provider who is licensed or registered by a health-related licensing board or the commissioner of health, if there is a reasonable likelihood that the client needs to be seen by a licensed or registered health care provider.

Subd. 2. **Less customary approach.** The fact that a complementary and alternative health care practice may be a less customary approach to health care shall not constitute the basis of a disciplinary action per se.

Subd. 3. **Evidence.** In disciplinary actions alleging a violation of subdivision 1, paragraph (b), (c), (d), or (h), a copy of the judgment or proceeding under the seal of the court administrator or of the administrative agency that entered the same is admissible into evidence without further authentication and constitutes prima facie evidence of its contents.

Subd. 4. **Examination; access to medical data.** (a) If the commissioner has probable cause to believe that an unlicensed complementary and alternative health care practitioner has engaged in conduct prohibited by subdivision 1, paragraph (h), (i), (j), or (k), the commissioner may issue an order directing the practitioner to submit to a mental or physical examination or chemical dependency evaluation. For the purpose of this subdivision, every unlicensed complementary and alternative health care practitioner is deemed to have consented to submit to a mental or physical examination or chemical dependency evaluation when ordered to do so in writing by the commissioner and further to have waived all objections to the admissibility of the testimony or examination reports of the health care provider performing the examination or evaluation on the grounds that the same constitute a privileged communication. Failure of an unlicensed complementary and alternative health care practitioner to submit to an examination or evaluation when ordered, unless the failure was due to circumstances beyond the practitioner's control, constitutes an admission that the unlicensed complementary and alternative health care practitioner violated subdivision 1, paragraph (h), (i), (j), or (k), based on the factual specifications in the examination or evaluation order and may result in a default and final disciplinary order being entered after a contested case hearing. An unlicensed complementary and alternative health care practitioner affected under this paragraph shall at reasonable intervals be given an opportunity to demonstrate that the practitioner can resume the provision of complementary and alternative health care practices with reasonable safety to clients. In any proceeding under this paragraph, neither the record of proceedings nor the orders entered by the commissioner shall be used against an unlicensed complementary and alternative health care practitioner in any other proceeding.

(b) In addition to ordering a physical or mental examination or chemical dependency evaluation, the commissioner may, notwithstanding section 13.384; 144.651; 595.02; or any other law limiting access to medical or other health data, obtain medical data and health records relating to an unlicensed complementary and alternative health care practitioner without the practitioner's consent if the commissioner has probable cause to believe that a practitioner has engaged in conduct prohibited by subdivision 1, paragraph (h), (i), (j), or (k). The medical data may be requested from a provider as defined in section 144.291, subdivision 2, paragraph (h), an insurance company, or a government agency, including the Department of Human Services. A provider, insurance company, or government agency shall comply with any written request of the commissioner under this subdivision and is not liable in any action for damages for releasing the data requested by the commissioner if the data are released pursuant to a written request under this subdivision, unless the information is false and the person or organization giving the information knew or had reason to believe the information was false. Information obtained under this subdivision is private data under section 13.41.

History: 1999 c 227 s 22; 2000 c 460 s 17; 2005 c 56 s 1; 2007 c 147 art 10 s 15; 2008 c 189 s 1; 2014 c 180 s 9

146A.09 Disciplinary Actions.

Subdivision 1. **Forms of disciplinary action.** When the commissioner finds that an unlicensed complementary and alternative health care practitioner has violated any provision of this chapter, the commissioner may take one or more of the following actions, only against the individual practitioner:

(1)   revoke the right to practice;
(2)   suspend the right to practice;
(3)   impose limitations or conditions on the practitioner's provision of complementary and alternative health care practices, impose rehabilitation requirements, or require practice under supervision;
(4)   impose a civil penalty not exceeding $10,000 for each separate violation, the amount of the civil penalty to be fixed so as to deprive the practitioner of any economic advantage gained by reason of the violation charged or to reimburse the office for all costs of the investigation and proceeding;
(5)   censure or reprimand the practitioner;
(6)   impose a fee on the practitioner to reimburse the office for all or part of the cost of the proceedings resulting in disciplinary action including, but not limited to, the amount paid by the office for

services from the Office of Administrative Hearings, attorney fees, court reports, witnesses, reproduction of records, staff time, and expense incurred by the staff of the Office of Unlicensed Complementary and Alternative Health Care Practice; or

(7)   any other action justified by the case.

Subd. 2. **Discovery; subpoenas.** In all matters relating to the lawful activities of the office, the commissioner may issue subpoenas and compel the attendance of witnesses and the production of all necessary papers, books, records, documents, and other evidentiary material. Any person failing or refusing to appear or testify regarding any matter about which the person may be lawfully questioned or failing to produce any papers, books, records, documents, or other evidentiary materials in the matter to be heard, after having been required by order of the commissioner or by a subpoena of the commissioner to do so may, upon application to the district court in any district, be ordered to comply with the order or subpoena. The commissioner may administer oaths to witnesses or take their affirmation. Depositions may be taken within or without the state in the manner provided by law for the taking of depositions in civil actions. A subpoena or other process may be served upon a person it names anywhere within the state by any officer authorized to serve subpoenas or other process in civil actions in the same manner as prescribed by law for service of process issued out of the district court of this state.

Subd. 3. **Hearings.** If the commissioner proposes to take action against the practitioner as described in subdivision 1, the commissioner must first notify the practitioner against whom the action is proposed to be taken and provide the practitioner with an opportunity to request a hearing under the contested case provisions of chapter 14. If the practitioner does not request a hearing by notifying the commissioner within 30 days after service of the notice of the proposed action, the commissioner may proceed with the action without a hearing.

Subd. 4. **Reinstatement.** The commissioner may at the commissioner's discretion reinstate the right to practice and may impose any disciplinary measure listed under subdivision 1.

Subd. 5. **Temporary suspension.** In addition to any other remedy provided by law, the commissioner may, acting through a person to whom the commissioner has delegated this authority and without a hearing, temporarily suspend the right of an unlicensed complementary and alternative health care practitioner to practice if the commissioner's delegate finds that the practitioner has violated a statute or rule that the commissioner is empowered to enforce and continued practice by the practitioner would create a serious risk of harm to others. The suspension is in effect upon service of a written order on the practitioner specifying the statute or rule violated. The order remains in effect until the commissioner issues a final order in the matter after a hearing or upon agreement between the commissioner and the practitioner. Service of the order is effective if the order is served on the practitioner or counsel of record personally or by first class mail. Within ten days of service of the order, the commissioner shall hold a hearing on the sole issue of whether there is a reasonable basis to continue, modify, or lift the suspension. Evidence presented by the office or practitioner shall be in affidavit form only. The practitioner or the counsel of record may appear for oral argument. Within five working days after the hearing, the commissioner shall issue the commissioner's order and, if the suspension is continued, schedule a contested case hearing within 45 days after issuance of the order. The administrative law judge shall issue a report within 30 days after closing of the contested case hearing record. The commissioner shall issue a final order within 30 days after receipt of that report.

Subd. 6. **Automatic suspension.** The right of an unlicensed complementary and alternative health care practitioner to practice is automatically suspended if (1) a guardian of an unlicensed complementary and alternative health care practitioner is appointed by order of a court under sections 524.5-101 to 524.5-502, or (2) the practitioner is committed by order of a court pursuant to chapter 253B. The right to practice remains suspended until the practitioner is restored to capacity by a court and, upon petition by the practitioner, the suspension is terminated by the commissioner after a hearing or upon agreement between the commissioner and the practitioner.

Subd. 7. **Licensed or regulated practitioners.** If a practitioner investigated under this section is licensed or registered by the commissioner of health or a health-related licensing board, is subject to the jurisdiction of the commissioner under section 146A.01, subdivision 6, clause (1), item (ii), and the commissioner determines that the practitioner has violated any provision of this chapter, the commissioner, in addition to taking disciplinary action under this section:

(1) may, if the practitioner is licensed or regulated in another capacity by the commissioner, take further disciplinary action against the practitioner in that capacity; or

(2) shall, if the practitioner is licensed or registered in another capacity by a health-related licensing board, report the commissioner's findings under this section, and may make a nonbinding recommendation that the board take further action against the practitioner in that capacity.

History: 2000 c 460 s 18; 2004 c 146 art 3 s 47; 2019 c 50 art 1 s 42

146A.10 Additional Remedies.

Subdivision 1. **Cease and desist.** (a) The commissioner may issue a cease and desist order to stop a person from violating or threatening to violate a statute, rule, or order which the office has issued or is empowered to enforce. The cease and desist order must state the reason for its issuance and give notice of the person's right to request a hearing under sections 14.57 to 14.62. If, within 15 days of service of the order, the subject of the order fails to request a hearing in writing, the order is the final order of the commissioner and is not reviewable by a court or agency.

(b) A hearing must be initiated by the office not later than 30 days from the date of the office's receipt of a written hearing request. Within 30 days of receipt of the administrative law judge's report, the commissioner shall issue a final order modifying, vacating, or making permanent the cease and desist order as the facts require. The final order remains in effect until modified or vacated by the commissioner.

(c) When a request for a stay accompanies a timely hearing request, the commissioner may, in the commissioner's discretion, grant the stay. If the commissioner does not grant a requested stay, the commissioner shall refer the request to the Office of Administrative Hearings within three working days of receipt of the request. Within ten days after receiving the request from the commissioner, an administrative law judge shall issue a recommendation to grant or deny the stay. The commissioner shall grant or deny the stay within five days of receiving the administrative law judge's recommendation.

(d) In the event of noncompliance with a cease and desist order, the commissioner may institute a proceeding in Hennepin County District Court to obtain injunctive relief or other appropriate relief, including a civil penalty payable to the office not exceeding $10,000 for each separate violation.

Subd. 2. **Injunctive relief.** In addition to any other remedy provided by law, including the issuance of a cease and desist order under subdivision 1, the commissioner may in the commissioner's own name bring an action in Hennepin County District Court for injunctive relief to restrain an unlicensed complementary and alternative health care practitioner from a violation or threatened violation of any statute, rule, or order which the commissioner is empowered to regulate, enforce, or issue. A temporary restraining order must be granted in the proceeding if continued activity by a practitioner would create a serious risk of harm to others. The commissioner need not show irreparable harm.

Subd. 3. **Additional powers.** The issuance of a cease and desist order or injunctive relief granted under this section does not relieve a practitioner from criminal prosecution by a competent authority or from disciplinary action by the commissioner.

History: 2000 c 460 s 19

146A.11 Complementary and Alternative Health Care Client Bill of Rights.

Subdivision 1. **Scope.** (a) All unlicensed complementary and alternative health care practitioners shall provide to each complementary and alternative health care client prior to providing treatment a written copy of the complementary and alternative health care client bill of rights. A copy must also be posted in a prominent location in the office of the unlicensed complementary and alternative health care practitioner. Reasonable accommodations shall be made for those clients who cannot read or who have communication disabilities and those who do not read or speak English. The complementary and alternative health care client bill of rights shall include the following:

(1) the name, complementary and alternative health care title, business address, and telephone number of the unlicensed complementary and alternative health care practitioner;

(2) the degrees, training, experience, or other qualifications of the practitioner regarding the complementary and alternative health care being provided, followed by the following statement in bold print:

"THE STATE OF MINNESOTA HAS NOT ADOPTED ANY EDUCATIONAL AND TRAINING STANDARDS FOR UNLICENSED COMPLEMENTARY AND ALTERNATIVE HEALTH CARE PRACTITIONERS. THIS STATEMENT OF CREDENTIALS IS FOR INFORMATION PURPOSES ONLY.

Under Minnesota law, an unlicensed complementary and alternative health care practitioner may not provide a medical diagnosis or recommend discontinuance of medically prescribed treatments. If a client desires a diagnosis from a licensed physician, chiropractor, or acupuncture practitioner, or services from a physician, chiropractor, nurse, osteopathic physician, physical therapist, dietitian, nutritionist, acupuncture practitioner, athletic trainer, or any other type of health care provider, the client may seek such services at any time.";

(3) the name, business address, and telephone number of the practitioner's supervisor, if any;

(4) notice that a complementary and alternative health care client has the right to file a complaint with the practitioner's supervisor, if any, and the procedure for filing complaints;

(5) the name, address, and telephone number of the office of unlicensed complementary and alternative health care practice and notice that a client may file complaints with the office;

(6) the practitioner's fees per unit of service, the practitioner's method of billing for such fees, the names of any insurance companies that have agreed to reimburse the practitioner, or health maintenance organizations with whom the practitioner contracts to provide service, whether the practitioner accepts Medicare or medical assistance, and whether the practitioner is willing to accept partial payment, or to waive payment, and in what circumstances;

(7) a statement that the client has a right to reasonable notice of changes in services or charges;

(8) a brief summary, in plain language, of the theoretical approach used by the practitioner in providing services to clients;

(9) notice that the client has a right to complete and current information concerning the practitioner's assessment and recommended service that is to be provided, including the expected duration of the service to be provided;

(10) a statement that clients may expect courteous treatment and to be free from verbal, physical, or sexual abuse by the practitioner;

(11) a statement that client records and transactions with the practitioner are confidential, unless release of these records is authorized in writing by the client, or otherwise provided by law;

(12) a statement of the client's right to be allowed access to records and written information from records in accordance with sections 144.291 to 144.298;

(13) a statement that other services may be available in the community, including where information concerning services is available;

(14) a statement that the client has the right to choose freely among available practitioners and to change practitioners after services have begun, within the limits of health insurance, medical assistance, or other health programs;

(15) a statement that the client has a right to coordinated transfer when there will be a change in the provider of services;

(16) a statement that the client may refuse services or treatment, unless otherwise provided by law; and

(17) a statement that the client may assert the client's rights without retaliation.

(b) This section does not apply to an unlicensed complementary and alternative health care practitioner who is employed by or is a volunteer in a hospital or hospice who provides services to a client in a hospital or under an appropriate hospice plan of care. Patients receiving complementary and alternative health care services in an inpatient hospital or under an appropriate hospice plan of care shall have and be made aware of the right to file a complaint with the hospital or hospice provider through which the practitioner is employed or registered as a volunteer.

(c) This section does not apply to a health care practitioner licensed or registered by the commissioner of health or a health-related licensing board who utilizes complementary and alternative health care practices within the scope of practice of the health care practitioner's professional license.

Subd. 2. **Acknowledgment by client.** Prior to the provision of any service, a complementary and alternative health care client must sign a written statement attesting that the client has received the complementary and alternative health care client bill of rights.

History: 2000 c 460 s 20; 2007 c 147 art 10 s 15; 2008 c 189 s 2; 2013 c 62 s 6; 2014 c 291 art 4 s 3; 2016 c 158 art 2 s 38; 2016 c 119 s 7

Appendix B

International Declaration of Health Freedom

World Health Freedom Assembly Passes
International Declaration of Health Freedom

On September 29 and 30, 2006, a World Health Freedom Assembly met in St. Paul, Minnesota, and adopted and proclaimed an International Declaration of Health Freedom, the full text of which appears below. Following this historic act, the assembly called upon all members of the human family, organizations, and countries present, and those others who wish to support this statement, to publicize the text of the declaration and "to cause it to be honored, implemented, disseminated, displayed, read and endorsed by signature, by all people."

International Declaration of Health Freedom

We Declare That:

Recognition of the inherent dignity and of the equal and inalienable rights of all members of the human family is the foundation of freedom, justice, and peace in the world.

Among the inalienable rights are not only the right to life, liberty, property, and the pursuit of happiness, but also the right to health, well-being, and survival.

Health is a state of physical, mental, spiritual, and personal social well-being, and not merely the absence of disease or infirmity.

In order to secure the right to health, a human being must be able to exercise their fundamental right to privacy and self-determination and the right to make personal choices in pursuit of health, healing, well-being, and survival.

The right to choose requires that every individual holds the right to ultimately decide whether to obtain or reject any health treatment, research, or advice.

In order to fully exercise the fundamental right of privacy and self-determination, full access to health care practitioners, healers, researchers, treatments, services, products, devices, substances, and information sources of their choice must be protected and preserved for each member of the human family.

Full access to health care practitioners, healers, researchers, treatments, services, products, devices, substances, and truthful information is an inherent and fundamental right and is independent of the actions of any government or other regulatory public or private bodies.

There exist worldwide diverse healing arts theories, practices, treatments, substances, and modalities that are deemed by the people to contribute to their health and well-being, whether by one human or by many, and these need to be protected and available to all members of the human family.

The global adoption of these principles will strengthen the foundation of freedom, justice, and peace in the world.

Organization	Invited voting delegates	Nation
Friends of Freedom International *	Peter Helagson	Canada
Live Longer Educational Foundation *	Trueman Tuck	Canada
Mayday *		Denmark
Kommittén för Alternativ Medicin *	Tamara Theresa Mosegaard	Sweden
Citizens for Health * Healthkeepers Alliance *	Birgitta Holmner	USA
National Health Federation * National Health Freedom Action * Sunshine Health Freedom Foundation * Native Americans *	Jim Turner	USA
	Wendell Whitman	USA
	Scott Tips	USA
	Clinton Miller Joan Vandergriff Mark	USA
Alliance for Health Freedom Australia Natural Health Care Alliance	Ravenhair Michael Bending Patricia Reed Ronald	Australia
	Modra Sepp	Australia
Salud Natural A.G.	Hasselberger David Sloan	Chile
		Italy
La Leva Assoc. for Freedom of Choice New Health	Rob Verkerk Brenna Hill	New Zealand
Alliance for Natural Health	Assembly Co-Chair Diane Miller	UK
American Association for Health Freedom	Assembly Co-Chair Karen Studders	USA
National Health Freedom Coalition *		USA
National Health Freedom Coalition *		USA

(*) The World Health Freedom Assembly met in St. Paul, Minnesota, USA, at the William Mitchell College of Law.

Eleven of the signing organizations attended in person (*), and nine organizations are signing via courier.

A motion was made to launch an ongoing assembly, and founders are now formalizing the assembly and meeting monthly by conferencing.

Appendix C

2012 US Health Freedom Congress Resolutions

(Accessible online at https://healthfreedomcongress.org/resolution1/)

Resolution 1A: Protecting Humanity from Mercury-containing Drugs
Resolution 2B: Resolution on Electromagnetic Health
Resolution 3A: Genetically Engineered Food Right to Know
Resolution 3B: Supporting the California Right to Know, Genetically
 Engineered Food
Resolution 4A: Dietary Supplement Protection
Resolution 5A: Misrepresentations of High-Fructose Corn Syrup (HFCS)
Resolution 6B: Food Freedom
Resolution 7A: Right to Refuse Vaccination
Resolution 8A: Water Fluoridation Resolution
Resolution 9A: Dental Amalgam (Mercury) Fillings
Resolution 11A: Autism
Resolution 13A: Protecting the Profession of Colon Hydrotherapy
Resolution 14A: Informed Consent
Resolution 15A: FDA Warning Letters
Resolution 16A: FDA Treatment of Synthetic Botanicals

Appendix D

Principles of Health Freedom

Principle 1

Freedom to Be Let Alone

Individuals and members of the human family have the inherent fundamental right of self-determination, to be let alone to survive on their own terms and in their own manner.

Principle 2

Freedom to Act

Individuals and members of the human family hold the fundamental right and freedom to act on their own behalf and as they choose to secure health and survival.

Principle 3

Freedom to Access

For freedom of choice to be implemented or meaningful, individuals and members of the human family hold the fundamental right and freedom to access their choices, whomever and whatever they deem necessary or prefer for their own health and survival.

Principle 4

Responsibility to Do No Harm

To maintain the health and survival of individuals, members of the human family, and the community as a whole, individuals and members of the human family have the responsibility to do no harm.

Principle 5

Responsibility of Tolerance

Because of the diverse nature of the human experience, members of the human family have the responsibility to show tolerance to the extent of avoiding hostile acts toward diverse health and survival options and toward those who choose those options.

Principle 6

General Responsibility of Corporations

Corporations have the potential of significantly affecting the health and survival of the human family and thus have the responsibility and duty to be trustworthy entities safeguarding health freedom rights and responsibilities.

Principle 7

Special Responsibilities of Corporations

In light of the special legal nature of corporate entities and their potential systemic impact on the health and survival of the human family, corporations have the following five responsibilities:

Principle 7-1

To honor and preserve the sovereign nature of individuals and the sovereignty of the United States and to avoid any negative impact on the sovereignty of other nation-states as it applies to health and survival.

<u>Principle 7-2</u>

To honor and preserve American financial and cultural diversity and multicultural systems that are abiding by and upholding American law, and avoid negative impact on the financial or cultural status of other nation-states as it applies to health and survival.

<u>Principle 7-3</u>

To avoid creating or being monopolies with large ownership of resources and allowing that status to dictate or dominate cultures, public policies, regulations, or laws that affect health and survival.

<u>Principle 7-4</u>

To avoid the dominant control of natural resources and the suppression of access to natural resources, and not to cause potentially harmful modifications or destruction of natural resources.

<u>Principle 7-5</u>

To avoid promotion of products, protocols, policies, regulations, or laws that would encourage unlimited dependence on corporations and institutions or that would discourage, prohibit, or otherwise negatively affect the ability or will of humans and local communities to survive and prosper without the existence of the corporation or institution.

Principle 8

Responsibility of Government

Government has the responsibility and duty to protect health freedom and to make no law or public policy abridging health freedom or its fundamental principles.

Appendix E

Minnesota Statute 12.39

12.39 Individual Treatment; Notice, Refusal, Consequence.

Subdivision 1. **Refusal of treatment.** Notwithstanding laws, rules, or orders made or promulgated in response to a national security emergency or peacetime emergency, individuals have a fundamental right to refuse medical treatment, testing, physical or mental examination, vaccination, participation in experimental procedures and protocols, collection of specimens, and preventive treatment programs. An individual who has been directed by the commissioner of health to submit to medical procedures and protocols because the individual is infected with or reasonably believed by the commissioner of health to be infected with or exposed to a toxic agent that can be transferred to another individual or a communicable disease, and the agent or communicable disease is the basis for which the national security emergency or peacetime emergency was declared, and who refuses to submit to them may be ordered by the commissioner to be placed in isolation or quarantine according to parameters set forth in sections 144.419 and 144.4195.

Subd. 2. **Information given.** Before performing examinations, testing, treatment, or vaccination of an individual under subdivision 1, a health care provider shall notify the individual of the right to refuse the examination, testing, treatment, or vaccination, and the consequences, including isolation or quarantine, upon refusal.

History: 2002 c 402 s 15,21; 2004 c 279 art 11 s 7; 2005 c 149 s 7; 2005 c 150 s 10,14

Appendix F

NHFA Model Right to Refuse

NHFA Model Draft Right to Refuse Bill Language

An Act to add Section [insert new section number] to the [insert name of code section] Code, relating to public health.

THE PEOPLE OF THE STATE OF [INSERT STATE NAME HERE] DO ENACT AS FOLLOWS:

Sec. 1. Section [insert state section of code here] is added to the [insert name of section of law code here] Code to read:

[New section number] (a) **Refusal of treatment.** Notwithstanding laws, rules, orders, or directives made or promulgated in response to an emergency, including but not limited to a national security emergency, statewide emergency, local or other health emergency, or any peacetime emergency, and notwithstanding existing laws and rules addressing outbreaks or potential outbreaks or epidemics of a contagious, infectious, or communicable disease, individuals retain the right to be free and independent and maintain their inalienable and fundamental right of self-determination to make their own health decisions, including but not limited to the right to refuse the following health related countermeasures:

1. medical treatments or procedures;
2. testing;
3. physical or mental examination;

4. vaccination;
5. experimental procedures and protocols;
6. collection of specimens;
7. participation in tracking or tracing programs;
8. the wearing of masks;
9. the maintaining of measured distance from other humans and animals that is not otherwise unlawful;
10. the involuntary sharing of personal data or medical information; and
11. other recommended or mandated countermeasures.

An individual who has been directed or ordered by a government or its designees, or a public or private business or entity, including but not limited to a commissioner or director of health, a local health officer, a sheriff or peace officer, or any designee of such commissioner, director or officer, to submit to a directive or order as described in this part, may choose to decline to comply, respond to, or participate with said directive or order.

For purposes of this Section [insert section number from above] parts (a)–(d), "individual" and "person" includes adults and minor children.

(b) Coercion. The government or its designees, or other employers, businesses, non-profits, institutions, churches, travel carriers, or other public or private entities, may not infringe upon, put conditions on, restrict, or take away a person's ability to fully participate in necessary and important services and lifestyle choices and preferences including but not limited to education, daycare, employment, travel, religion, hobbies, entertainment, sports, and lifestyle preferences, based on a person choosing to decline countermeasures as described in part (a).

(c) Persons needing care. A person who is infected with, or reasonably believed to be infected with, or who has been exposed to a toxic agent that can be transferred to another individual, or who has been exposed to a communicable disease, and the agent or communicable disease is the basis on which an emergency has been declared, or is the basis of a non-emergency order, law, or rule, and who refuses to submit to countermeasure as described in part (a), may participate in isolation or quarantine according to the parameters set forth in sections [Insert citation to the State's Existing Section of Code for isolation and quarantine].

Notwithstanding existing isolation and quarantine laws, all said isolation or quarantine must be of the least restrictive means possible, include reasonable notice and due process, be protective of the right of the individual to remain in their home, live with family members, friends or significant others at all times, and not require homes to be altered or renovated such as adding additional bathrooms.

The quarantining of a non-infected person must be based on sufficient credible evidence of contact or close proximity with an infected person and may not be imposed upon an individual based on third party location data.

Treatment, testing, tracking, or prevention orders must not be imposed as a requirement for the ending of isolation or quarantine of a person. A person in isolation or quarantine has the right to utilize the health care treatments of their choice and to have a consenting person of their choice with them and attending their needs at all times.

Quarantine or isolation may not take away or alter the legal or medical custody of a person who is under a parent or legal guardian. A minor child may not be forcibly removed from their parent or home.

(d) Information given. Before a health care provider or an individual who has been directed or ordered by a government or its designees, or a public or private business or entity, including but not limited to a commissioner or director of health, a local health officer, a sheriff or peace officer, or any designee of such commissioner, director or officer, performs a countermeasure included in an order or directive or requests participation in a countermeasure that is included in an order or a directive including but not limited to the countermeasures listed in part (a) of this section, he/she shall notify the person of his/her rights as described herein by reading aloud to him/her both part (a) and part (b) of this section.

If the person being ordered is a minor, then parts (a) and (b) must be read to the person's parent or legal guardian. A copy of this section must be provided to the person, or the person's parent or legal guardian, in writing.

The provider, commissioner, director, officer or any designee shall also obtain a signature of acknowledgement of receipt of notification from a person, or the person's parent or legal guardian, who declines to participate or who exercises his/her right to refuse.

Appendix G

Model Physician Expanded Practice Act, Introduced in Minnesota in 2006

Minnesota House File 3213
In the Eighty-Eighth Legislative Session (2006–2007)

1.1   A bill for an act

1.2   relating to health; authorizing expanded health care practices for health care

1.3   professionals; proposing coding for new law as Minnesota Statutes, chapter

1.4   146B.

1.5   BE IT ENACTED BY THE LEGISLATURE OF THE STATE OF MINNESOTA:

1.6   Section 1. **[146B.01] Minnesota Expanded Health Care Practices**

1.7   **Act.**

1.8   Subdivision 1. **Citation.** This chapter may be cited as the "Minnesota Expanded

1.9   Health Care Practices Act for Licensed Health Care Professionals."

1.10 Subd. 2. **Purpose.** The purpose of this chapter is to:

1.11 (1) protect a person's right to seek health care of the person's choice;

1.12 (2) ensure that the people of Minnesota maintain access to all health care options

1.13 including conventional treatment methods and other treatment modalities designed to

1.14 complement or substitute for conventional treatment methods; and

1.15 (3) permit health care professionals licensed or registered by the state to offer

1.16 expanded and complementary or alternative health care treatments according to this

1.17 chapter.

1.18 Subd. 3. **Definitions.** For the purposes of this chapter, the terms in this section

1.19 have the meanings given them.

1.20 (a) "Expanded health care practices and services" means health care and healing

1.21 methods, modalities, treatments, procedures, or protocols that have not been generally

1.22 adopted by a profession, or that are not generally considered to be within the prevailing

1.23 minimum standards of care of a profession, or that are not standard practices of a

1.24 profession in a particular community.

2.1 (b) "Licensed health care practitioner" means a health care practitioner licensed or

2.2 registered by the state to practice a health care profession under a licensing board or

2.3 the Department of Health.

2.4 (c) "Patient" shall include a patient's parent, guardian, or conservator, as appropriate.

2.5 Subd. 4. **Right to provide expanded health care.** Notwithstanding Minnesota

2.6 statutes, administrative rules, and other laws governing or authorizing health-related

2.7 professionals to practice their professions, a licensed health care practitioner may provide

2.8 expanded health care practices and services to patients as long as the treatments or
services:

2.9 (1) have a reasonable basis for potential benefit to the patient;

2.10 (2) do not pose a greater risk of direct and significant physical or emotional harm

2.11 to a patient when used as directed than that of conventional treatment that would have

2.12 been recommended;

2.13 (3) are provided with reasonable skill and safety according to the practitioner's

2.14 knowledge, education, experience, and training in the expanded health care practice or

2.15 service.

2.16 A licensed health care practitioner providing expanded health care practices and services

2.17 must comply with the disclosure requirement in subdivision 5.

2.18 Subd. 5. **Disclosure guidelines for expanded practice.** Prior to administering or

2.19 treating a patient with an expanded health care practice or service, a practitioner
shall:

2.20 (1) disclose in writing to the patient an explanation in plain terms of the theoretical

2.21 approach for the treatment or service and the practitioner's education, training,
experience,

2.22 and credentials regarding the expanded health care practice and service being
provided or

2.23 recommended;

2.24 (2) obtain informed consent from the patient according to Minnesota law for

2.25 providing medical treatments including the nature and purpose of the proposed

2.26 expanded practices and services, the expected benefits, the significant and material risks

2.27 associated with the proposed expanded practices and services, and any other truthful

2.28 and nonmisleading information that a patient or client would reasonably require in

2.29 order to make an informed determination regarding whether to undertake or refuse the

2.30 recommended expanded practice and services; and

2.31 (3) obtain written acknowledgment from the patient that the patient or client has

2.32 received the information required by this section.

2.33 Subd. 6. **Evidence.** For any investigation or disciplinary proceeding regarding

2.34 a healing or health care practitioner performing expanded health care practices and

2.35 services, the authorized licensing board or regulatory authority shall use experts who

2.36 have specialized knowledge, training, and clinical competence in the practice method

3.1 or treatment used by the professional being investigated. The majority of the expert's

3.2 practice must be the same as that of the professional being investigated.

3.3 Subd. 7. **Complaints; investigations.** A practitioner's license or registration shall

3.4 not be revoked, suspended, or conditioned, or have any other form of reprimand imposed

3.5 or be denied a license or registration if the practitioner is practicing in compliance with

3.6 this chapter and the practitioner has:

3.7 (1) recommended or utilized expanded health care practices;

3.8 (2) referred a patient to, or comanaged a patient or client with, a practitioner of

3.9 expanded health care practices or a practitioner who is practicing in compliance with

3.10 chapter 146A.

3.11 Subd. 8. **Burden of proof.** In any proceeding under this section, the authorized

3.12 licensing board or regulatory authority having jurisdiction over the practitioner bears the

3.13 burden of proof regarding the practitioner's deviation from the requirements established

3.14 in this chapter.

Endnotes

Preface

1   Minn. Stat. 147.081, Subd. 3 (3), accessed November 17, 2020, https://www.revisor. mn.gov/statutes/cite/147/pdf.

Chapter 1: The Arrest of Herbert Saunders

1   Dan Haley, *Politics in Healing: The Suppression and Manipulation of American Medicine* (Washington, DC: Potomac Valley Press, 2000), 209.
2   Ibid.

Chapter 2: Changing the Minnesota Law

1   Minnesota Senate File 561, Eightieth Legislature (1997–1998), accessed August 29, 2020, https://www.revisor.mn.gov/bills/text.php?number=SF561&version=0&session= ls80&session_year=1997&session_number=0.
2   Minnesota Senate File 1908, Eightieth Legislature (1997–1998), accessed August 29, 2020, https://www.revisor.mn.gov/bills/text.php?number=SF1908&version= 3&session=ls80&session_year=1997&session_number=0.
3   *Complementary Medicine: A Report to the Legislature: January 15, 1998*, Minnesota Department of Health, Health Economics Program, accessed August 29, 2020, https:// www.leg.state.mn.us/docs/pre2003/mandated/980251.pdf.
4   Ibid., 3.
5   Monica Miller, National Health Freedom Coalition, archived hard-copy audio.
6   Minnesota Senate Bill 689 (introduced February 11, 1999), accessed July 2018, https://www.revisor.mn.gov/bills/text.php?number=SF689&version=0&session_ year=1999&session_number=0.
7   Minnesota House File 537 (introduced February 8, 1999), accessed July 2018, https:// www.revisor.mn.gov/bills/bill.php?f=HF537&y=1999&ssn=0&b=house.
8   *Complementary Medicine, A Final Report to the Legislature*, 2.
9   Minn. Stat. 214.001, Subd. 2(a), accessed July 19, 2018, https://www.revisor.mn.gov/ statutes/cite/214.001.

10 Minn. Stat. 147.081, Practicing without License; Penalty, Subd. 3. Practice of medicine
    defined, accessed July 2018, https://www.revisor.mn.gov/statutes/cite/147.081.
11 M. Artus, P. Croft, and M. Lewis, "The Use of CAM and Conventional Treatments
    among Primary Care Consulters with Chronic Musculoskeletal Pain," *BMC Family
    Practice* 8 (2007): 26. https://doi.org/10.1186/1471-2296-8-26.
12 Minn. Stat. 146.15, Discrimination against Systems of Healing, accessed July 19,
    2018, https://www.revisor.mn.gov/statutes/cite/146.15.
13 Minn. Stat. 146A, Complementary and Alternative Health Care Practices, 2019,
    accessed August 30, 2020, https://www.revisor.mn.gov/statutes/cite/146A/pdf.

Chapter 3: Health Freedom Going Forward

1   National Health Freedom Coalition, "Previous Congresses," accessed May 29, 2020,
    https://nationalhealthfreedom.org/health-freedom-congress/previous-congresses
2   "International Declaration of Health Freedom," accessed May 25, 2020, https://
    nationalhealthfreedom.org/wp-content/uploads/Internatinal.pdf.
3   National Health Freedom Coalition, "Previous Congresses," 2012 United
    States Health Freedom Congress, Resolutions, accessed May 25, 2020, https://
    nationalhealthfreedom.org/health-freedom-congress/previous-congresses.
4   "US Health Freedom Congress goals," accessed November 30, 2020, https://
    nationalhealthfreedom.org/health-freedom-congress.
5   Codex Alimentarius, "International Food Standards: What Is Codex?," accessed July
    7, 2020, http://www.fao.org/fao-who-codexalimentarius/en/.
6   World Health Organization, "International Code of Marketing of Breast-milk
    Substitutes," Geneva, 1981, accessed November 30, 2020, https://www.who.int/
    nutrition/publications/code_english.pdf.
7   National Health Federation, "Codex," accessed July 7, 2020, https://thenhf.com/
    codex/our-work-at-codex/.
8   Diane Miller, "Understanding Codex and Its Impact on Health Freedom," with grateful
    thanks for the very helpful comments of Suzanne Harris, JD, and David Hinde,
    solicitor, July 2004, accessed May 29, 2020, https://nationalhealthfreedom.org/wp-
    content/uploads/Codex-Draft-9.-8.12.04-Final-Master-with-acknowledgement-for-
    Techstarters.doc.pdf.
9   NHFA comments on the FDA draft guidance entitled "Guidance for Industry on
    Complementary and Alternative Medicine Products and Their Regulation by the
    Food and Drug Administration," May 15, 2007, accessed May 29, 2020, https://
    nationalhealthfreedom.org/wp-content/uploads/FDA-comments-draft-3-Final-
    Submission-CAM-Products-2007.pdf.
10 Ibid.
11 NHFA comments on the CDC Notice of Proposed Rulemaking: "Control of
    Communicable Disease," September 16, 2016, accessed May 29, 2020, https://
    nationalhealthfreedom.org/wp-content/uploads/CDC-2016-NHFA-Response-to-
    NPRM-Control-of-Communicable-Disease-Sept-19-2016-FINAL.pdf.
12 NHFA comments to FDA on the draft guidance document entitled "Drug Products
    Labeled as Homeopathic: Guidance for FDA Staff and Industry," March 8, 2018,

accessed May 29, 2020, https://nationalhealthfreedom.org/wp-content/uploads/FDA-2018-NHFA-FINAL-Comments-Draft-Guidance-Homeopathy-3.8.2018.pdf.

Chapter 4: Health Freedom—a Fundamental Right

1   National Archives, Declaration of Independence, accessed August 29, 2020, https://www.archives.gov/founding-docs/declaration-transcript.
2   Id. Declaration of Independence
3   "America's Founding Documents: The Bill of Rights" National Archives, accessed April 3, 2021, https://www.archives.gov/founding-docs/bill-of-rights
4   Id. Bill of Rights
5   Encyclopedia.com, s.v. "Slippery Elm, Description," accessed May 29, 2020, https://www.encyclopedia.com/medicine/encyclopedias-almanacs-transcripts-and-maps/slippery-elm.
6   National Institute of Health Office of Dietary Supplements, Dietary Supplement Health and Education Act of 1994, Public Law 103-417, 103rd Cong, accessed July 19, 2018, https://ods.od.nih.gov/About/DSHEA_Wording.aspx.
7   Dr. Benjamin Rush, Lecture, University of Pennsylvania, November 3, 1801, published 1811, accessed July 2018, https://ia800306.us.archive.org/2/items/2569048R.nlm.nih.gov/2569048R.pdf.
8   Cruzan v. Director, Missouri Department of Health, 110 S.Ct. 2841, 2865 (1990).
9   Ibid.
10 Cruzan Justice Brennan, with whom Justice Marshall and Justice Blackmun join, dissenting, citing Snyder v. Massachusetts, 291 U.S. 97, 105 (1934).
11 Cruzan Justice Brennan, Marshall Blackmun dissent, p. 78; see Ante at p. 270.
12 Ibid.
13 Ibid., citing Natanson v. Kline, 186 Kan. 393, 406–7 (1960).
14 Ibid. at 2866, citing Tune v. Walter Reed Army Medical Hospital, 602 F.Supp. 1452, 1455 (DC 1985).
15 Griswold v. Connecticut, 381 U.S. 479 (1965). See Poe v. Ullman, 367 U.S. 497, 516–22 (dissenting opinion), accessed July 19, 2018, https://www.law.cornell.edu/supremecourt/text/381/479.

Chapter 6: Health Freedom Principle 1—Freedom to Be Let Alone

1   Cruzan v. Director, Missouri Department of Health 110 S.Ct. 2841, 2865 (1990).
2   2018 US Health Freedom Congress, Story of Courage, Michelle Krinsky, RN, 2018, accessed May 31, 2020, https://nationalhealthfreedom.org/wp-content/uploads/2018-Congress-Summary-FINAL_071118-3.pdf; WPCO 9, "Christ Hospital Fires Nurse for Refusing Flu Vaccine," December 26, 2017, video, accessed August 29, 2020, https://www.youtube.com/watch?v=SDBCEJYNgeA.
3   NBCNews.com, "Judge Rules Family Cannot Refuse Chemotherapy for Boy," May 19, 2009, accessed May 31, 2020, http://www.nbcnews.com/id/30763438/ns/health-childrens_health/t/judge-rules-family-cant-refuse-chemo-boy/#.XtRovEBFzIU.

4   California Senate Bill No. 277, 2015, accessed May 31, 2020, http://www.leginfo. ca.gov/pub/15-16/bill/sen/sb_0251-0300/sb_277_bill_20150630_chaptered.pdf.

5   Fla. Stat. 456.41, Complementary and Alternative Health Care Treatments, accessed June 13, 2020, http://www.leg.state.fl.us/Statutes/index.cfm?App_mode=Display_ Statute&Search_String=&URL=0400-0499/0456/Sections/0456.41.html.

6   Environmental Protection Agency, "Cases and Settlements," accessed July 5, 2020, https://www.epa.gov/enforcement/cases-and-settlements.

7   Kathryn Paul, "Monsanto-Bayer Gets Bitten. But the Fight Is Far from Over," Organic Consumers Association Kathryn Paul, July 2, 2020, accessed July 5, 2020, https:// www.organicconsumers.org/blog/monsanto-bayer-gets-bitten-fight-far-over.

8   Ibid.

9   Organic Consumers Association, accessed July 18, 2020, https://www.organic consumers.org/usa.

10   Arthur Firstenberg, "Putting the Earth in a High-Speed Computer," June 3, 2020, accessed July 5, 2020, https://nationalhealthfreedom.org/wp-content/uploads/ Putting-the-Earth-inside-a-High-Speed-Computer_ArthurFirstenburg.pdf.

11   Ibid.

12   Ibid.

13   Ibid.

14   Minn. Const. art. I, sec. 1, adopted October 13, 1857, generally revised November 5, 1974, accessed June 13, 2020, https://www.revisor.mn.gov/constitution/#article_1.

15   Minn. Stat. 12.03, Subd. 3, 2019, accessed June 13, 2020, https://www.revisor.mn.gov/ statutes/2019/cite/12.03.

16   Minnesota Senate File 2669, introduced February 2002, Section 31, Subd. 2., accessed June 13, 2020, https://www.revisor.mn.gov/bills/text.php?number=SF2669&version= 0&session=ls82&session_year=2002&session_number=0.

17   Minnesota House File 3031, Conference Committee Report, Eighty-Second Legislature (2001–2002), chapter 402, accessed June 13, 2020, https://www.revisor. mn.gov/laws/2002/0/402/.

18   "Q and A on the Model State Health Emergency Powers Act," ACLU, accessed June 13, 2020, https://www.aclu.org/other/model-state-emergency-health-powers-act.

19   California Health and Safety Code Section 120140, accessed June 13, 2020, http://leginfo.legislature.ca.gov/faces/codes_displaySection.xhtml?lawCode= HSC&sectionNum=120140.

20   California Health Coalition Advocacy, 2020 proposed Right to Refuse Legislation Bill draft, accessed August 29, 2020, https://californiahealthcoalitionadvocacy.org/ civilliberties/.

21   Wisconsin Legislature v. Secretary of Wisconsin Department of Health Services, 2020 Wis. 42 (May 13, 2020) (4–3 decision) (quoting Grassl Bradley, J., concurring), accessed June 13, 2020, https://nationalhealthfreedomaction.org/wp-content/ uploads/2020/05/Corona-Virus-Supreme-Court-Wisconsin.pdf.

22   Upper Midwest Law Center, Summary of Northland Baptist Church of St. Paul Minnesota, et al., v. Governor Tim Walz, et al. (COVID-19 Orders Case), accessed June 13, 2020, https://www.umwlc.org/lawsuits.

Chapter 7: Health Freedom Principle 2—Freedom to Act

1   United States Congress, Committee on Financial Services, hearing, October 23, 2019, "An Examination of Facebook and Its Impact on the Financial Services and Housing Sectors," witness testimony, Mark Zuckerberg, accessed July 7, 2020, https://financialservices.house.gov/calendar/eventsingle.aspx?EventID=404487.

2   Ibid.

3   Federal Trade Commission, Protecting America's Consumers website, "FTC Sends Letters Warning 30 More Marketers to Stop Making Unsupported Claims that Their Products and Therapies Can Effectively Prevent or Treat COVID-19," June 18, 2020, accessed July 7, 2020, https://www.ftc.gov/news-events/press-releases/2020/06/ftc-sends-letters-warning-30-more-marketers-stop-making.

4   Ibid.

5   Massachusetts Law, Powers of the Commissioner upon Declaration of an Emergency, Mass. Part I, Title II, Chapter 17, Section 2A, accessed July 7, 2020, https://malegislature.gov/Laws/GeneralLaws/PartI/TitleII/Chapter17/Section2A.

6   Colorado Statute 12-235-110, Massage Therapy, 2020, accessed July 7 2020, https://advance.lexis.com/documentpage/teaserdocument/?pdmfid=1000516&crid=a8e3f713-d3d1-460b-b59a-0924a5e82fcb&config=014FJAAyNGJkY2Y4Zi1mNjgyLTRkN2YtYmE4OS03NTYzNzYzOTg0OGEKAFBvZENhdGFsb2d592qv2Kywlf8caKqYROP5&pddocfullpath=%2Fshared%2Fdocument%2Fstatutes-legislation%2Furn%3AcontentItem%3A5YWF-4WB1-F60C-X279-00008-00&pddocid=urn%3AcontentItem%3A5YWF-4WB1-F60C-X279-00008-00&pdcontentcomponentid=234176&pdteaserkey=h1&pditab=allpods&ecomp=f5w_kkk&earg=sr0&prid=01e86c44-a4b9-4337-91ce-10645f6025c9.

7   Texas Massage Law, TX Chapter 455, Subchapter D, Licensing, Sec. 455.151. License Required, accessed July 7, 2020, https://www.tdlr.texas.gov/mas/maslaw.htm#455151.

Chapter 8: Health Freedom Principle 3—Freedom to Access

1   Dan Healy, *Politics in Healing: The Suppression and Manipulation of American Medicine* (Washington, DC, Potomac Valley Press, 2000).

2   Minn. Stat. 147.091, Subd. 1(k), 2020, accessed July 11, 2020, https://www.revisor.mn.gov/statutes/2019/cite/147.091.

3   Health and Safety Code Division 105. Communicable Disease Prevention and Control, Part 2. Immunizations, Chapter 1. Educational and Child Care Facility Immunization Requirements, 120370 (a) (1), 2020, accessed July 11, 2020, http://leginfo.legislature.ca.gov/faces/codes_displaySection.xhtml?lawCode=HSC&sectionNum=120370.

4   Health and Safety Code, Division 105. Communicable Disease Prevention and Control, Part 2. Immunizations, Chapter 1. Educational and Child Care Facility Immunization Requirements, 120325, 2020, accessed July 11, 2020, http://leginfo.legislature.ca.gov/faces/codes_displaySection.xhtml?lawCode=HSC&sectionNum=120325.

Chapter 9: Health Freedom Principle 4—Responsibility to Do No Harm

1   "Use of Placebos," National Cancer Institute, February 2020, accessed July 11, 2020, https://www.cancer.gov/about-cancer/treatment/clinical-trials/what-are-trials/placebo.

2   Ibid.

3   Ibid.

4   "Can Measles Vaccine Cause Injury and Death?" National Vaccine Information Center (NVIC), accessed July 12, 2020, https://www.nvic.org/vaccines-and-diseases/measles/measles-vaccine-injury-death.aspx.

5   Physicians for Informed Consent.

6   "Study Suggests Medical Errors Now Third Leading Cause of Death in the U.S.," Johns Hopkins, May 3, 2016, accessed December 1, 2020, https://www.hopkinsmedicine.org/news/media/releases/study_suggests_medical_errors_now_third_leading_cause_of_death_in_the_us.

7   *Encyclopedia Britannica*, s.v. "Hippocratic Oath, Ethical Code," accessed July 11, 2020, https://www.britannica.com/topic/Hippocratic-oath.

8   Ibid.

9   Ibid.

10 Ibid.

Chapter 10: Health Freedom Principle 5—Responsibility of Tolerance

1   International Declaration of Health Freedom, accessed July 18, 2020, https://nationalhealthfreedom.org/wp-content/uploads/International-Declaration-of-Health-Freedom-for-Techstarter.pdf.

Chapter 11: Health Freedom Principles 6 and 7—Responsibility of Corporations

1   "Evaluation of Five Organophosphate Insecticides and Herbicides," World Health Organization, International Agency for Research on Cancer, Monographs vol. 112, March 2015, accessed October 2019, https://www.iarc.fr/wp-content/uploads/2018/07/MonographVolume112-1.pdf.

2   Baum, Hedlund, Aristei, and Goldman, attorneys for the plaintiff, Dewayne Johnson v. Monsanto Company, California State Court, accessed August 29, 2020, https://www.baumhedlundlaw.com/toxic-tort-law/monsanto-roundup-lawsuit/dewayne-johnson-v-monsanto-company.

3   Ibid.

4   Maria Armental, "Monsanto Hit by $289 Million in Cancer Case," *Wall Street Journal*, August 10, 2019, https://www.wsj.com/articles/monsanto-hit-by-289-million-verdict-in-cancer-case-1533949524.

5   Baum, Hedlund, Aristei, and Goldman, attorneys for the plaintiff, *Dewayne Johnson v. Monsanto Company*, California State Court, accessed August 29, 2020,

https://www.baumhedlundlaw.com/toxic-tort-law/monsanto-roundup-lawsuit/
dewayne-johnson-v-monsanto-company.

6   US District Court, Northern District of California, regarding Dewayne Johnson
    v. Monsanto, California State Court, Pretrial Order Number 141, mediation order
    for Roundup Products Liability Litigation, all actions, Stevick v. Monsanto, April
    11, 2019, Honorable Vince Chhabrias, accessed August 29, 2020, https://usrtk.org/
    wp-content/uploads/bsk-pdf-manager/2019/04/Judge-vacates-Stevick-trial-orders-
    mediation.pdf.

7   "Monsanto Roundup Trial Tracker," US Right to Know, accessed August 29, 2020,
    https://usrtk.org/monsanto-roundup-trial-tracker-index/.

8   Carey Gillam, "Court Frowns on Bayer's Proposed Roundup Class-Action
    Settlement," US Right to Know, July 6, 2020, accessed August 29, 2020,
    https://usrtk.org/monsanto-roundup-trial-tracker   /court-frowns-on-bayers-
    proposed-roundup-class-action-settlement/.

9   Ibid.

10 Ibid.

11 Centers for Disease Control and Prevention, Vaccine Information Statements (VISs),
    MMR (measles, mumps, and rubella) VIS, accessed December 2, 2020, https://www.
    cdc.gov/vaccines/hcp/vis/vis-statements/mmr.html.

12 Arthur Allen, "Questions for Barbara Loe Fisher on the Costs of Vaccines," *New York
    Times Magazine*, May 6, 2001, http://archive.is/5MZYk#selection-763.0-763.497.

13 National Vaccine Information Center, "Biography of Barbara Loe Fisher," accessed
    December 3, 2020, https://www.nvic.org/about/barbaraloefisher.aspx.

14 Stephen Engelberg, "Maker of Vaccines Quits the Market," *New York Times*,
    December 14, 1984, https://www.nytimes.com/1984/12/12/us/maker-of-vaccine-
    quits-the-market.html.

15 Ibid.

16 Ibid.

17 Ibid.

18 S. 1744 (Ninety-Ninth Congress): State Comprehensive Mental Health Services Plan
    Act of 1986, Section 301, the National Childhood Vaccine Injury Compensation Act
    of 1986, https://www.govtrack.us/congress/bills/99/s1744/text.

19 Ibid.

20 Bruesewitz v. Wyeth LLC, 562 U.S.C. 223 (2011), https://casetext.com/case/
    bruesewitz-v-wyeth-llc.

21 *National Vaccine Injury Compensation Program Data Report*, US Health Resources
    and Service Administration, August 1, 2020, https://www.hrsa.gov/sites/default/files/
    hrsa/vaccine-compensation/data/data-statistics-report.pdf.

22 Wayne Rhode, *The Vaccine Court: The Dark Truth of America's Vaccine Injury
    Compensation Program* (New York: Skyhorse, 2014).

23 "Report Vaccine Reactions. It's the Law!" National Vaccine Information Center,
    https://www.nvic.org/reportreaction.aspx.

24 "CDC Recommended Vaccine Schedule," Children Defense Fund.

25 Christiane Northrup, "Should You Get the Flu Shot This Year?" October 6,
    2020, accessed December 3, 2020, https://www.drnorthrup.com/should-you-get-
    the-flu-shot-this-year/.

26 42 U.S.C. § 300aa–27—Mandate for safer childhood vaccines, accessed July 19, 2020, https://www.law.cornell.edu/uscode/text/42/300aa-27.

27 Ibid.

28 ICAN v. US Department of Health and Human Services, US Dist. Ct., Southern District of New York, Stipulation, 18-cv-03215-(JMF), July 6, 2018 (Stipulated Order Confirming Noncompliance with 42 U.S.C. Sec 300aa-27), accessed July 19, 2020, https://www.icandecide.org/ican_lawsuits/his-lawsuit/.

29 Bertrand Russell, *The Impact of Science on Society* (New York: AMS Press, 1953).

30 Kate Vinton, "These Fifteen Billionaires Own America's News Media Companies," *Forbes*, June 1, 2016, https://www.forbes.com/sites/katevinton/2016/06/01/these-15-billionaires-own-americas-news-media-companies/#6b86952e660a.

Chapter 12: Health Freedom Principle 8—Responsibility of Government

1 "Quotations on the Jefferson Memorial, Panel Four," Jefferson Memorial, accessed July 22, 2018, https://www.monticello.org/site/jefferson/quotations-jefferson-memorial#Panel_Four.

2 Jonathan W. Emord, *The Rise of Tyranny* (Washington, DC: Sentinel, 2008), 77–78.

3 "Branches of the U.S. Government," USA.gov, accessed July 21, 2020, https://www.usa.gov/branches-of-government.

4 Public Health Emergencies, Public Readiness, and Emergency Preparedness Act, US Department of Health and Human Services, accessed August 30, 2020, https://www.phe.gov/Preparedness/legal/prepact/Pages/default.aspx.

5 "Notices: Declaration under the Public Readiness and Emergency Preparedness Act for Medical Countermeasures against COVID–19," *Federal Register* 85, no. 52 (March 17, 2020): 15198, https://www.govinfo.gov/content/pkg/FR-2020-03-17/pdf/2020-05484.pdf.

6 Ibid, Section XIV. Countermeasures Injury Compensation Program.

7 Ibid.

8 Medical Mission Sisters, "It's a Long Road to Freedom," published 1966, Hymnary.org, accessed August 30, 2020, https://hymnary.org/text/i_walked_one_morning_by_the_sea.

Chapter 13: People at Risk

1 "Cancer Statistics," National Institute of Health (NIH), National Cancer Institute, last modified April 2018, https://www.cancer.gov/about-cancer/understanding/statistics.

2 Centers for Disease Control and Prevention (CDC), National Center for Chronic Disease Prevention and Health Promotion, accessed January 12, 2020, https://www.cdc.gov/chronicdisease/index.htm.

3 Ibid.

4 *World Health Report 2000—Health Systems: Improving Performance*, World Health Organization, accessed January 12, 2020, https://www.who.int/whr/2000/en/.

5   World Health Organization Report 2016: *Noncommunicable Diseases and Mental Health*, statistical data, accessed July 19, 2018, http://apps.who.int/gho/data/node. sdg.3-4.

6   World Health Organization Report 2016, *Newborn and Child Mortality*, statistical data, accessed July 19, 2018, http://apps.who.int/gho/data/node.sdg.3-2.

7   Ibid.

8   World Health Organization Report 2016, *Mortality from Environmental Pollution, Subcategory, Unintentional Poisoning*, statistical data, accessed July 19, 2018, http:// apps.who.int/gho/data/node.sdg.3-9-viz-3?lang=en.

9   "Growing Evidence of Harm from GMOs," Institute for Responsible Technology, accessed January 12, 2020, https://responsibletechnology.org/docs/IRT-Health-RisksBrochure-2014-web%282%29.pdf, p. 2.

10   Ibid.

11   "Statistics from the National Health Interview Survey," National Institute of Health: National Center for Complementary and Integrative Health, accessed August 30, 2020, https://www.nccih.nih.gov/health/statistics-from-the-national-health-interview-survey.

12   "Campaign to Restore Child's Health, Parents Speak Out on Vaccine Injuries," Children's Health Defense, October 16, 2017, accessed December 20, 2020, https://childrenshealthdefense.org/news/campaign-restore-child-health-parents-speak-vaccine-injuries/.

13   "America's Founding Documents: The Constitution of the United States," National Archives, accessed August 30, 2020, https://www.archives.gov/founding-docs/constitution.

14   "Jefferson Quotes and Family Letters," Jefferson Monticello, accessed August 30, 2020, http://tjrs.monticello.org/letter/334.

15   "Jefferson Quotes and Family Letters," Jefferson Monticello, accessed August 30, 2020, http://tjrs.monticello.org/letter/407.

Index

bold denotes photo

A

access
    freedom to, 121–127
    impact of licensing laws on,
        122–127
    underpinnings of, 121–122
acupressure, 30, 175
Adams, Francis, 133
Advisory Committee on
    Immunization Practices (US
    Department of Health and
    Human Services), 126
Advisory Council Task Force, study
    on scope of complementary
    medicine, 21–22
air pollution, negative effects of,
    96, 128alternative cancer
    treatments
    availability of outside US,
        129–130
    parents as wishing to choose, 94
American Academy of Family
    Physicians, 126
American Academy of Pediatrics, 126
anthroposophy, 30, 175
aromatherapy, 30, 175
Ayurvedic medicine, 30, 175

B

Barbara (MNHC member), 28
Bayer, lawsuits against for exposure
    to Roundup, 96, 140–142, 148
Bedell, Berkley, viii, 8, **14**, 16n,
    25–26, 163
Berg, Mr., 6
Berglin, Linda, 29, 52
Beyer, Marillyn, 23, 27, 35
bodily autonomy, viii, 103, 145
bodily integrity, 78, 92
bodywork, 28, 31, 117, 176
Boudreau, Lynda, 26, 29, 31, 33, 41,
    42, 48, 53
Bradley (representative), 41
burden of proof, 70, 119–120, 157
Burzynski, Stanislaw, 24–25

C

California Health Coalition Advocacy
    (CHCA), 103
California Senate Bill 277 (2015), on
    recommended vaccines, 94, 95,
    125–126, 155–157
California Statute Health and Safety
    Code Section 120140 (health
    emergencies), 102–103

223

cancer. *See also* chemotherapy
    treatments
  alternative treatments for, 34, 94,
    129–130
  hyperimmune colostrum as
    treatment for, 2, 4, 6, 8
  lawsuit against Bayer by people
    suffering from, 96,
    140–142
  National Cancer Institute
    projection on estimates
    of new cases and deaths,
    162–163
  non-Hodgkin's lymphoma (NHL),
    140, 141
  treatment options, 35–36,
    124, 129
Carruthers (representative), 39, 48, 55
Cashman, Leo, 23, 27, 32, 61
Cell Phone Task Force, 96
cell phones, negative effects of
    exposure to, 97
Centers for Disease Control and
    Prevention (CDC)
    "Control of Communicable
    Disease," 70–71
  on vaccines, 145, 155
change, resistance to, 152–153
CHCA (California Health Coalition
    Advocacy), 103
chemicals in industrial agricultural
    practices, negative effects of,
    96, 129
chemotherapy treatments
  forcing family to accept, 63
  medical boards as enforcing
    conventional standard of
    care based on, 124
  options for persons choosing not
    to undergo, 35–36
  parents as wishing to stop,
    94, 135

side effects of, 129–130
Chhabria, Vince, 141
chronic diseases, statistics on, 163
CICP (Countermeasure Injury
    Compensation Program), 157
Clark, Karen, 30
Clifford, Dr., 8
Coalition for Natural Health, 29
Codex. *See* United Nations Codex
    Alimentarius
Colorado, protections of many healing
    practices in, 117
colostrum
  power of, 5
  sales of by Herb Saunders, 1–3
  therapy with, 2, 4, 30
  use of in China, 8
communicable disease, CDC's
    "Control of Communicable
    Disease," 70–71
Complementary and Alternative
    Health Care Freedom of
    Access Act (HF 537). *See also*
    Minnesota Statute 146A (MN
    146A)
  introduction of, 29–31
  path of, 32–56, **54**
  prohibited acts as listed in, 21,
    43, 46
  protected practices as listed in,
    30–31
Complementary and Alternative
    Health Care Freedom of
    Access Act (SF 689). *See also*
    Minnesota Statute 146A (MN
    146A)
  introduction of, 29–31
  path of, 32–56, **54**
  prohibited acts as listed in, 21,
    43, 46
  protected practices as listed in,
    30–31

224

complementary and alternative health care/complementary and alternative medicine
    FDA's "Guidance for Industry on Complementary and Alternative Medicine Products and Their Regulation by the Food and Drug Administration," 69–70
    Minnesota bill to study, 21–22
    protections for physicians using, 126
    statistic on use of, 36
    US states with laws allowing licensed doctors to practice, 94
Complementary Medicine: A Report to the Legislature, 22
consumer movement, mobilization of, 16, 17–18
coronavirus
    response to and personal freedom, 102–104
    warning letters from FDA regarding treatment/ prevention products, 113–114
corporations
    accountability of, 140, 142, 148–149
    health seekers and, 149
    legal liability of, 149
    as owning information and media outlets, 146–148
    responsibility of, 138–150
Coult, Lyman H., 23
Coulter, Harris, 143
Countermeasure Injury Compensation Program (CICP), 157
COVID-19. *See* coronavirus
craniosacral therapy, 30

"the crossing of the skin barrier," use of term, 94
Cruzan case (1990), 77–78, 92–93
cultural traditions, role of in practice of healing, 12, 30, 107
culture, and law, 152–154

D

David (MNHC member), 28
Dean, Caroline, 132
Death by Modern Medicine (Dean and Tuck), 132
Dempsey (district court judge), 9, 10, 12
denial
    breaking out of, 165
    foundation of, 162–164
detoxification practices and therapies, 30
DeVries, Ray, 11
Dewayne Johnson v. Monsanto Company (2018), 140–141
dietary ingredients, FDA's "Draft Guidance for Industry; Dietary Supplements: New Dietary Ingredient Notifications and Related Issues; Availability," 70
Dietary Supplement Health and Education Act (1994), xxiii, 67, 70, 76
dietary supplements
    access to, xxiii, 73
    author's use of, xii
    foods regulated and sold as, 76
    labeling restrictions on, 114
    NHFC and NHFA as supporting access to, 73
    right to make truthful claims about, 64
    setting upper limits of dosage for, 66

do no harm, 88, 128–133, 149, 203

DPT: A Shot in the Dark (Fisher and Coulter), 143

drugs, prescription, and Minnesota Statute 146A, 43, 46

E

Eckstein, Tony, **14**, 16n

electromagnetic microwave radiation, from utility meters, 66, 93, 127, 129, 150

elm tree bark, use of during Revolutionary War, 75–76

emergencies

agency power to declare corporate liability shield in, 157–158

health freedom during, 98–104

emergency power acts, 98–102

Emord, Jonathan, 154

energetic healing, 30, 175

enumerated rights/freedoms, 77, 78

environmental medicine, 30

erythrocythemia, use of colostrum on case record of man with, 4–5

exemptions (to laws/rules), vii, 20, 22, 23, 24, 25, 30, 31, 45, 95, 125, 127, 130, 145

F

FAO (Food and Agricultural Organization), 67

Farmers Amendment, 9

FDA (Food and Drug Administration). *See* Food and Drug Administration (FDA)

fear, foundation of, 161–162

Federal Advisory Board on Alternative Medicine, 8

federal agencies, list of, 155

Federal Communications Commission, SpaceX application with, 97

Federal Trade Commission (FTC), warning letters regarding coronavirus prevention/ treatment products, 113–114

Firstenberg, Arthur, 96–97

Fischbach, Michelle, 29

Fisher, Barbara Loe, 142–143

Florida

coronavirus response, 104

law regarding complementary and alternative health care treatments, 94–95

fluoridation (of water), 64, 90, 93

folk medicine, 30

Food and Agricultural Organization (FAO), 67

Food and Drug Administration (FDA)

"Draft Guidance for Industry; Dietary Supplements: New Dietary Ingredient Notifications and Related Issues; Availability," 70

"Drug Products Labeled as Homeopathic: Guidance for FDA Staff and Industry," 71–72

"Guidance for Industry on Complementary and Alternative Medicine Products and Their Regulation by the Food and Drug Administration," 69–70

investigation of Herb Saunders, 1

food sovereignty, NHFC and NHFA as supporting, 73

food supplies, local, NHFC and NHFA as supporting protection to access of, 73

Nancy Hone as practitioner of,
18, 27
NHFC and NHFA as supporting
access to, 73
and "practice of medicine," 7
role of in practice of healing, 12
and safe harbor practitioner
exemption law, vii
Hone, Nancy, 18, 23, 27, 50, 57
Hottinger, John, 29, 40, 41, 46
Huntley (representative), 36

I

iatrogenesis, 132
immune system
Dr. Fudenberg's work
involving, 6
natural methods to boost health
of, 131
potential cure for, 13
The Impact of Science on Society
(Russell), 147
inalienable rights, xxi, 12, 60, 74, 97,
104, 105, 116, 134, 151, 153
infant formula, WHO resolution
on, 68
information
corporation-owned information,
146–148
seeking health care
information, 115
informed consent, 43, 71, 78, 92, 142,
143, 167
Informed Consent Action Network
(ICAN), 145
insecticides, use of, 93
integrative practices/approaches
as growing, 133, 166
protections for, 94, 126
International Agency for Research on
Cancer (WHO), 140

International Declaration of Health
Freedom, 64–65, 134, 198–200
International World Health Freedom
Assembly (2006), 64–65
invasive testing and treatments,
having the right to refuse, 92
iridology, 30, 176

J

Jan (MNHC member), 28
Jefferson, Thomas, 153–154, 168–169
Johnson, Calvin, xiii, xv, xvi–xvii, 2,
3, 4–5, 6, 7, 11, **14**, 15
Johnson, Dewayne (Lee), 141
Johnson, Janet, 16–17, 21, 33, 39, 41
Johnson, Jerri, 18, 22, 27, 47, 50,
61, 62
Joint FAO/WHO Food Standards
Programme, 67

K

Kiscaden, Sheila, 47, 51, 55

L

LaDonna (MNHC member), 28, 57
law(s)
about vaccines, 130–131, 155–157
culture and, 152–154
licensing laws, 19, 122–127
that infringe on access to health
care, 118
Leach, Mr., 37
Libby (MNHC member), 28
licensing laws
impact of on access, 122–127
in Minnesota, 19
as needing to include
exemptions, 127
life support, maintenance of, Cruzan
case (1990), 77–78, 92–93
lobbying efforts

debriefings as secret Ingredient of, 47

formation of Minnesota Natural Health Legal Reform Project, 32

lobbying training day, 41

photo of lobbying team, **56, 57**

Louisiana House Bill 642 (introduced February 2020), on right of employees to decline vaccines, 94

Lyme disease, use of colostrum on case record of man with, 8

M

Mandate for Safer Childhood Vaccines clause, 145

mask mandates, 104

massage/massage therapy, 28, 30, 117–118, 165, 176

MDH (Minnesota Department of Health)

rulemaking capacity of, 55

study on scope of complementary medicine, 21–22

Mead, Margaret, 31

media outlets, corporation-owned, 146–148

medical boards

involvement of in public policy, 124–125

Minnesota Board of Medical Practice, 15, 36, 42–46

medicine

compared to healing, 12, 109–110

environmental medicine, 30

iatrogenesis as death caused by, 132

meditation, 30, 176

Metzen (senator), 52

Meyers, Michael, 35–36, 62

Miller, Clinton, 83

Miller, Diane, photo of, **14**

Miller, Marylu, 62

Miller, Monica, 23, 25

mind–body healing practices, 30, 119, 176

Minnesota

disciplining of physicians in, 125

professional licensing laws, 19

Minnesota Appeals Court, certified question for appeal, 9–10

Minnesota Board of Medical Practice

cease and desist papers served to Helen Healy by, 15

opposition to House File 537, 36, 42–46

Minnesota Bureau of Criminal Apprehensions, investigation of Herb Saunders, 1, 5

Minnesota Department of Health (MDH)

rulemaking capacity of, 55

study on scope of complementary medicine, 21–22

Minnesota Department of Health Study on Complementary Medicine (1998), 32

Minnesota Emergency Powers Act, 102

Minnesota Freedom of Access to Complementary and Alternative Health Care Act, 24

Minnesota HF 2699 omnibus bill, 50, 52, 53

Minnesota HF 3213 (2006–2007), on protections for physicians who use complementary, alternative, integrative, holistic, and other practices, 126

Minnesota HF 3839 omnibus bill, 56

Minnesota Medical Association, 36

Minnesota Medical Practice Act

negative effects on by
    corporations, 122
NHFC and NHFA as supporting
    protection to access of, 73
naturopaths/naturopathic practices
    David as, 28
    Helen Healy as, 15, 18
    licensing of, 19–20, 21, 24, 34
    Lyman Coult as, 23
    in Minnesota, 20
    and Minnesota Statute 146A, vii,
        31, 176
    Nancy Hone as, 27
    and "practice of medicine," 7
    protections for, vii, 115, 120
    public interest in getting licensing
        for in Minnesota, 19
NCVIA (National Childhood Vaccine
    Injury Act) (1986), 145
New York Natural Health
    Coalition, 42
NHFA (National Health Freedom
    Action). See National Health
    Freedom Action (NHFA)
NHFC (National Health Freedom
    Coalition). See National Health
    Freedom Coalition (NHFC)
NOAH (National Organization for
    Alternative Health), Legal
    Defense and Education
    Fund, 16n
non-Hodgkin's lymphoma (NHL),
    140, 141
noninvasive healers/practices, 21, 31,
    35, 45–46, 71, 118, 131
noninvasive instrumentalities, 31
Nornes, Bud, 30
Northrup, Christine, 145
NVIC (National Vaccine Information
    Center), 142, 143

NVICP (National Vaccine Injury
    Compensation Program) (1988),
    142, 144

O

occupational boards, and licensing
    laws, 123
Office of Alternative Medicine
    (OAM), 16n, 25
Organic Consumers Association, 96
organic food movement
    access to pesticide-free foods, 66
    author's participation in, xiv
    growth of organic farming, 167
    infringements on freedom of
        access in, 127
    NHFC and NHFA as
        supporting, 72
    protections for food standards
        in, 64
    support for, 96
Otremba, Mary Ellen, 30

P

parental rights, xvii, 63, 66, 72, 94,
    95, 97, 130, 131, 144–145,
    155–157, 167
Pawlenty (representative), 54
personal liberty
    basic view of, 77
    NHFC and NHFA as supporting
        continued vigilance to
        protect, 73
    protections for, 86, 97, 103
    self-determination as bedrock of,
        91–93
    testing of concept of, 171
pesticides
    access to pesticide-free foods, 66
    laws against use of dangerous
        ones, 166–167